D0965787

Language for Hearers

LANGUAGE & COMMUNICATION LIBRARY

Series Editor: Roy Harris, *University of Oxford*

A Related Pergamon Journal

Language & Communication*

An Interdisciplinary Journal
Editor: Roy Harris, *University of Oxford*

The primary aim of the journal is to fill the need for a publicational forum devoted to the discussion of topics and issues in communication which are of interdisciplinary significance. It will publish contributions from researchers in all fields relevant to the study of verbal and non-verbal communication. Emphasis will be placed on the implications of current research for establishing common theoretical frameworks within which findings from different areas of study may be accommodated and interrelated.
By focusing attention on the many ways in which language is integrated with other forms of communicational activity and interactional behaviour it is intended to explore ways of developing a science of communication which is not restricted by existing disciplinary boundaries.

*Free specimen copy available on request.

NOTICE TO READERS

Dear Reader

An invitation to Publish in and Recommend the Placing of a Standing Order to Volumes Published in this Valuable Series

If your library is not already a standing/continuation order customer to this series, may we recommend that you place a standing/continuation order to receive immediately upon publication all new volumes. Should you find that these volumes no longer serve your needs, your order can be cancelled at any time without notice.
The Editors and the Publisher will be glad to receive suggestions of outlines of suitable titles, reviews or symposia for editorial consideration: if found acceptable, rapid publication is guaranteed.

ROBERT MAXWELL
Publisher at Pergamon Press

tm

(Language for Hearers)

Edited by

GRAHAM McGREGOR
University of Newcastle upon Tyne

PERGAMON PRESS

OXFORD · NEW YORK · BEIJING · FRANKFURT
SÃO PAULO · SYDNEY · TOKYO · TORONTO

WILLIAM MADISON RANDALL LIBRARY UNC AT WILMINGTON

U.K.	Pergamon Press, Headington Hill Hall, Oxford OX3 0BW, England
U.S.A.	Pergamon Press, Maxwell House, Fairview Park, Elmsford, New York 10523, U.S.A.
PEOPLE'S REPUBLIC OF CHINA	Pergamon Press, Qianmen Hotel, Beijing, People's Republic of China
FEDERAL REPUBLIC OF GERMANY	Pergamon Press, Hammerweg 6, D-6242 Kronberg, Federal Republic of Germany
BRAZIL	Pergamon Editora, Rua Eça de Queiros, 346, CEP 04011, São Paulo, Brazil
AUSTRALIA	Pergamon Press Australia, P.O. Box 544, Potts Point, N.S.W. 2011, Australia
JAPAN	Pergamon Press, 8th Floor, Matsuoka Central Building, 1-7-1 Nishishinjuku, Shinjuku-ku, Tokyo 160, Japan
CANADA	Pergamon Press Canada, Suite 104, 150 Consumers Road, Willowdale, Ontario M2J 1P9, Canada

Copyright © 1986 Pergamon Books Ltd.

All Rights Reserved. No part of this publication may be reproduced, stored in a retrieval system or transmitted in any form or by any means: electronic, electrostatic, magnetic tape, mechanical, photo-copying, recording or otherwise, without permission in writing from the publishers.

First edition 1986

Library of Congress Cataloging in Publication Data
Language for hearers.
(Language & communication library; v. 8)
Includes index.
1. Listening. 2. Oral communication. 3. Linguistics
I. McGregor, Graham. II. Series.
P95.46.L36 1986   001.54′2   86-4977

British Library Cataloguing in Publication Data
Language for hearers. — (Language &
communication library; v. 8)
1. Psycholinguistics. 2. Oral communication
I. McGregor, Graham II. Series
401′.9   BF455

ISBN 0-08-031852-5

Printed in Great Britain by A. Wheaton & Co. Ltd., Exeter

P95
.46
.L36
1986

In memory of my brother David

Contents

Contributors

Anthony Bladon
Phonetics Laboratory, University of Oxford, 41 Wellington Square, Oxford OX1 2JF, U.K.

James Bradac
Communication Studies Program, University of California, Santa Barbara, CA 93106, U.S.A.

Roger Brown
Department of Modern Languages, University of Aston in Birmingham, Gosta Green, Birmingham B4 7ET, U.K.

Evan Friedman
Communication Arts and Sciences, University of Southern California, Grace Salvatori Hall, 344, Los Angeles, CA 90089-1694, U.S.A.

Howard Giles
Centre for the Study of Communications and Social Relations, University of Bristol, 8–10 Berkeley Square, Bristol BS8 1HH, U.K.

Charles, F. Hockett
Cornell University, Ithaca, New York (Address for correspondence 145 North Sunset Drive, Ithaca, NY 14850, U.S.A.)

Claire Humphreys-Jones
School of English Language and Literature, University of Newcastle upon Tyne, NE1 7RU, U.K. (*Address for correspondence:* 81[A] Friary Park, Ballabeg, Isle of Man)

Graham McGregor
School of English Language and Literature, University of Newcastle upon Tyne, NE1 7RU, U.K.

John Pellowe
Department of English, National University of Singapore, Kent Ridge, Singapore 0511.

H. Stephen Straight
Department of Linguistics, State University of New York at Binghampton, Binghampton, NY 13901, U.S.A.

Talbot J. Taylor
Department of English, College of William and Mary, Williamsburg, Virginia 23185, U.S.A.

Introduction

"We speak in order to be heard and need to be heard in order to be understood" (Jakobson and Waugh, 1979, p. 95).

A conventional view of the speech communication process provides for a sender (speaker) and a receiver (hearer) as Jakobson and Waugh suggest, and as scholars like Lyons (1977, Chapter 2), have outlined. However, although increasing recognition has been given to the cooperative nature of this process, vis-à-vis investigation of the activities of which "speaking" and "hearing" are part, various different scholars have been wont to point out that research has tended to focus on the question of what it is to be a "speaker" of a language rather than on the question of what kinds of contribution are made by those to whom spoken language is addressed, namely, the "hearers" or "listeners" of this world.[1]* As Parker-Rhodes (1978, p. xiii) would have it, "Ours is a speakers' civilization and our linguistics has accordingly concerned itself almost solely with the speaker's problems . . . The skilful speaker wins praise; the skilful listener, despite the mystery of his achievement, is ignored."[2]

Whilst Parker-Rhodes does not make any attempt to provide evidence for his claim (it would in any case require a vast, possibly impracticable, exercise in linguistic historiography to provide such evidence), the challenge of the laconism is nonetheless pertinent for that. "What *skills* do listeners possess and what *is* the mystery of their achievement?"

By bringing together work from various different disciplines which share as their theme a "hearer"- or "listener"-oriented approach to language study (research in phonetics, theoretical linguistics, sociolinguistics, social psychology and discourse analysis is represented), this volume has two major aims. Firstly, it aims to exemplify something of the rich diversity of issues, both theoretical and methodological, that may be raised as a consequence of attempts to investigate or model the achievement and skills to which Parker-Rhodes alludes; the fact that these issues often overlap across and within the disciplines that are represented bears witness to the considerable research potential that a "hearer"-oriented approach offers. Secondly, by the very act of presenting such material within the context of a single volume, it also aims to serve as a means of attenuating redress of balance in the very important sense of recognizing that one cannot be a "speaker"

* Superscript numbers refer to notes at end of chapter.

without also being a "hearer" of language; hence the title of the volume.

Since each contributor states clearly the issues s/he is dealing with, I have attempted by way of introduction to offer only a broad outline of what I know of the general orientation of each paper.

The first three chapters of the volume are linked in the sense in which they are all essentially concerned with auditory and discriminatory ability, albeit from very different perspectives. Since the theme of the volume is based on the role of the hearer, the nature of auditory capacity seems as good a place to start as any.

Anthony Bladon's paper is based on the premise that in the context of working towards a theory of speech perception, considerable progress can be made by attempting to build on and improve models of the auditory processing of speech. Since attempts to investigate auditory capacity by various different instrumentation techniques are problematic,[3] Bladon points out that it is hardly surprising that the traditional frameworks and terminology of phonetics are derived on the basis of largely articulatory observations. What then does an auditory-based phonetics have to offer?

By tracing developments in auditory-based research over the last 40 years or so, Bladon is able to identify some of the most promising principles that have emerged as a result of work involving experimental methods in phonetics. These principles are usefully enumerated in Section B of the paper, at the end of which Bladon concludes "that auditory analysis can offer a novel and often revealing idea of the representation of speech sounds to the hearer". The linguistic implications of these principles are then weighed in terms of their implications upon language systems (Section C) and language in use (Section D).

Whilst recognizing that much needs still to be done, the paper positively affirms that a hearer-oriented phonetics not only offers important theoretical insights but also offers considerable research potential for future work. In sketching out some possible directions that this work might take, Bladon is able to aver, with not unjustified optimism, that as a consequence of developing its auditory base "phonetic theory can hope to gain a new methodology".

The prospect for a new methodology, though in a rather different disciplinary context, is echoed in the following chapter written by John Pellowe. Whilst this paper was written some 17 years ago in circumstances that Pellowe explains in his prefatory note, I would suggest that the idea upon which it is based maintains its originality and relevance today.

The paper lays the theoretical foundations for a hearer-based model of urban linguistic variation. It was written in the context of an emerging sociolinguistics largely pioneered by the work of William Labov and which in Pellowe's terms ". . . seemed and (still seems) unable to grasp its own proper subject matter because of its atomism and its inability to comprehend and incorporate the nature of individual differences" (Pellowe, 1984, p. 37).

By attempting to analyse data in accordance with the discriminatory abilities of hearers, the model was conceived as a set of methods that would help to establish salient features of linguistic and social diversity in urban Tyneside speech where the features concerned would be empirically determined by, rather than presupposed in, the model. Since the need for an explicit and unbiased methodology to account for these features was considered paramount, the notion of a multidimensional "variety space" was employed, the nature and properties of which Pellowe outlines in Sections 4 and 5 of the paper.

The consequent research which evolved from this initial circumscription of the model is detailed in various publications that followed the *Lingua* article to which Pellowe refers in his preface (see references cited in Jones-Sargent, 1983, and Pellowe, 1984). This research is characteristic of the basic orientation of Pellowe's work, that is "it is hearers, rather than speakers, who give social meaning to linguistic variation".

Unfortunately the theoretical and methodological ramifications of this approach have never been made as publicly explicit as they might; nor have they been fully explored.[4] Indeed this state of affairs seems unlikely to change since the Tyneside Linguistic Survey lost its effective director with the departure of John Pellowe from Newcastle in 1979. However, Pellowe maintains a keen interest in the creative capacities of hearers. His current work is based on the conjecture that "hearers create the meanings of utterances" (Pellowe, 1984; 1986) and readers who wish to pursue the development of this idea are referred to the publications cited in the preface to the present essay. It remains singularly my opinion, however, that the challenge of analysing sociolinguistic data in accordance with the perceptions of hearers remains.

Something of the problems facing the researcher wishing to investigate such perceptions further is dealt with by Roger Brown.[5] As its title suggests, this paper is concerned with the particular ability of individuals to identify other speakers on the basis of hearing samples of their speech. The process of recognition involves what Brown terms "a pattern-matching technique" which enables the listener to reach a decision about who the speaker might be. As part of what it might be to apply this technique, listeners are modelled as working within an analytic framework based on two major reference factors. These factors essentially involve (a) the invocation of long-term and short-term memory systems, and (b) the possible set of reference voices from which the listener might choose.

However, whilst these factors appear to be appropriate in categorizing recognition tasks in experimental situations, Brown argues that they need to be revised in the context of "real-world" application; say in circumstances where the telephone rings in one's office. The major revision that is required relates to "listener expectation' which Brown suggests is constrained by the number of probable reference candidates, and hence reference voices, who may wish to make contact through the telephone in question.

Other everyday occurrences which involve speaker recognition are also considered, and these raise a number of extremely interesting issues for sociolinguistic practitioners in particular. Apart from problems connected with the tasks of voice identification and differentiation, Brown brings into question the use of tape-recorded evidence for purposes of verifying a suspect's voice in courtroom situations. This issue is in fact taken up in a paper by James Milroy which reports on the trial in Belfast of a County Derry man charged with blackmail. The accused was convicted on the basis of positive voice identification by witnesses who ". . . had sworn under oath that the voice (or voices) heard on several tape-recordings was/were one and the same voice, and that the voice was that of the accused" (Milroy, J., 1984, p. 52). In offering a detailed consideration of the linguistic status of this evidence, Milroy is able to cast doubt on the verdict of guilt since, in his words, he is ". . . completely convinced that *at least* two different speakers were involved" (Milroy, J., 1984, p. 1970). We would suggest, therefore, that the issues that Brown raises are not only interesting from a linguistic perspective but also of consequence for society at large.[6]

The following two chapters address the issue of "language for hearers" within the context of a modern, theoretical linguistic framework and the first of these constitutes the earliest attempt, of which I am aware, to explicitly incorporate the hearer in a formal theory of language.

Charles Hockett's paper first appeared in print some 25 years ago. Since, in the context of his prefatory statement, he effectively provides his own review of the paper, I feel it is unnecessary to do more than let it speak for itself. I would like to say, however, that despite his brutally frank dismissal of large sections of the paper as "mostly pompous trivia", its title and content were to contribute in no small part to the idea of producing the volume. Given Hockett's endorsement that "what listeners do in trying to comprehend what is said to them" forms an important element of linguistic study, we might now move on to consider something of how and why it is important in this respect.

Stephen Straight's paper considers the implications for a theory of language of recognizing the inherent separability of processes of listening and processes of speaking. Working from the basis that language structure is neutral with respect to comprehension and production, Straight argues that speakers monitor their own output and listeners anticipate input as part of two different kinds of activity whose dynamic interplay is crucial to our understanding of the communicative process of which they are part.

The implications of this "dialectical–processural" view of language, as he terms it, are set in the context of a linguistics which has yet to exploit the explanatory value of this dichotomy, or indeed a possible theory of interaction between them. Evidence for the large and promising new areas of research that may be explored by advocating irreducibility of the comprehension/production distinction is then presented in the form of a substantial exposition on the nature of lexical development in child language. This exposition, in turn, paves the way for a consideration of the functionality of the dialectic in adult language use where its manifestations pose no less of a problem for the analyst but offer equal opportunities for further research, one of which is how or where we might begin to investigate the question of what has been "understood" by the participants in some communicative context.

In an often-quoted phrase, Wittgenstein was to aver "that the tacit conventions on which the understanding of everyday language depends are enormously complicated". Further grist to Wittgenstein's mill, if indeed it is needed, is provided in the following three papers which deal with various different aspects of the hearer's role in the interactional and interpersonal management of everyday verbal exchange.

In the first of these, Talbot Taylor argues that we do not need to find out whether the hearers with whom we interact arrive at the same interpretations of speech which are equivalent to our own in order to know if we are communicating successfully. Since "understandings" as such are not observable phenomena, "speakers cannot be sure if the hearer's understanding of an utterance is what the speaker intends them to be" (cf. Bradac, Friedman and Giles's notion of the "crafty/sceptical" communicator in Chapter 8 of this volume), evidence for the criteria of understanding in everyday verbal interaction has to be sought as a *product* of what speaker-hearers jointly achieve.

By considering something of what these products might be in the context of data that derive from various invented instances (whilst he is aware of the limitations of such data he has good arguments for its use on this occasion), Taylor is able to suggest evidence that might be invoked as criterial support for an "understanding-claim". This evidence is cited in the form of various different criteria that speakers may apply in the process of coordinating everyday verbal exchange to the effect that they have or have not "understood" what has been said.

In recommending an approach which focuses on the nature of such evidence, Taylor rejects the idea that communication can be viewed as a form of telementation. Subsequently, he draws attention to the need for a "lay, common sense theory of understanding" that realistically reflects the goals and principles of everyday verbal interaction where these are not so much the products of private, shared mental events but rather the results of coordinated and cooperative public activities.

Whilst speakers may not regularly question the existence of "understanding" as such, as Taylor points out, the communicative results of failure to "understand", or "misunderstand" are more obviously amenable to empirical analysis, and it is this approach which is taken up in the following paper by Humphreys-Jones.

This paper is part of an extensive corpus-based study (Humphreys-Jones, 1986) which seeks to develop an analytic framework for determining the types and structure of misunderstandings that may occur in the context of everyday verbal exchange. The framework is based on the notion that in the course of attempts by speakers to communicate successfully with their interlocutors three basic possibilities present themselves. These possibilities are based on the perceived communicative effect of some speaker's utterance in terms of whether the consequent discourse structure suggests that there has been (a) correct understanding, (b) lack of understanding or (c) misunderstanding. By careful analysis of her data, Humphreys-Jones is able to provide tangible evidence for how misunderstandings can be detected, and also of course what happens when they are not detected or resolved.

The analytic scheme which she outlines is based on the role of the hearer who has failed in some respect to understand the propositional content of some speaker's utterance, where the nature of the proposition is identified as the "originating" source of the misunderstanding, the effect of the misunderstanding is "manifested" in the hearer's response and where appropriate the individuals concerned come to "realize" that something has gone wrong. Whilst helping to identify the fact that a misunderstanding has occurred, these "primary components" do not account for how the participants may go on to resolve or fail to resolve the misunderstanding as the case may be. Consequently, further analytical constructs are required to account for what happens next; these are described in terms of secondary components or "devices" which may combine with each other in various different ways which Humphreys-Jones specifies.

This analytic framework is then applied to selected instances of misunderstandings taken from her corpus enabling Humphreys-Jones not only to demonstrate the considerable complexity of the phenomenon that is involved[7] but also to provide empirically based evidence of the crucial role that hearers play in determining and monitoring the relative communicative success of everyday verbal interaction.

The paper by James Bradac, Evan Friedman and Howard Giles is described by them as "an initial foray moving use beyond the rule-bound dominance of communication-based information processing". The basic thrust of this "foray" is an attempt to map out certain belief states which speakers may invoke prior to the undertaking of communicative actions of the propositional sort.[8] These states are particularly linked to interactional behaviour that for whatever social reason leads individuals to adopt a kind of "communicative camouflage" in order to hide, or at least disguise, their true "intentions" and/or feelings from their immediate interlocutors. In order to account for the nature of this "camouflage", speakers are modelled as being more communicatively devious than perhaps professional analysts, at least, have given them credit for.

Four major types of belief are identified that may potentially affect some message that is selected in undertaking communicative actions of a propositional sort. These are: beliefs about self, about the world, about the hearer and about communication. Two further types are also specified, "intentional beliefs" and "perloctionary beliefs" to account for particular cases within this larger set, providing a basic typology from which four axioms and subsequently a series of twelve theorems are derived. The theorems describe twelve states of mind "which constitute a cognitive code exploited by the speaker as s/he communicates propositionally". But what of the hearer in this scheme of things?

As Bradac *et al.* are quick to point out, "speakers do not lie or evade in a social vacuum". Thus we not only need to consider "speakers' *beliefs about* the hearer" but also "beliefs about the latter's beliefs concerning the former". In order to begin to explore hearers' beliefs within a theory of propositional communication, Bradac *et al.* suggest that an "attributional" approach could be adopted in which the hearer might try to assess whether the speaker has been truthful or not, for example. Whilst I think this approach may prove to be more problematic than Bradac *et al.* indicate, it does offer exciting possibilities for undertaking empirically based work perhaps of the kind that John Gumperz (1982a,b) has begun to develop in advancing a sociolinguistic theory of "conversational inferencing". This possibility is clearly recognized by the present authors, who in fact make reference to Gumperz's research, but the issue of precisely how we can establish hearers' inferences about speakers' beliefs is clearly tantalizing enough to warrant further research.

In the final paper of the volume, my own contribution considers the role of the hearer as "listener judge". I have argued elsewhere (see, for example, McGregor, 1985) that it is important to recognize that there are different kinds of listener to talk since the listening role we adopt is likely to affect the nature of any interpretive work we might undertake. Thus, for example, in conversational contexts where we are ratified participants, we presumably listen to talk in order to make use of it in some way; let's say for purposes of comprehension and recall. However, in circumstances where we are overhearers or third-person eavesdroppers, of the kind I have in mind in the current work, our motivation for listening must be different. In such circumstances the listening we undertake might be best thought of as "critical" or "evaluatory" listening; we listen in order to make judgements about the talk of others. What actually motivates our listening is clearly crucial in this respect, since I take it that the interpretive work of the professional analyst is stimulated by a very different purpose than that which may be required by the lay judge. It is something of this difference which is explored in the present paper.

By comparing the analyses of two professional linguists with those of lay listener judges, a framework for inferencing is suggested based upon an examination of the ways in which different individuals arrive at particular judgements in regard to the same body of data.

Particular consideration is given to the functional significance of prosodic and paralinguistic features and discussion centres upon explaining variations that were discovered to exist across and within lay eavesdropper judges and the analysts in question. The need to consider such differences is considered paramount since I argue that analysts ought to provide a framework for inferencing that goes beyond their own subjective platforms. It is also considered to be paramount because in the absence of an adequate conceptualization, analysts always run the risk of either simplifying or falsifying the data. In order to avoid such a risk I argue in conclusion for an interpretive sociolinguistic approach to the analysis of everyday talk that includes listener effect and listener variability as important elements in any interpretive work or interpretive theory that involves the analysis of utterances taken from everyday verbal exchange.

The material presented in this volume does not exhaust either the research possibilities,[9] or disciplinary perspectives,[10] that "language for hearers" raises. However, as a consequence of paying greater heed to the skills and achievements of human ears, the contributions will, I trust, have served to identify and elucidate some of the most critical sites for methodological and theoretical development that language study faces. In choosing to pick up the gauntlet thrown down by Parker-Rhodes I would like to think, in conclusion, that the current series of papers will prove to be only the beginnings of a response. In a phrase, and as I recall Allen Grimshaw urging, "Let's hear it for H!"

Finally, I would like to make some brief but necessary acknowledgements. To Roy Harris grateful thanks are due for encouragement and help to launch the volume in the first place. Thanks are also due to all the contributors, both for their support and of course for providing such stimulating and well-prepared papers. John Pellowe was instrumental in drawing my attention to the importance of hearers some ten years ago, and hence warrants particular mention. Last, but by no means least, I owe special thanks to my family, without whose support I would have enjoyed neither the time nor energy to undertake such a project; I am very much in their debt.

University of Newcastle upon Tyne   Graham McGregor
November 1985

Notes

1. We cite both these terms on this occasion because whilst we recognize that they may be distinguished (as might their associate verbs "hearing" and "listening") according to, say, physiological aspects of audition on the one hand and socio/psycholinguistic aspects of perception and comprehension on the other, they are often simply used interchangeably. The terms may also reflect differing degrees of intentionality in communicative settings. One might well be a "hearer", for example, without necessarily "listening" to what is being said, and of course various different kinds of "listeners" can also be distinguished according to the nature of their role as either "receivers" (a person who receives and interprets the message) or "addressees" (a person who is an *intended* receiver of a message) (Lyons, 1977, p. 34).

Yet although "hearers" can clearly be different kinds of "listener" (a fuller discussion of the kinds of distinction that can be made is presented in McGregor, 1985), it may be worth pointing out that in order to be a "listener" one must *always* be a "hearer". Whilst we acknowledge that there might be a terminological problem here, usage on this occasion is simply left to the practices and/or purposes of individual contributors.

2. Stephen Straight, in personal correspondence, has rightly drawn my attention to the fact that this speaker-oriented bias in linguistic study has been counteracted by a listener bias in much of the rest of what has become known as "cognitive science", even when obviously speaker-orient(at)ed models of grammar have shaped the investigations (see, for example, the papers presented in Freedle, 1977, 1979). One might also make particular note of the hearer-oriented approach of Howard Giles and his associates within the context of their research on language attitude studies (see, for example, Ryan and Giles (1982), wherein there is also an extensive bibliography).

3. The ear does not act like a sound spectrograph, for example, as Bladon (1985) convincingly demonstrates in considering the physical properties of the speech signal of male and female speakers for which the human ear systematically compensates but instrumental analysis does not.

4. Cf. Milroy (1984, p. 207), who points out "that an imbalance of interest in favour of methodology and theory has led to a relative weaknesss of results", though what results have been published are duly recognized as "stimulating and innovatory". A detailed account of the computational methods that were ultimately adopted by the survey and the consequent classification of many of the variables, both linguistic and social, may partially help to offset this criticism, and readers are referred to Jones-Sargent (1983) for details.

5. Roger Brown has now changed his name to Adam Brown. To alleviate confusion all references within this volume are cited in his old name. However, readers interested in contacting him are asked to address any correspondence in his new name.

6. Two further matters related to speaker recognition within legal contexts may be worth raising. The first concerns the use of spectrograms as evidence of speaker identity. In this respect we recall Bladon's remarks on the analytic capacities of instruments compared to the human ear. The second relates to an issue of sociolinguistic methodology which must have confronted the various linguistic experts who were consulted by the police investigating the so-called Yorkshire Ripper case. Whether the tape-recordings sent to the police were hoax or not, one wonders exactly how many and what kind of linguistic variables (phonological, non-segmental, syntactic, lexical) one would need in order to identify a particular individual and/or characterize or locate their accent in terms of regional origin.

7. Something of the difficulties facing the analyst of misunderstandings is presented in Grimshaw (1982), where it is salutory to note that his role as participant in the data extract in question does not aid his *post hoc* analysis. He notes, "As a participant I did not, apparently, know 'what was going on'. As an analyst I believe *something* was going on – I still don't know exactly *what* it was" (Grimshaw, 1982, p. 37).

8. On the particular role of the hearer in speech act design, see Clark and Carlson (1982), who analyse a wide range of situations and speech acts in which the notion of "audience design" is shown to be "a fundamental property of utterances" (1982, p. 342). A revision of speech act theory is consequently proposed to take this property into account. The notion of "audience design" is also the subject of an impressive paper by Bell (1984), who demonstrates how this design affects speaker style.

9. Roy Harris (personal correspondence) has suggested, for example, the need to address the problem of what it might be to attempt to reconstruct discourse rules for a hearer (in the manner of say Labov and Fanshel, 1977), since the nature of this attempt must inevitably face up to the issue of infinite regress. In other words, however the hearer was to gloss his own interpretation of what had gone on in some discourse, this gloss would be in turn subject to further unstated but expected glosses.

10. One thinks of research in applied language studies, artificial intelligence, cognitive psychology, language pathology and sociology for instance.

References

Bell, A. (1984) "Language style as audience design", *Language in Society*, **13**, 145–204.
Bladon, R. A. W. (1985) "Acoustic phonetics, auditory phonetics, speaker sex and speech recognition: a thread". In Fallside, F. and Woods, W. (eds), *Computer Speech Processing*, ch. 2. Cambridge: Cambridge University Press.
Clark, H. H. and Carlson, T. B. (1982) "Hearers and speech acts", *Language*, **58**, 332–373.
Freedle, R. O. (ed.) (1977) *Discourse Production and Comprehension*. New Jersey: Ablex.
Freedle, R. O. (ed.) (1979) *New Directions in Discourse Processing*. New Jersey: Ablex.
Grimshaw, A. D. (1982) "Comprehensive discourse analysis: an instance of professional peer interaction," *Language in Society*, **11**, 15–47.
Gumperz, J. J. (1982a) *Discourse Strategies*. Cambridge: Cambridge University Press.
Gumperz, J. J. (ed.) (1982b) *Language and Social Identity*. Cambridge: Cambridge University Press.
Humphreys-Jones, C. (1986) *A Study of the Types and Structure of Misunderstandings*. Unpublished Ph.D. thesis, University of Newcastle upon Tyne.
Jakobson, R. and Waugh, L. R. (1979) *The Sound Shape of Language*. Brighton: Harvester.
Jones-Sargent, V. (1983) *Tyne Bytes: A Computerised Sociolinguistic Study of Tyneside*. Frankfurt am Main: Verlag Peter Lang.
Labov, D. and Fanshel, D. (1977). *Therapeutic Discourse: Psychotherapy as Conversation*. New York: Academic Press.
Lyons, J. (1977) *Semantics*, vol. 1. Cambridge: Cambridge University Press.
McGregor, G. (1985) "Listening between the lines: towards a model of conversational inferencing", *Belfast Working Papers in Language and Linguistics*, **7**, 44–59.
Milroy, J. (1984) "Sociolinguistic methodology and the identification of speakers' voices in legal proceedings". In Trudgill, P. (ed.), *Applied Sociolinguistics*. London: Academic Press.
Milroy, L. (1984). "Urban dialects in the British Isles". In Trudgill, P. (ed.), *Language in the British Isles*. Cambridge: Cambridge University Press.
Parker-Rhodes, A. F. (1978) *Inferential Semantics*. Sussex: Harvester.
Pellowe, J. (1984) "For our selves we are silent". In Nicholson, C. and Chatterjee, R. (eds), *Tropic Crucible: Self and Theory in Language and Literature*, pp. 37–63. Singapore: Singapore University Press.
Ryan, E. B. and Giles, H. (eds) (1982) *Attitudes towards Language Variation*. London: Arnold.

1

Phonetics for hearers

ANTHONY BLADON

A. The scope of auditory phonetics

A familiar presentation in introductory works on phonetics (e.g. Denes and Pinson, 1963; Gimson, 1980) is in terms of the "speech chain": a visualization of the spoken signal as a chain of events which connects the speaker's idea to the hearer's comprehension of it. Breaking into the speech chain can be done by the investigator at various points, yielding different kinds of data and allowing us to recognize divisions of the field of phonetic (and, indeed, neurolinguistic) enquiry. In the more strictly phonetic parts of the speech chain, a useful and familiar primary distinction can be drawn between articulatory and acoustic phonetics; further subdivisions are also possible. For example, among levels of articulatory analysis we might think experimentally in terms of a level of speech motor programming and control, a level of muscle-unit firings in the speech articulators themselves (involving, probably, electromyographic recordings), and a level of gross articulator position and movement (as observed by X-rays, ultrasound, fibreoptics, palatography and so on).

What of the hearer's ear and brain in this scheme of things? Investigating human speech as it is represented to (or, actually processed by) the hearer is a much less familiar concept. Can we assume that this is because the ear is not amenable to experimental access in a comparable way?

It is of course true that as hearers we do not have sensory feedback enabling us to feel which part of the basilar membrane, for instance, is being excited by a given sound. We cannot use a mirror, as we can in the mouth, to look at the movements of the middle ear ossicles. Even with instrumental assistance and some massive magnification, the eardrum vibrations (which could be observed) would not be easily resolvable into visually distinct patterns. Worse still, to inspect the auditory nerve, while the density of its electrical discharge changes in response to incoming speech, would require anaesthesia and invasive surgery.

It is no surprise, then, that the frameworks and terminology which phonetics has established are based overwhelmingly on articulatory observations. So it is no accident that the vowels [i] and [o] are usually referred to as "front" and "back", in a quasi-articulatory way, even though a much more theoretically satisfactory basis for their classification would be an auditory one.

This chapter will argue, however, that phonetics is now beginning to detach itself from this articulatory bias, and to affirm and develop a new, hearer-orientated base. As a result, phonetic theory should emerge the richer. The familiar maps of phonetic territories (vowel space, distinctive features, properties of phonological systems, etc.) should start to look somewhat different. They will look, it is hoped, more like the ear hears them. But what has changed to make this a feasible programme? There are several factors.

1. Historical limitations of acoustic phonetics

Acoustic phonetics, as epitomized by more than 30 years of work with the sound spectrograph, is not nearly as hearer-orientated as might be thought. Acoustic phonetics has the limitation that it analyzes the sound wave intercepted in air, not in the hearer's ear. The picture of the sound wave which we obtain has consequently been distorted (relative to the hearer) by our analysis instrumentation. We now know that the spectrograph does not bring out too well the properties of the speech signal which the ear attends to. Klatt has recently expressed this rather strongly:

As far as speech perception research is concerned, it is not inconceivable that the sound spectrograph has had an overall detrimental influence over the last 40 years by emphasizing aspects of speech spectra that are probably not direct perceptual cues (and in some cases may not even be resolved by the ear) (Klatt, 1982: 181).

Some examples of auditorily relevant aspects which are not well brought out by conventional spectrography include the spectral filtering characteristics of the ear, and the temporal smear caused by auditory-nerve adaptation. It will be part of the purpose of this paper to survey such matters and, importantly also, the effect they have on the sounds used in languages.

2. Auditory constraints on phonological form

As hinted in the previous sentence, a second reason for strengthening an auditory approach to phonetics is that the ear, just like the mouth and the vocal cords, can be expected to contribute to moulding the form of languages. Phoneticians are often asked why, from the vast inventory of sounds and sound combinations theoretically available to them, languages actually use only a very restricted set. Why do five-vowel systems predominate so? Why is preaspiration so rare? One answer to this kind of question is an auditory answer: it is that the human auditory system can only do so much, and it does some things better than others. Studying these constraints helps us further to understand why languages behave the way they do. This orientation will determine the central objective for Section C (if not, indeed, the whole) of this paper.

3. Auditory analysis: the new context

Things have changed quite a lot since 1950 when Heffner had to leave experimental auditory methods out of his book *General Phonetics* because he was still not equipped with the necessary knowledge:

Clearly, we cannot now describe these integrated auditory and neuromuscular patterns scientifically in terms of the numbers of nerve impulses distributed over various nerve channels and in accordance with a definite sequence in time (Heffner, 1950: 62).

Indeed at that time there was another, quite different, conception of hearer-orientated phonetics. For Pike in 1943, and for a generation of traditional phoneticians after him, "auditory phonetics" was used to mean an impressionistic, listening skill: "to give labels to different types of tone quality as perceived by the ear" (Pike, 1943: 26).

In due course, as related research progressed, some scholars noted the potential within phonetics for an emphasis "both in terms of the physiology of the ear and associated organs of hearing, and in terms of the psychology of perception" – as Robins defined "auditory phonetics" in 1964 (p. 84). Today, as Fant (1984: 15–16) says in his keynote address to the 10th International Congress of Phonetic Sciences,

Phonetics has been computerized and has gained new efficient instrumentation and advanced speech processing methods. . . . Phonetics has now attained somewhat of a technical profile.

Computer models of the auditory processing of speech are therefore now a standard tool (see for example, Karnickaya *et al.*, 1975; Searle *et al.*, 1979; Bladon and Lindblom, 1981; Dolmazon, 1982; Linggard and McCullagh, 1982; Lyon, 1984). The sources of knowledge for these auditory-phonetic models have been cross-disciplinary. Electrophysiological experiments on the mammalian auditory system have had, for the reasons outlined earlier, to be based not on man but on the ear of cat and guinea-pig; but this is an adequate analogue. The work of the past 15 years or so has, at long last, now moved on to using speech stimuli. As a result, much has been learned quite recently about how speech is encoded, both spectrally and temporally, in the cochlea, the auditory nerve, and even beyond. At the same time speech stimuli (together with human listeners) have now come to be more widely used in psycho-acoustic research. There is an encouraging consensus between these two differing paradigms of enquiry.

Simplifying a little, we can say that these hearer-orientated models, in so far as they have direct physiological correlates, are still principally models of the peripheral part of the auditory system. There is much to be learned from simulating computationally how the ear, taking in a speech signal (as conventionally analysed using acoustic methods), warps it. This warping takes numerous forms, including a rescaling and a smearing of information in the frequency domain, as well as a smearing and some sharpening of temporal effects. If the experimenter transforms speech signals in these ways, the output versions ought to look more like those the auditory system passes on to the brain. Using the analogy of the structure of the ear itself, we might say that the observer then sees speech "through an oval window". The results of the auditory transformation exercise ought to stand evaluation against what we know of listeners' perceptual abilities with speech sounds (e.g. which sounds get confused most easily, which artificial stimuli best match a speech sound, and so on).

This chapter is not the forum for the detailed examination of any hearer-orientated model of speech processing. Rather, we will concentrate on the implications upon language systems (in Section C) and upon language use (in Section D). First, though, it may be helpful to have a referenced overview, without full explanation of technicalities, of what seem to this author to be the most promising principles emerging from experimental auditory phonetics, selected in terms of their potential contribution to our linguistic discussion.

B. Principles of auditory phonetics

A first physical principle of the hearer's processing of speech is that information is subjected to more than one kind of analysis at any time. One such analysis is the binaural integration of signals arriving with different phase at each ear, a mechanism which assists with localizing the sound source, but upon which we shall have no more to say.

1. The dynamic processing of the phonetic content of the speech wave runs in parallel in the auditory system, by
   (a) detection of spectral change, and
   (b) analysis of spectral shape (Chistovich et al., 1982).
   First we can expand on (1a).
2. Spectral change in the stream of speech may be of two kinds:
   (a) where its own rate-of-change is important to the hearer;
   (b) where the changing spectrum is of little importance itself, acting instead to emphasize neighbouring regions which are of spectral interest.
   Rapid consonant transitions signalling place of articulation in stops and nasals could exemplify the first type of change; but diphthongs, and probably glides too, are suggestive of interpretation (b) (Bladon, 1984).

Some relevant physiological support comes from Delgutte and Kiang (1984).

3. On/off response asymmetry: spectral changes whose response in the auditory nerve is predominantly an onset of firing are much more perceptually salient than those producing an offset (Tyler *et al.*, 1982).

4. Short-term adaptation: after a rapid onset of auditory nerve discharge at a particular frequency, there is a decay to a moderate level of discharge, even though the same speech sound is continuing to be produced (Delgutte, 1982). An estimate of the decay time constant is 30 ms (Smith, 1979).

5. Neural recovery: silent intervals in speech sounds give rise to a rapid, high-amplitude discharge when interrupted (Delgutte, 1982).

This behaviour can be illustrated in the phonetic contrast between an affricate and a fricative. The affricate [tʃ], for example, contains a silent interval which allows auditory nerve fibres to recover (from earlier responses), and this promotes a very rapid increase in discharge rate at the start of the [ʃ] element of [Vtʃ], as opposed to at the start of the [ʃ] in [Vʃ] (Delgutte and Kiang, 1984).

Principles 2 to 5 have in common that they relate to the temporal organization of dynamically changing speech events. At the same time, we must examine the effects of passing a relatively static spectrum (such as a vowel or a fricative) through the ear as a frequency analyser. The auditory system remoulds the acoustic spectrum in three main ways, all of them non-linear.

6. Frequency warping: a first approximation to the frequency selectivity of the ear is the Bark scale of critical bands (Zwicker and Terhardt, 1980). This scale effects a drastic compression of the high frequencies, in comparison with the familiar Hertz (Hz) scale. This step is such an important one that something like it deserves to be standard practice in all acoustic measurements used by linguists. The conversion to Bark value z from a Hz frequency f can be carried out by a formula, viz .:

$$z = [26.81\,f/(1960 + f)] - 0.53 \qquad \text{(Bark)}$$

(This formula is very accurate in the range 200 to 6700 Hz, Traunmüller, 1983.) For introductory material on the critical band scale and its importance in hearer-orientated phonetics, one can suggest Moore (1982).

7. Amplitude warping: the sound pressure level of a spectrum expressed in dB (as on conventional spectrum analysers) forms a poor basis for the modelling of how vowels are heard (Plomp, 1970; Bladon and Lindblom, 1981). As a first step, which takes into account the ear's frequency-dependent "equal loudness contours", a conversion to loudness level in

phons is recommended. No simple formula exists, but the conversion table is well reported (e.g. Moore, 1982: 45).

8. The filtering (smoothing) characteristics of the ear: an "auditory filter". These reflect the ear's properties of masking, notably the behaviour where a component renders inaudible an adjacent one of higher frequency (the "upward spread of masking", see Zwicker and Feldtkeller, 1967). An auditory filter's shape should at the same time mirror some physiological facts, such as the asymmetric shape of the frequency tuning curves of auditory nerve fibres (Evans, 1972). For some detailed suggestions regarding the implementation of an auditory filter see Houtgast (1974), Patterson (1976), Moore and Glasberg (1983a), Bladon (1985).

   Much debate surrounds the appropriate bandwidth of the auditory filter for speech. In this presentation we shall take a fairly novel position, opting for a very broad bandwidth. This idea, which is spelled out further in Section C, is of extremely great potential for understanding the hearer's considerable role in shaping the speech segments and structures which languages use.

9. Speaker type is, first and foremost, a function of the displacement of the spectrum in auditory space (but not a function of the spectrum shape which is reasonably constant) (Bladon *et al.*, 1984).

   The practical meaning of this as follows. Acoustic comparison of the speech sounds of male and female speakers is a routine requirement for dialectologists, speech therapists, and speech technology researchers. This has not, however, been an easy requirement to meet. The sex-based physical differences are extensive and, as many earlier researchers (e.g. Fant, 1975) have had to conclude, frustratingly non-uniform. Suppose, however, that male/female spectra are re-scaled in auditory space. Then, as established empirically and embodied in the above principle, it turns out that the representation of male/female spectra can be characterized in a straightforward way, which matches the hearer's ability to call them the same or different.

These then, in brief, are the main principles which a hearer-based approach to the analysis of speech sounds can currently offer to phonetics. We have given a summary of information which risks being over-condensed and yet is still by no means exhaustive. But the abiding impressions we would wish to reinforce in the reader's mind are just two. The first is to note just how different the profiles of auditory-nerve activity are, from ordinary spectrograms of the corresponding speech. A simple [i] vowel, for instance, produced continuously and looking continuous on a spectrogram, excites the auditory nerve in a decidedly varying fashion, over time. The neural fibres respond initially very strongly, but then quickly suffer adaptation which lowers their response density. The auditory–spectral pattern of the [i], given the analysing filter of the ear, will be smoother and have just two peaks (all formants above the first being integrated into a single centre of gravity).

The second realization should be the auditory importance of phonetic context. Thus, in one instance, a weakly produced sound can yield a weak temporal response in the ear (such as many instances of [h]); or, in a different context, it can yield a strong response (for example, the comparably weak energy in the aspiration phase of an aspirated stop, which auditorily is greatly boosted by the recovery-permitting silence). In such a case, it could be argued, traditional phonetics has done us a disservice by transcribing both sounds with the same symbol [h].

A general conclusion would be that auditory analysis can offer a novel and often revealing idea of the representation of speech sounds to the hearer. Space, and the priorities of our subject-matter, demand that we turn now to exploring the linguistic implications of these matters. Our procedure in Section C will be to re-examine a number of familiar linguistic phenomena and, by visualizing them through the "oval window", try to illuminate them in terms of hearer-based explanation.

C. Hearer-based effects on sound systems

1. Preaspiration

Beginning with dynamic auditory considerations, and continuing the theme of the [h]-like illustrations just introduced, it is easy to see, for example, that preaspiration is not going to be very auditorily robust. Preaspiration of a stop means, of course, that a preceding vowel will give way to an aspirated phase prior to the stop closure. It would be hard to imagine a speech pattern less favourably designed for the hearer. The aspiration spectrum has essentially the same shape as that of the preceding vowel; there is therefore widespread short-term adaptation (Principle 4) following that vowel. There is no apparent prospect of neural recovery during the preaspiration. Such temporal information as is imparted by preaspiration must in any case depend wholly on the detection of offsets – which does not make for a robust outlook (Principle 3). And so, given that preaspiration suffers from an accumulation of auditory handicaps, it would not be a risky prediction that languages would rarely make use of this auditory-phonetic dinosaur. Indeed, from the 317 languages of the UCLA database (Maddieson, 1981), preaspiration is attested in only 2 or 3.

2. The glottal fricative

The same arguments apply also to the distributional asymmetry of /h/ in languages. It has often been said that syllable-final and word-final occurrences of [h] are much rarer than initial [h] (Holmberg and Gibson, 1979). A related fact is the well-attested report (Lindblom, 1978) from languages having /h/, that a word ending in a vowel (with no glottal stop after it), when played to listeners in reverse, is heard as having an initial [h]. Now there probably is a physiological based tendency for the vocal folds to open, at vowel end, more gradually than they approximate for a vowel beginning; this would contribute to the impression (in the reversal condition) of an initial [h]. However this does not explain why we do not hear the vowel offset as a final [h]. But there is a perfectly good auditory-phonetic reason for these /h/ behaviours. Like preaspiration in the previous paragraph, /h/ after a vowel is highly non-salient, to the hearer. With its vowel-like spectrum it suffers heavily from short-term adaptation by the preceding vowel, and it depends on offset detection, which is inefficient. In short, temporal auditory smear prevents a final [h] from being easily heard. Hence, presumably, its rarity.

3. Nasalization of vowels

A frequent cross-language observation has been that vowels nasalize over-whelmingly more readily before a nasal consonant then they do after it (which is only "occasional", Ruhlen, 1978). Numerous articulatory explana-tions for this asymmetry have been sought (e.g. in differential velocities of velum opening versus closing), but none is really persuasive (Al-Bamerni, 1983). Is there then a hearer-related reason? We suggest that there is. It can be noted that the vowel-to-nasal transition consists much more predomi-nantly of (weak) spectral offsets, with some adaptation, than the reverse sequence nasal-to-vowel does. The vowel-to-nasal transitions can therefore be assumed to be more vulnerable to auditory temporal smear. If this is so, it will more readily provoke a spread of nasalization and thus assert itself in the phonetic pattern of languages.

4. Vocalization of laterals

A very comparable case is provided by the sequence vowel + lateral. Acoustically, the tendency is for a lateral's spectrum to adopt something of the quality of the adjacent vowel, while being somewhat weaker in energy level (Bladon and Al-Bamerni, 1976). Now it can be noted that the transition onto a postvocalic lateral is coded auditorily as mostly neural offsets (whereas a lateral + vowel sequence consists mainly of the more salient onsets). Thus one might predict in vowel + lateral sequences some overt evidence of an extra tendency towards assimilation. Indeed this is just what is observed. We suggest that this is precisely why laterals vocalize so much more readily after a vowel (e.g. in Cockney, Old French, Dutch,

Portuguese, etc.) then they do before a vowel. To the hearer, the lateral quality is less distinct in the postvocalic position.

5. Formation of syllabic consonants

The last two cases demonstrated that where auditory transitions between somewhat similar sounds are temporally indistinct, language can be expected to show an assimilatory effect. If the syllable in question is unstressed, one might predict that the effect would go further. In these respects, conditions are just right for the generation of syllabic consonants. A vowel which "overnasalizes" could readily be heard as a (syllabic) nasal; a vowel + lateral sequence could readily by heard as a "lateral-like vowel", from which the step to a perceived syllabic consonant is indeed short. One would expect these syllabic consonants to form most readily after vowels (because of adaptation), and with nasals and laterals rather than other consonants because their auditory spectra are more similar to a vowel's. Now, from Bell's study (1978) of 85 languages, it is noticeable how well this scenario is borne out. Bell shows (a) that syllabic consonants tend to occur in unstressed positions; (b) that much the commonest syllabic consonants are nasals, followed by laterals; and (c) that these syllabic consonants inevitably result from vowel syncope. It seems fair to conclude that dynamic auditory phonetics can predict this behaviour rather well. Notice in particular the asymmetry: syllabic consonants arise commonly from the syncope of a preceding vowel, but very rarely from the syncope of a following vowel, e.g. in such a sequence as NVC– – –. This can of course be attributed to the relatively greater auditory strength of the spectral onsets, in the NV transition.

6. Dissimilation

Of the observed cross-language trends in consonant cluster types, a few (though obviously not all) can be seen to have a hearer-orientated base. The phenomena which seem most consistently to be attributable to the hearer's role in speech are those of epenthesis and of dissimilation.

Greenberg (1978), from a 104-language sample, showed a strong tendency for sibilants not to combine in sequence. A familiar illustration of this is provided in English which inserts an epenthetic vowel to separate the sibilants in /wɪʃɪz, wɪtʃɪz/ but not otherwise /wɪts, wɪfs/. Now the articulatory difficulty argument does not seem very attractive here, since English happily tolerates /θs/, a sequence with a nonsibilant but surely as difficult to produce as /ʃs/. Rather, we can draw on our knowledge of the auditory-spectral properties of sibilants, and suggest that the succession of sibilant sounds is disfavoured for hearers, because of excessive auditory adaptation. Sibilants have a similar spectral shape to each other, much more so than a sibilant does adjacent to a (low-intensity) front fricative. In this way the hearer's identification of a second sibilant in a sequence of two of them is prejudiced.

A second escape route which languages use, apart from epenthesis, to avoid a succession of sibilants, is dissimilation. For example, German *sechs* [zɛks] "six" shows a dissimilation of sibilant [ç] to [k] before [s]. Compare, however, *sechzehn* [zɛçtse:n] "sixteen" which keeps [ç] before [ts]. This example fits rather neatly with auditory expectations. While the adjacent sibilants dissimilate, the non-adjacent sibilants [ç–s] in *sechzehn* do not: they are robust enough to the hearer, because the intervening plosive permits the necessary neural recovery.

Ohala has advanced the interesting view that dissimilations are all to be laid at the hearer's door. More particularly they are, he claims, the product of the listener's (mistaken) compensations.

I believe it is possible to explain all cases of dissimilation proper, even so-called "distance dissimilation", . . . as due to a misapplication of listeners' reconstructive rules (Ohala, 1981: 188).

Ohala's presentation is worth closer study as a source of evidence for hearer-based phonetics. However we shall not further elaborate Ohala's reasoning here; rather, it seems more important to note a reservation about it. Our dissimilating sibilants cited above are suggestive of an altogether less exotic line of thinking (which, nevertheless, still implicates the hearer). Dissimilations such as our illustration, which concern sounds immediately adjacent and hence within the range of temporal smear effects, may arise not (as Ohala assumes) out of some active compensation process hypothetically attributed to listeners, but, much more probably, as a way simply to avoid an auditory insufficiency. We need suppose no more than that hearers (passively) need to maintain some temporal auditory distinctiveness. Dissimilation can be an expedient to that end.

This discussion of dissimilation combines with the discussions of the preceding sections to form a consistent picture. They all give evidence of an underlying hearer-based influence on the long-term syntagmatic properties of phonetic systems. We saw how auditory adaptation and failure to achieve neural recovery can lead to temporal smear, which hearers resolve in a variety of phonological ways. We also saw illustrations of how the temporal asymmetry, by which adaptation follows (but does not precede) a neural event, and by which energy onsets are much more salient than offsets, turn out to be relatable, in the sound patterns of languages, to a variety of structural asymmetries.

7. Steady-state sounds: general

Turning now to hearer-relevant properties of steady-state sounds, we must first comment further on the general question of the auditory bandwidth within which speech signals are spectrally integrated. Alternatively, put, what is the width of the frequency band, for speech sounds, which the ear can resolve?

The hypothesis we wish to adopt is that energy present in a speech sound spectrum will be integrated together, when it falls within a range of about 3.5 Bark. Only outside the band will the frequency resolution of components of a speech sound be possible. We may also expect that, in passing outside the 3.5 Bark "umbrella", sudden discontinuities will be found in hearers' judgements of appropriate stimuli.

This broad-bandwidth view of auditory integration is still in the early stages of experimental support. It derives initially from Chistovich and Lublinskaya (1979), who reasoned for this analysing filter bandwidth in speech, on the basis of a series of psychoacoustic experiments in which discontinuities were observed at 3.5 Bark intervals, in listeners' judgements of what they termed the "centre of gravity" in vowel sounds. Subsequent evidence from masking studies conducted on vowels (Moore and Glasberg, 1983b; Sidwell and Summerfield, 1985) is also indicative of a broad integration of close-lying formants. Traunmüller's work (1981) on the perception of vowel openness points very strongly in the same direction. Details of these experiments will not be reviewed here.

We move instead to the linguistic implications. If the spectral resolution of the human hearer is constrained in this quite severe way, when analysing speech, then it could be expected that some reflections of it would precondition the nature of sound systems. Phonologies are, in part at least, the servant of their transmission channel. Articulatory capabilities are of course not being denied a role; but auditory robustness must be a prime determinant of a language subsystem which is stable over time.

8. Fricatives

Jassem (1979) investigated the five (voiceless) fricatives of Polish [f ʃ s ç x], which are known to be strongly cued by spectral (not temporal, transitional) information. He used statistical discriminant analysis to determine the border frequencies which would, purely numerically, best enable these five fricatives to be kept apart. His findings broke up the fricatives according to three centres of gravity, of low, medium and high frequency. Now, if we go a stage further and plot the fricatives, thus analysed, on a Bark scale, the picture which emerges is as in Figure 1. The inference is clear, and interesting: the border frequencies detemined by Jassem in Hz turn out to fall very close to 3.5 Bark apart. The language seems to be making use of the internal resolution characteristic of the ear. The spectral shapes of the five fricatives are ergonomically arranged for their distinctiveness to be auditorily resolved, and hence, perhaps, for stability over time.

Perhaps even more interesting to the linguist, however, is that this analysis

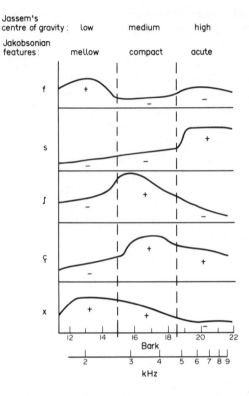

FIG. 1. Polish fricatives, their acoustic spectra and the border frequencies which best separate them, according to Jassem (1979). Thus we derive low, medium and high centres of gravity. Subsequently, the Jakobsonian feature specifications were added. The coincidences suggest an auditorily defined basis for those features.

of Polish fricatives brings out a motivation, previously unsuspected, for the feature system of Jakobson, Fant and Halle. It is well known that, relevant to these fricatives, Jakobson *et al.* (1952) defined the features mellow, compact and acute (each with an oppositely valued member also). Now what relationship is there between the Jakobsonian feature specifications for Polish fricatives and the Jassem analysis (as Bark-scaled by us)? Suppose that we assign to the fricative envelopes of Figure 1 a plus or minus value in accordance with a simple integration principle, determined by the size of an area bounded by a curve and a 3.5 Bark line. The outcome is striking and encouraging to our thinking. The assignment of plus and minus specifications defines three "features" whose function is entirely consistent with the Jakobsonian definitions of mellow, compact and acute. Indeed, the definitions of mellow, compact and acute in fricatives are sharpened up somewhat, because we can now specify their frequency location in auditory space.

The actual feature coefficients (the + and − values) which the Jakobsonian system uses for the Polish fricatives are just those predicted by the integrated energy within those locations.

There are signs here, then, that our newly won knowledge about the hearer may enable us, in part, to define deductively (rather than postulate for linguistics *a priori*) what woud be a likely set of phonetically motivated features. The belief that energy is integrated within a wide band of about 3.5 Bark means that, given the fricative-producing capabilities of the vocal tract, a trio of centres of gravity is a reasonable maximum. This limitation constrains a biologically favoured feature system which languages could be predicted to use. Polish happens to exploit the system rather fully. There are signs, in fact, that the Jakobsonian features can gain an external justification. In addition, they can gain in precision because we can specify boundaries for them in auditory space.

9. Liquids

A fruitful source of acoustic data on liquids is Lehiste's (1964) study of American English /r/ and /l/ allophones. The spectra of these sounds were recently subjected, by Syrdal (1982a), to a hearer-based reanalysis using a 3.5 Bark integration band. Data were taken from 6 male speakers × 15 contexts × 3 allophones [ɫ l ɹ]. Syrdal was interested to discover whether the formant peaks in these liquids would be integrated together or not.

What this analysis revealed was a striking clustering of each of the three sounds in auditory space: dark [ɫ] was set distinctly apart from the other two liquids by having a F2–F1 distance of less than 3.5 Bark, i.e. by those two peaks being integrated together. The postalveolar approximant [ɹ] on the other hand was distinguished from both the /l/ allophones by the auditory integration of its F3–F2 peaks. In this way, exactly as with the Polish fricatives, it could be argued that the auditory space for liquids in American English is optimized.

This is undeniably an appealing kind of interpretation; but how much generality can we allow it? Although based on just one language (unavoid-ably, given the dearth of acoustic data on liquids), there are indications that these data are not untypical. Maddieson (1980) found from a survey of 321 languages that two liquids is much the commonest system size, and that 84 per cent of languages have no more than three liquids. This looks quite consistent with the present analysis.

10. Vowel features

It has just been suggested that there is some evidence to support a hearer-based method for deducing Jakobsonian features. This evidence can now be

TABLE 1. *The patterning of auditory integration in vowels of American English (after Syrdal, 1982b).*

	Auditory spectral definition	
	Integration <3.5 Bark	Resolution >3.5 Bark
F1–F0	i u ɪ ʊ (ɚ)	ɑ a ʌ ɔ ɛ
F3–F2	i ɪ ɛ a ɚ	ɑ ɔ ʊ u ʌ
F4–F3–F2	i	remainder
F4–F3	remainder	ɚ

added to further. Of the features applied to fricative spectra, certain are also said to characterize the vowels. How far are those characterizations predictable from an assumption that vowel energy will be integrated when located within a 3.5 Bark range? This question was posed by Syrdal (1982b), and her interesting findings are reorganized as Table 1. This table is a reanalysis of the male vowel data on American English by Peterson and Barney (1952). Syrdal found that, in these data, vowels were separated into classes by the criteria of auditory integration versus resolution of their formants. Several noteworthy correlations can be seen.

(a) To assume the auditory integration of F1–F0 yields a set of vowels which coincides with the Jakobsonian definition of *"diffuse"*.

(b) When, however, F1–F0 are not integrated, a *"compact"* vowel results. Jakobson's definition of "compact", as having a centrally located formant, is then interpretable as F1 being high enough in frequency to escape the auditory skirt of F0.

(c) The F3–F2 integration defines for us the Jakobsonian *"acute"* vowels. When, however, F2 and F3 are separately resolvable, the "grave" feature is defined.

(d) The *retroflexed* vowel is picked out by the presence of an F4–F3 integration.

These coincidences are quite impressive. The auditory integration hypothesis seems to point to the possibility that vowel features are, in part, biologically determined for the hearer.

We can perhaps look forward to a further bonus for phonological theory. Recall that Jakobson's feature definitions lack quantification. Close vowels are "the most diffuse"; acute vowels have "F2 closer to F3" than do grave ones. But how much closer? Is there a borderline after which a grave vowel quality becomes acute? Is there, in other words, a Jakobsonian "natural class" of grave vowels? The acoustic knowledge of Jakobson's time did not equip him with the wherewithal to answer these questions constructively.

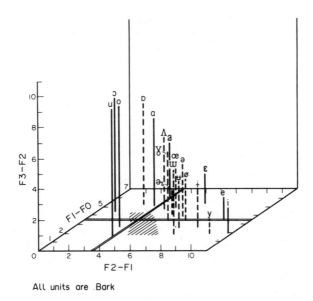

FIG. 2. Cardinal vowels visualized in a three-dimensional space defined by whether there is integration or resolution of their various spectral peaks, within a 3.5 Bark band. Primary cardinal vowels appear with solid lines, secondary ones with dashed lines.

But now it can be seen that the hypothesis of auditory integration permits the formulation of a quantified answer to these questions. For in the psychoacoustic experiments conducted by Chistovich, a sudden perceptual shift took place when formants moved outside the 3.5 Bark bandwidth. There would, therefore, be the expectation of a natural, auditorily determined borderline at such points. In this way an auditory definition of "natural class" can be provided for phonology.

11. Properties of vowel systems

In a forthcoming publication we shall explore these possibilities further. By way of a preview, some preliminary observations can be made here. Figure 2 shows how a set of cardinal vowels, spoken by the author, would be represented in a certain three-dimensional auditory space. The dimensions themselves are not really the most interesting question. We will say no more here than that their choice is motivated by aspects of the preceding discussion, by the work of Fant (1983), and also by the speaker-normalization hypothesis (Bladon *et al.*, 1984) of constant spectral shape (and hence constant inter-formant distances) in a Bark space.

What is important in Figure 2 is that, following the reasoning of the previous section, each of the three dimensions is quantized into zones of integration and of resolution. These define potential borderlines, areas of discontinuity and instability for vowels, as represented to the hearer. Some preliminary observations on this notion can be encapsulated into a rather programmatic summary.

(a) A large "hole" is apparent in the hatched region. This is not due to an articulatory impossibility; nor to an undersampling of vowel space. The alert eye will have noticed that the empty region contains the auditory borderlines on more than one decision. Such a vowel, its formants neither clearly resolved nor integrated, would be predicted to be disfavoured by hearers. Will this auditory discontinuity help us to explain the residual problem shared by all those who have undertaken efforts to simulate and predict vowel systems, namely that they always predict more close vowels (of an [ɨ, ʉ] type) than languages actually use?

(b) The non-retroflexed vowels all tend to line on a surface, visualizable as sloping downward from left to right in the figure. Now, despite the preconceptions of a phonetician's training, the only dimension of arrangement for vowels which investigators have consistently been able to extract from naive listeners, is that of *brightness* (Fischer-Jørgensen, 1967; Butcher, 1974). A ternary division of brightness groupings has been suggested. Will this brightness dimension correlate with the sloping surface described; and will the ternary division have to do with integration/resolution boundaries on this dimension?

(c) The number of *height* distinctions generally observed in back vowels is less than or equal to the number in front vowels (Crothers, 1978: 22). Can this be predicted from our figure, in terms of the number of integration zones coursed through?

(d) *Interior vowels* in Figure 2 are strongly disfavoured in languages; three-quarters of the languages in Crothers' (1978) sample have none at all. Is there a justification for Daniel Jones' term 'secondary' (cardinal vowel) in terms of these interior vowels in the figure? Is it relevant that these vowels are more densely packed, nearer to auditory regions of uncertainty and hence less distinctive to hearers?

(e) Numerous *asymmetries* have been observed in the historical tendencies of pure vowels to *change* in quality. To take an example from many, it is relatively common to find a change [u] > [y] (as in the history of French, Provençal, Norwegian, Swedish and Attic Greek), but rather rare to find the reverse [y] > [u]. Can this be accounted for in terms of the auditory integration hypothesis? Specifically, can we implicate the [u] vowel's proximity to an auditory region of uncertainty, where it is more easily capable of being misheard as "more front" (while [y] is safely anchored far from a point where ambiguity would threaten)?

In the future work which will explore these questions, we expect to answer all of them in the affirmative.

This rather extensive section has drawn together many instances which illustrate how phonetic theory and the understanding of long-term trends in language systems can be enriched from taking the hearer's perspective. The hearer's constraints on speech output are such as to permit a methodological gain also: it becomes feasible for numerous phonetic properties and phenomena to be defined deductively, without the need for them to be postulated *a priori*.

D. Hearers' influence on speech use

A somewhat different complexion can be put on the notion "Phonetics for Hearers" by taking the standpoint, not (as hitherto) of long-term effects upon the patterning of sounds, but of short-term adjustment due to the current communicative context. In this section we will review some of the relevant work under this second head, but only briefly and selectively since some of it falls more naturally into the scope of other contributions to this volume.

One fruitful area of hearer-based phonetic adjustment forms a pivotal part of what has been termed "*accommodation theory*" (Giles and Powesland, 1975). The most commonly observed cases of accommodation have been where a speaker's usage adapts to be more like that of the interlocutor (so-called "convergence"); in other cases, for such reasons as maintaining distance or formality, a speaker may shift divergently towards a less similar style. A great deal of the theoretical progress in this area has been made, and will continue to be made, by social psychology rather than by linguistics or phonetics. Nonetheless, a considerable descriptive phonetic task lies ahead. Some of the most important findings so far, for a hearer-orientated phonetics, have identified numerous speech parameters which subjects modify according to the social context defined by their hearers. The speech variables include (as reviewed and referenced by Giles and Smith, 1979): segmental sounds, especially vowels in English; articulation rate; pause length; utterance length; and overall intensity level.

Let us pick up some of these phonetic variables for further comment. First, *speech tempo*, as expressed by articulation rate and pausing rate. Quite a lot of observed data demonstrating speech tempo change would have to be excluded as irrelevant here, because they are not predominantly hearer-orientated. Among such instances would be the sports (especially racing) commentary with its accelerando markers of speaker excitement (Fónagy and Magdics, 1960). In part, this same exclusion should probably apply to tempo markers of speech styles such as ceremonial language, official announcements, formal addresses (Crystal, 1975: 88), elliptical versus explicit style (in Russian, Shapiro, 1968), and folk tales (which in Mojave have to be in rapid, staccato tempo – Devereux, 1949). All of these are communicative contexts where the tempo adaptations are style-defining but not predominantly for the hearer's benefit. What, then, are we left with? Communicative contexts which do illustrate speech tempo modifications primarily for the hearer's benefit include speaking against a noisy background, speaking to foreigners, and speaking to babies. Against noise, a reduction in speech tempo has not consistently been confirmed (Hanley and Steer, 1949; Pisoni *et al.*, 1985): it seems to be an optional strategy. Likewise, in adapting one's speech to foreigner listeners, changes in tempo for the recipient's benefit are reported only in sporadic cases (Katz, 1981; Clyne, 1981). In talking to babies and young children it is more consistently found that speech tempo is changed – as has been reported in Marathi (Kelkar, 1964) and in several other languages (the contributions of Snow and Ferguson, 1977). However this lento phenomenon is never the most striking baby-talk feature which authors report, and sometimes its occurrence is only "occasional" (Rūķe- Draviņa, 1977).

Such reductions in speech tempo as do occur in foreigner talk and in baby talk, are apparently not so much in articulation rate itself, as in total speaking rate, due to increases in pausing time (results summarized by Freed, 1981). This is consistent, of course, with tempo variations in speech in general (as shown classically by Goldman-Eisler, 1961). These observations jointly suggest that rate of articulation is not one of the variables which is strongly constrained by hearers' needs and capabilities. A clue to the reason for this lies in the observation that, under most conditions, speech remains intelligible even when speeded up by a factor of three. Hearers have a substantial inbuilt safety margin in coping with rapid articulation, and so hearers are unlikely to be a factor in defining its gross limits. In addition to this, hearers are apparently well able to handle the spontaneous demands for time-normalization in speech, due to the fact that lento and allegro versions of words or utterances are an integral, everyday part of prosodic and of inter-speaker differences. The discussion can be summed up by saying that there is little, but not much, evidence of a role for the hearer in shaping the observed patterns of adjustments of speech tempo.

Let us turn next to *whispered speech*. Here, clearly, the hearer is a main determinant of its use – whether due to extreme proximity, a need for confidentiality, voice disguise (Conklin, 1959), or in baby talk (Garnica, 1977). To help us to judge the value of whisper material to phonetic theory, let us look first at some descriptive phonetic facts. Phoneticians have traditionally been content to consider that, in whispered speech, voiceless sounds are not altered (Abercrombie, 1967: 28). In terms of what the hearer hears, this claim seems uncontentious (though at the physiological detail level there is undoubtedly more to say). Voiced segments, of course, become noise-excited, losing their harmonic structure but (with a slight proviso to be addressed in a moment) retaining the resonance shaping of the spectrum. Unlike in shouted speech, very marked formant frequency shifts are not seen in whispered speech. The spectral differences due to speaker sex are maintained (Schwartz and Rine, 1968). Formant bandwidths tend to increase, due to a greater transglottal coupling (Fant, 1972), but these are known to be of little perceptual significance.

Consequently, the hearer-motivated compensations in whispered speech are essentially restricted to those made due to a loss of pitch information. Compensating for lost pitch can be done only to a limited extent: the two main mechanisms (Meyer-Eppler, 1957) are increased intensity in the form of inter-formant noise (with a consequently smoother spectral envelope); and spectral shift. The spectral shifts, however, are not large: from our analysis of the data of Meyer-Eppler and that of Kallail and Emanuel (1984), the shifts are normally less than 1 Bark. Since male/female speech spectra are 1 Bark different (Bladon *et al.*, 1984), we see that a mechanism exists in whisper such that speaker-sex information can be protected from disruption. Conceivably, there could be some social purposiveness in this.

Apart, however, from this interesting matter of speakers' attempts to compensate in whispered speech for lack of pitch information, it does seem from this summary of knowledge about whispered speech that the area does not promise much else in the way of development ground for new aspects of phonetic theory, strictly interpreted. On the other hand, sociolinguistic theory may have more to gain from studying whispered speech: the social contexts of the use of whisper are probably partly but not wholly universal and they remain a research issue.

We turn next to a generally more fruitful area of hearer-based phonetic adjustment: that of *loud speech*. Numerous everyday conditions require the use of loud speech, including speaking against a noisy background, from a long way away, over a poor telephone line, to a foreigner, or to a hearing-impaired person. It is known that variations in loudness of output have profound, nonlinear consequences on the speech spectrum. Yet hearers compensate for them. Consequently, for those engaged in research on applied questions in this area, such as the design of hearing aids, digital coding of speech, or automatic speech recognition, an understanding of the perceptual compensations invoked by the hearer is of great importance.

At the time of writing, we are still some considerable way from that understanding. The modest effort that has taken place, has been directed primarily at a description of the actual properties of loud speech itself. Even that work has been restricted to vowels; we know nothing of the changes undergone by consonants in loud speech.

Most often identified has been the substantial increase in F1 frequency in loudly spoken vowels (Rostolland, 1982; Kiukaanniem *et al.*, 1982;

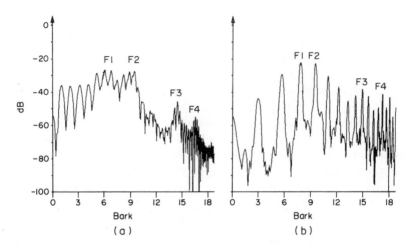

FIG. 3. Narrow-band spectra of a vowel [a] in "fire", (a) at normal loudness and (b) shouted; microphone distances 15 cm and 100 cm respectively. See text for comment on the substantial spectral differences.

Schulman, 1985). The jaw opens more widely in loud speech, bringing with it a lowering of tongue height, which is consistent with the F1 increase (Schulman, 1985). At the same time, loud speech invariably results in a higher voice pitch; and, indeed, the predictable increase in fundamental frequency (F0) does occur, and has approximately the same magnitude as the F1 increase (Kiukaanniem *et al.*, 1982, Traunmüller, 1985). Upper formants, including F2, do not substantially move in frequency. In Figure 3 these various effects can be detected in a normal versus loud (shouted) version of an [a] vowel. In the loud version, panel (b), the harmonics become more widely spaced, as F0 (and F1) increase by about 1.8 Bark; at the same time, since F2, F3 and F4 increase only slightly, the F2–F1 distance is reduced by some 2 Bark.

How, in the face of these non-uniform spectral shifts, does the hearer maintain a constancy of vowel identification? There is no problem with vowel openness, since the best correlate of openness, the F1–F0 distance in Bark space, remains largely unchanged (Traunmüller, 1981). But, as is illustrated in Figure 3, the F2–F1 distance reduces markedly in loud speech, perhaps by several Bark. This ought, *prima facie*, to present a direct conflict with the cueing of retraction or rounding of vowels. However, it does not. Hearers resolve the conflict.

The answer to how they do this is not yet known. Figure 3 guides us, however, towards one possible speculation. It is noticeable that a further concomitant of loud speech is a change in spectral balance or tilt. The shouted vowel has an envelope in which the high-frequency components, say between 12 and 19 Bark, fall off much less steeply. We may suppose that this tilt cue (which otherwise plays a very minor role for the speech listener) can be recruited to signal a speech loudness decision; and that, if loud, the hearer can scale the F2–F1 distance accordingly. The experiment, manipulating spectral tilts so as to test this idea, currently remains to be done.

E. Conclusion

This chapter has tried to illustrate what a "Phonetics for Hearers" can contribute to linguistic theory and description. As such, "phonetics for hearers" does not stand instead of, but alongside, a more traditional methodology of "phonetics for speakers". Both orientations have an important part to play in explaining speech behaviour.

We have argued that a hearer-based phonetics, distilled into a set of principles which derive from cross-disciplinary research in auditory physiology, psychoacoustics and social psychology, is making useful progress in specifying the hearer's role in defining important properties (including the boundary conditions) of phonological structure and speech output. Equipped with this improved "window on the ear", we have found new possibilities to help answer the question why languages favour certain aspects of vowel, liquid and fricative systems, while disfavouring others; why dissimilation occurs; why there are directional asymmetries in a variety of processes such as vowel nasalization, pre- and postaspiration, syllabic consonant formation, and vowel change. We were able to suggest an (auditory) biological basis for the definition and refinement of a number of distinctive features. We have also begun to understand more about listeners' compensations for short-term changes to the speech signal, in different communicative contexts: for example, compensations for a change of speaker sex, or of speech loudness.

Much remains to be done, both in analytical terms and in respect of further implications of this orientation. A personal view of some of the most interesting missing links would include the incorporation of a hearer-based theory of the analysis of linguistic pitch; numerous cases of the integration of multiple cues; and the validation of constructs of phonological theory such as markedness and strength hierarchies. Meanwhile, considering the auditory insights still in prospect and those outlined in this chapter, it may not be unreasonable to say that phonetic theory can hope to gain a new methodology.

References

Abercrombie, D. (1967) *Element of General Phonetics*. Edinburgh: Edinburgh University Press.
Al-Bamerni, A. H. A. (1983) "Oral, velic and laryngeal coarticulation across languages". D.Phil. thesis, University of Oxford.
Bell, A. (1978) "Syllabic consonants". In Greenberg J. H. (ed.), *Universals of Human Language*, vol. 2: *Phonology*. Stanford: Stanford University Press, pp. 153–201.
Bladon, R. A. W. (1984) "Rapid versus slow spectral change: implications for dynamic auditory processing of speech", *Proc. Inst. Acoust* **6**, 275–280.
Bladon, R. A. W. (1985) "Acoustics phonetics, auditory phonetics, speaker sex and speech recognition: a thread". In Fallside, F. and Woods, W. (eds), *Computer Speech Processing*, ch. 2. Cambridge: Cambridge University Press.
Bladon, R. A. W. and Al-Bamerni, A. (1976) "Coarticulation resistance in English /l/. *J. Phonetics*, **4**, 137–150.
Bladon, R. A. W. and Lindblom, B. (1981) "Modeling the judgement of vowel quality differences", *J. Acoust. Soc. Am.* **69**, 1414–1422.
Bladon, R. A. W., Henton, C. G. and Pickering, J. B. (1984) "Towards an auditory theory of speaker normalization", *Lang. Communication*, **4**, 59–69.
Butcher, A. (1974) "Brightness, darkness and the dimensionality of vowel perception", *J. Phonet.*, **2**, 153–160.
Chistovich, L. A. and Lublinskaya, V. V. (1979) "The center of gravity effect in vowel spectra and critical distance between the formants: psychoacoustical study of the perception of vowel-like stimuli", *Hearing Res.*, **1**, 185–195.
Chistovich, L. A., Lublinskaya, V. V., Malinnikova, T. G., Ogorodnikova, E. A., Stoljarova, E. I. and Zhukov, S. J. (1982) "Temporal processing of peripheral auditory patterns of speech. In Carlson, R. and Granström, B. (eds), *The Representation of Speech in the Peripheral Auditory System*, pp. 165–180. Amsterdam: Elsevier Biomedical.
Clyne, M. (1981) "Second generation foreigner talk in Australia", *Int. J. Soc. Lang.*, **28**, 69–80.
Conklin, H. C. (1959) "Linguistic play in its cultural context", *Language*, **35**, 631–636.
Crothers, J. (1978) "Typology and universals of vowel systems. In Greenberg, J. H. (ed.), *Universals of Human Language*, vol. 2: *Phonology*, pp. 93–152. Stanford: Stanford University Press.
Crystal, D. (1975). *The English Tone of Voice*. London: Arnold.
Delgutte, B. (1982) "Some correlates of phonetic distinctions at the level of the auditory nerve". In Carlson, R. and Granström, B. (eds), *The Representation of Speech in the Peripheral Auditory System*, pp. 131–150. Amsterdam: Elsevier Biomedical, 131–150.
Delgutte, B. and Kiang, N. Y. S. (1984). "Speech coding in the auditory nerve: IV. Sounds with consonant-like dynamic characteristics", *J. Acoust. Soc. Am.*, **75**, 897–907.
Denes, P. B. and Pinson, E. N. (1963) *The Speech Chain*. Bell Telephone Labs.
Devereux, G. (1949) "Mohave voice and speech mannerisms", *Word*, **5**, 268–272.
Dolmazon, J.-M. (1982) "Representation of speech-like sounds in the peripheral auditory system in the light of a model". In Carlson, R. and Granström, B. (eds), *The Representation of Speech in the Peripheral Auditory System*, pp. 151–163. Amsterdam: Elsevier Biomedical.
Evans, E. F. (1972) "The frequency response and other properties of the guinea-pig cochlear nerve", *J. Physiol.*, **226**, 262–287.
Fant, G. (1972) "Vocal tract wall effects, losses and resonance bandwidths", *RIT Stockholm, STL-QPSR* 2-3/1972, 28–52.
Fant, G. (1975) "Non-uniform vowel normalization", *RIT Stockholm, STL-QPSR* 2-3/1975, 1–19.
Fant, G. (1983) "Feature analysis of Swedish vowels: a revisit", *RIT Stockholm, STL-QPSR* 2-3/1983, 1–19.
Fant, G. (1984) "Phonetics and speech technology". In Van den Broecke, M. P. R. and Cohen, A. (eds), *Proceedings of the Tenth International Congress of Phonetic Sciences*, pp. 13–24. Dordrecht: Foris.

Fischer-Jørgensen, E. (1967) "Perceptual dimensions of vowels", In *To Honor Roman Jakobson*, **1**, 667–671.
Fonagy, I. and Magdics, K. (1960). "Speed of utterance in phrases of different lengths", *Lang. Speech*, **4**, 179–192.
Freed, B. F. (1981). "Foreigner talk, baby talk, native talk", *Int. J. Soc. Lang.*, **28**, 19–39.
Garnica, O. K. (1977). "Some prosodic and paralinguistic features of speech to young children". In Snow, C. E. and Ferguson, C. A. (eds), *op. cit.*, pp. 63–88.
Giles, H. and Powesland P. F. (1975) *Speech Style and Social Evaluation*. London: Academic Press.
Giles, H. and Smith, P. (1979) "Accommodation theory: optimal levels of convergence". In Giles, H. and St. Clair, R. N. (eds), *Language and Social Psychology*, pp. 45–65. Oxford: Blackwell.
Gimson, A. C. (1980) *An Introduction to the Pronunciation of English*. London: Arnold.
Goldman-Eisler, F. (1961) "The significance of changes in the rate of articulation", *Lang. Speech*, **10**, 122–132.
Greenberg, J. H. (1978) "Some generalizations concerning initial and final consonant clusters". In Greenberg, J. H. (ed.), *Universals of Human Language*, vol. 2: *Phonology*, pp. 243–279. Stanford: Stanford University Press.
Hanley, T. D. and Steer, M. D. (1949) "Effect of level of distracting noise upon speaking rate, duration and intensity," *J. Speech Hearing Disorders*, **14**, 363–368.
Heffner, R. M. S. (1950) *General Phonetics*. Madison: University of Wisconsin Press.
Holmberg, E. and Gibson, A. (1979) "On the distribution of [h] in the languages of the world", *Phonet. Exper. Res. Inst. Ling. Univ. Stockholm*, **1**, 68–82.
Houtgast, T. (1974) "Auditory analysis of vowel-like sounds", *Acustica*, **31**, 320–324.
Jakobson, R., Fant, G. and Halle, M. (1952) *Preliminaries to Speech Analysis*. Cambridge, Mass.: MIT Press.
Jassem, W. (1979). "Classification of fricative spectra using statistical discriminant functions". In Lindblom, B. and Öhman, S. (eds), *Frontiers of Speech Communication Research*, pp. 77–91. London: Academic Press.
Kallail, K. J. and Emanuel, F. W. (1984) "Formant frequency differences between isolated whispered and phonated vowel samples produced by female subjects", *J. Speech Hearing Res.*, **27**, 245–251.
Karnickaya, E. G., Mushnikov, V. N., Slepokurova, N. A. and Zhukov, S. J. (1975) "Auditory processing of steady-state vowels". In Fant, G. and Tatham, M. A. A. (eds), *Auditory Analysis and Perception of Speech*, pp. 37–53. London: Academic Press.
Katz, J. T. (1981) "Children's second-language acquisition: the role of foreigner talk in child-child interaction", *Int. J. Soc. Lang*, **28**, 53–68.
Kelkar, A. (1964). "Marathi baby-talk", *Word*, **20**, 40–54.
Kiukaanniem, H., Siponen, P. and Mattila, P. (1982) "Individual differences in the long term speech spectrum", *Folia Phoniatrica*, **34**, 21–28.
Klatt, D. H. (1982) "Speech processing strategies based on auditory models". In Carlson, R. and Granström, B. (eds), *The Representation of Speech in the Peripheral Auditory System*, pp. 181–196. Amsterdam: Elsevier Biomedical.
Lehiste, I. (1964) *Acoustical Characteristics of Selected English Consonants*. Bloomington: Indiana University Press.
Lindblom, B. (1978). "Phonetic aspects of linguistic explanation", *Studia Linguistica*, **32**, 137–153.
Linggard, R. and McCullagh, P. (1982) "Neural firing model of the basilar membrane, *Proc. Inst. Acoust. (Autumn Conference)*, A6.1–A6.4.
Lyon, R. F., (1984) "Computational models of neural auditory processing", *IEEE Trans. ASSP*, 36.1.1–36.1.4.
Maddieson, I. (1980) "A survey of liquids", *UCLA Working Papers in Phonetics*, **50**, 93–112.
Maddieson, I. (1981) "UPSID: The UCLA Phonological Segment Inventory Database: Data and Index", *UCLA Working Papers in Phonetics*, **53**.
Meyer-Eppler W. (1957) "Realization of prosodic features in whispered speech", *J. Acoust. Soc. Am.*, **29**, 104–106.
Moore, B. C. J. (1982) *An Introduction to the Psychology of Hearing*. London: Academic Press.

24   Anthony Bladon

Moore, B. C. J. and Glasberg, B. R. (1983a) "Suggested formulae for calculating auditory-filter bandwidths and excitation patterns", *J. Acoust. Soc. Am.*, **74**, 750–753.

Moore, B. C. J. and Glasberg, B. R. (1983b) "Masking patterns for synthetic vowels in simultaneous and forward masking", *J. Acoust. Soc. Am.*, **73**, 906–917.

Ohala, J. (1981) "The listener as a source of sound change". In Masek, C. S., Hendrick, R. A. and Miller, M. F. (eds), *Papers from the Parasession on Language and Behavior* (Chicago, Chicago Linguistic Society), pp. 178–203.

Patterson, R. D. (1976) "Auditory filter shapes derived with noise stimuli", *J. Acoust. Soc. Am.*, **59**, 640–654.

Peterson, G. E. and Barney, H. (1952) "Control methods used in a study of the vowels", *J. Acoust. Soc. Am.*, **24**, 175–184.

Pike, K. L. (1943) *Phonetics*. Ann Arbor: University of Michigan Press.

Pisoni, D. B., Bernacki, R. H., Nusbaum, H. C. and Yuchtman, M. (1985) "Some acoustic-phonetic correlates of speech produced in noise", *IEEE Proc.* ICASSP 1985, pp. 1581–1584.

Plomp, R. (1970) "Timbre as a multidimensional attribute of complex tones". In Plomp, R. and Smoorenburg, G. F. (eds), *Frequency Analysis and Periodicity Detection in Hearing*, pp. 397–414. Leiden: Sijthoff.

Robins, R. H. (1964) *General Linguistics: An Introductory Survey*. London: Longman.

Rostolland, D. (1982) "Acoustic features of shouted voice", *Acustica*, **50**, 118–125.

Ruhlen, M. (1978) "Nasal vowels". In Greenberg, J. H. (ed.), *Universals of Human Language*, vol. 2, Phonology, pp. 203–241. Stanford: Stanford University Press.

Rūķe-Draviņa, V. (1977) "Modifications of Latvian speech to young children. In Snow, C. E. and Ferguson, C. A., *op. cit.*, pp. 237–253.

Schwartz, M. F. and Rine, H. E. (1968) "Identification of speaker sex from isolated whispered vowels", *J. Acoust. Soc. Am.*, **44**, 1736–1737.

Schulman, R. (1985) "Articulatory targeting and perceptual constancy of loud speech". Paper given at Franco-Swedish Seminar on Speech, Grenoble, April 1985.

Searle, C. L., Jacobson, J. Z. and Rayment, S. G. (1979) "Stop consonant discrimination based on human audition", *J. Acoust. Soc. Am.*, **65**, 799–809.

Shapiro, M. (1968) *Russian Phonetic Variants and Phono-stylistics*. University of California Press.

Sidwell, A. and Summerfield, Q. (1985) "The effect of enhanced spectral contrast on the internal representation of vowel-shaped noise", *J. Acoust. Soc. Am.*, **78** (to appear).

Smith, R. L. (1979) "Adaptation, saturation and physiological masking in single auditory-nerve fibers", *J. Acoust. Soc. Am.*, **65**, 166–178.

Snow, C. E. and Ferguson, C. A. (1977). *Talking to Children*. Cambridge: Cambridge University Press.

Syrdal, A. K. (1982a) "Frequency analyses of syllable initial and final liquids spoken by American English talkers", *J. Acoust. Soc. Am.*, **71**, S105.

Syrdal, A. K. (1982b) "Frequency analyses of American English vowels", *J. Acoust. Soc. Am.*, **71**, S105.

Traunmüller, H. (1981) "Perceptual dimension of openness in vowels", *J. Acoust. Soc. Am.*, **69**, 1465–1474.

Traunmüller, H. (1983) *On Vowels: Perception of Spectral Features, Related Aspects of Production and Sociophonetic Dimensions*. Stockholm: University of Stockholm.

Traunmüller, H. (1985) "The role of the fundamental and the higher formants in the perception of speaker size, vocal effort and vowel openness. Paper given at Franco-Swedish Seminar on Speech, Grenoble, April 1985.

Tyler, R. S., Summerfield, Q., Wood, E. J. and Fernandes, M. A. (1982) "Psychoacoustic and phonetic temporal processing in normal and hearing-impaired listeners", *J. Acoust. Soc. Am.*, **72**, 740–752.

Zwicker, E. and Feldtkeller, R. (1967) *Das Ohr als Nachrichtenempfänger*. Stuttgart: Hirzel.

Zwicker, E. and Terhardt, E. (1980) "Analytical expressions for critical-band rate and critical bandwidth as a function of frequency", *J. Acoust. Soc. Am.*, **68**, 1523–1524.

2

Establishing speech varieties of conurbations. I: Theoretical position[1]*

Note from John Pellowe, July 1985

(1) This paper is reprinted exactly in the form in which it was first circulated underground in 1970 (but with typographical and stylistic errors silently emended). Together with its two companions, referred to as "Pellowe, forthcoming *a, b*", it formed the core of a successful application to the SSRC (UK), and of a Seminar on Urban Speech Surveying held in Newcastle upon Tyne in 1970. Considerable parts of it reappeared in Pellowe *et al.* (1972) A dynamic modelling of speech variation: the urban (Tyneside) linguistic survey, *Lingua* **30**, 1–30 which itself had been prepared at J. B. Pride's request for his and Holmes' *Sociolinguistics: selected readings*, but which was rejected by him on the grounds of being too difficult for a student audience. (The appropriation of other minds!) The paper was based on doctoral research which remains unsubmitted to the establishment machinery.

Whilst "Pellowe, forthcoming *a, b, d*" may be read as "Pellowe, 1970*a, b, d*" since they were produced and circulated (their place of publishing and "publisher" being "Newcastle upon Tyne: University School of English"), "Pellowe forthcoming *c*" was never written.

In Section 2 the reader may prefer to save time by skipping "A simplified picture . . . as well as whole-system variation", i.e. the single-spaced summary of Libermann *et al.*, 1967.

(2) I do not seem to have substantial disagreements with the person who wrote this 15 years ago, or with the thinking which was its source and which was done 17 years ago.

It seems simple-minded to write it, but a given speaker, speaking on a particular occasion, is construed differently by different hearers who are co-present on that occasion. Failure to think through the consequences of this truism is what prevents one of the relevant understandings of what is written here from being created by the reader.

My currently active selves (those I am aware of) are less interested in methodological rigour and in data than those former ones; having too slowly come to realize that our subconscious assumptions about the world (which

Copyright of this article rests with the author.

* Superscript numbers refer to notes at end of chapter.

determine both "method" and "data") are where creativity can have its best effects. Let us not forget the inherent analyticity of Nietzsche's remark: "I mistrust all systematisers and avoid them. The will to a system is a lack of integrity."

My present thinking about hearers is expressed in: Pellowe, J. (1984) For our selves we are silent. In Nicholson, C. and Chatterjee, R. (eds), *Tropic Crucible: self and theory in language and literature*. Singapore: Singapore University Press, pp. 37–63; Pellowe, J. (1986) Hearers' intentions. In McGregor, G. and White, R. S. (eds), *The Art of Listening*. London: Croom Helm, pp. 1–12.

0. The Tyneside Linguistic Survey (T.L.S.) was first planned by Professor Barbara Strang in 1963, and a programmatic outline was published later (Strang, 1968). A pilot feasibility study was conducted between 1966 and 1967 (Pellowe, 1967). The T.L.S. seeks as its general goals:

(1) to establish a synchronically exhaustive description of the speech varieties of the Tyneside conurbation;
(2) to examine the degree of overlap or co-extensiveness between the system of varieties and the dispersion of informants on social attributes;
(3) to assess changes, through time, to either (1) or (2);
(4) to apply, where relevant, these findings and methods to specific situations, groups and organizations.

In this paper I explore the theoretical position which is relevant to the prosecution of research under (1) and (2) above. In two subsequent papers (Pellowe, forthcoming *a*, *b*), I shall try to show the relationship between this theoretical position and the actual procedures developed from it and used in the T.L.S., and to indicate the relationship between the theoretical position with its associated methods and wider sociolinguistic considerations.

A "speech variety" is here treated as an analytic construct, and therefore I shall only characterize it operationally as I proceed.

1. The theoretical position depends upon a model of the discriminatory abilities of the ("naive") hearer. Hearers derive rather specific non-linguistic information about their interlocutors from characteristics of the apprehended acoustic signal. It may be information about the social status of the speaker relative to that of the hearer (Labov, 1966); or about the geographical origin of the speaker; or about the value which the speaker is ascribing to the hearer's company (Pellowe, forthcoming *c*); or about the psychological or physiological state of the speaker (Pittenger *et al.*, 1960); or about the unique (known) identity of an unseen speaker; or about the high similarity (in one or more linguistic systems) between the speaker and the unique, well-known profile of another speaker's realization string; or any combination of these various kinds of information. (This is not an exhaustive list, it entirely omits, for instance, the hearer's understanding of affect. I do not claim that *all* hearers are equally proficient, nor that those who are proficient derive all this information all the time: there is much research in analogue modelling of neurophysical function which suggests multiple modes of selective (means–ends) perception. These abilities pose subtle problems of interpretation for the linguist. For instance, suppose that a hearer encounters a variety which contains some localized variants, but that he has neither knowledge, nor linguistic experience, of the locality in question: nevertheless the hearer still seems to be capable of deducing information (whether reliable or not) about the relative social status of the speaker. That is, even if he does not know either the systematic value of an item (in terms of its contrastivity), or its local social relevance, he still effects some comparison between that part of the speaker's variety and his own, and makes some judgement as a result of the comparison. The mechanism involved may be a probabilistic estimate of "equivalence" (in some undefined sense) to a localized variety whose distribution and social meanings he knows well. I return to a finer examination of these interpretative problems in the third paper (Pellowe, *b*) and return now to the impact which these sensitive, auditorily based judgements have on models of the hearer. I shall, for the moment, make one relatively weak, general assumption, namely: that much non-linguistic information is derived from a function of dissimilarity between the acoustic signal and the hearer's linguistic experience as a speaker. This dissimilarity function obtains its non-linguistic value by being mapped into an array of homologous functions with known non-linguistic correlates.

2.   I want now to examine, in some detail, the consequences of this assumption with respect to one model of the hearer as a *decoder*, that is a model which does not overtly account for the derivation of *non*-linguistic information from a linguistic, continuous signal. The model proposed by Liberman *et al.* (1967) is perhaps the most central to my purpose here, since it incorporates much of the acoustic and articulatory knowledge that we have; their account is less specifically a machine-analogue model than that of Stevens (1960), though the two models have underlying characteristics in common.

A simplified picture of their model (Liberman *et al.*, 1967) is provided by the following considerations:

(1) The temporal resolving power of the ear could not process a simple linear string of phonemes at the rate they are normally emitted in conversation.

(2) The phonemes are restructured in the realization string by means of acoustic cues. That is, the phonemes are *encoded* by transforming linearity to simultaneity. These transformations appear to be necessary for some phonemic elements (stops e.g.) to a greater extent than for others (vowels e.g.).

(3) Fully encoded phonemes seem to depend for their decoding upon some

left-hemisphere-specific mechanism.[2] Steady-state vowels, whether synthetic or natural, together with non-speech sounds, are not hemisphere specific. However, vowels in normal conversation probably are encoded, and thus also depend on a specific mechanism for decoding.

(4) In terms of this hemisphere-specific mechanism, "research with some of the encoded phonemes has shown that they are categorical, not only in the abstract linguistic sense, but as immediately given in perception. Consider, first, that in listening to continuous variations in acoustic signals, one ordinarily discriminates many more stimuli than he can absolutely identify. Thus, we discriminate about 1200 different pitches, for example, though we can absolutely identify only about seven. Perception of the restructured phonemes is different in that listeners discriminate very little better than they identify absolutely; that is to say, they hear the phonemes but not the intraphonemic variations" (Liberman et al., 1967).

(5) The production–perception mechanism is postulated with four sets of rules, each of which, through their sequence, ultimately depends on phonemes being represented by sets of sub-phonemic features which, in turn, are "assumed to exist in the central nervous system as implicit instructions to separate and independent parts of the motor machinery" (op. cit.). These sets of rules are here merely listed.

1. Phonemic rules.
2. Neuromotor rules (impulses to muscles) ⎫ 1 to 1
3. Myomotor rules (muscle contractions) ⎱ 1 to 1
4. Articulatory rules (tract shapes) ⎰ many to few
5. Acoustic rules (wave form) ⎰ 1 to 1

The crucial point is that the asymmetrical relationship between muscle contractions and tract shapes is precisely the kind of situation in which information compression could take place.

This is a, possibly violent, abbreviation of a long article, but it provides enough information against which to measure the possible ways in which the hearer uses intra-phonemic (and in general within-element), as well as whole-system, variation.

For my purposes, however, this model leaves certain abilities of the hearer unaccounted for. In particular, one has to ask:

(a) how is it that the hearer has apparently neither more nor less difficulty in deriving non-linguistic information from speakers with very different phonemic rules from himself, than he has in deriving it from speakers with slightly different phonemic rules from himself?;

(b) how is that two varieties which differ in a similar degree from the hearer's, and have similar social meaning, can nevertheless be diagnosed by radically different kinds of variants?

That is, firstly, the point on the way up the decoding hierarchy at which a disparity between incoming and "own" realizations occurs, does not seem to affect the confidence with which the hearer voices an opinion; and secondly, the discriminable range of a particular element does not seem to bear any simple predetermining relationship to its diagnostic power.

I want here to propose and expand three further characteristics of the model of the hearer, to cover my weak assumption of a dissimilarity function for which, however, Liberman *et al.* (1967) are not responsible; the implications of these further postulates cover the above-mentioned hearer abilities.

Firstly, the H is not constrained to *de*code by means of using the sets of rules in the reverse order to that in which he uses them to *en*code. Chomsky and Miller (1963) write "identifying an observed acoustic event as such-and-such a particular phonetic sequence is, in part, a matter of determining its syntactic structure (to this extent, understanding it)".

Secondly, if an equivalent amount of non-linguistic information is obtained by a given hearer, no matter what the value of the dissimilarity function between the hearer and the speaker, and if hearers discriminate "very little better than they identify absolutely", then one must postulate that continuum discriminations take place in some other part of the cortex, but that such discriminations occur in parallel with, and are linked to, the absolute identifications.

Thirdly, and underlying the whole model, the decoding process must depend continuously upon a Bayesian *estimation* of probabilities; that is, hypotheses are entertained, modified, introduced or rejected on the basis of neither *a priori* nor *a posteriori* grounds, but on the basis of intermediate odds (Good, 1965). In any given interactive situation, the hearer will form a complex of hypotheses $(h_1 \ldots h_n)$ concerning the precise nature of the semantic, syntactic, phonological and phonetic aspects of the continuous signal; and whether or not h_k is confirmed, but especially if $h_h \ldots h_n$ are modified or rejected, then specific information is obtained outside the meanings of the code as a code, since these cases are monitored as perceptual "strains". (Strain is sometimes too strong a term since a single dissimilar token when all others – at a given decoding level – match the hearer's own, is sufficient to markedly change the confidence placed on the intermediate probabilities hitherto attached to that particular hypothesis, and to correspondingly alter the sampling method on which these probabilities were based.)

3.   I now summarize certain features of this hearer model from a slightly different point of view.[3] The hearer is modelled as having:

(a) an internalized representation of certain fundamental features of language, together, possibly, with their associated variants when these recur very frequently;

(b) methods of sampling the incoming signal relevant to (c) and (d) below.

Clearly, insofar as the hearer's experience of the places of origin of localized variants and/or his range of social experience decreases, he will have increasing difficulty in either assigning a variant to its structural element, or to its place relative to other variants of the same element. To overcome this he must be able

(c) to establish the overall linguistic resemblance between speakers.

Conversely, when a speaker's signal is close to the hearer's own production patterns, an economic sampling (for the derivation of non-linguistic information) would be effected by having some way

(d) to determine a small number of 'key diagnostics' for frequently encountered varieties.

Thus although the realization of any given phonological element may be shown, by machine acoustic analysis, to be infinitesimally continuous over the population, such continuity is segmented into discrete variants, which individually or in bundles can bear a fairly stable relationship to attributes or the non-linguistic world (social or psychological attributes, e.g.).

It is clear, then, that because neither the number nor the nature of varying elements, from which the hearer derives non-linguistic information about the speaker, can be known in advance of decoding the message, that his methods of classification and allocation are necessarily *ad hoc.*[4] There is reason to suppose (Wittgenstein, 1958) that such a classification may be characterized by its groups or classes having neither necessary nor sufficient criteria for group membership, by their being dependent on overall measures of resemblance between members, and by their showing a continuous connectedness internally in spite of considerable differences between their most egregious members (Beckner, 1959; Cattell *et al.*, 1966).

By drawing together various strands off the preceding discussion one can say that a speech variety is a product of the hearer's perceptual processes, that at the least it must be a constellation of linguistic variants assumed to be continuously and normally available to a speaker, that it resembles the constellations of a single group of others, and that it differs from the constellations of all other groups of others. (Notice that the specification of a "single group of others" to which a variety is similar, does not preclude the *individual* from having more than one variety).

In addition to a speech variety (V), which is a mode of linguistic performance of the individual speaker, there is here the notion of a set of speech varieties which resemble each other in some general way and which I shall call simply a variety cluster (VC).

At a particular level of analysis (from that of idiosyncrasies to that of overall language structure) the speech variety is the set of coded variants of the individual speaker. The variety cluster is then a dense swarm of speakers in an otherwise sparsely populated space whose dimensions are defined by precisely the level of analysis adopted. A particular subset of the variants of a VC which indicate that a newly sampled V is in or out of that VC, I shall call diagnostics (D) or, collectively, a diagnostic profile (DP). I emphasize that all these terms refer to potential analytic constructs. Insofar as the actual methods of the T.L.S. are reflections of both the postulates of the model and of these constructs, the data may be distorted by the methods to give apparent support for the constructs. Such support – in the form of definitions of VCs by their DPs, and of a statement of the distribution of the VCs – should be rigorously tested both by hearers themselves, and by further sampling and controlled changes of method.

4. Generalization from the model for an individual hearer leads directly into methodological considerations, and in particular to the notion of *variety space*.[5] Before going into the necessary properties of the variety space (V-space), it is necessary to introduce two other pieces of terminology. Firstly, by a *criterion*, I shall mean some part of the linguistic structure which shows at least two linguistically non-contrastive variants across the population under consideration which are not *logically* predetermined by the nature of any other criterion in the set of criteria currently in use. I discuss the precise nature of criteria in the next paper (Pellowe, forthcoming *a*). Secondly, the Vs of British English are, broadly, either localized or non-localized. A non-localized variety is one whose "speakers can be placed as English or educated in an English milieu but [whose] speech does not indicate what part of England they are associated with" (Strang, 1968: 790). (The notion of non-localized varieties thus incorporates R.P. without the notion of homogeneity which is often attached to that term.)

I return now to the properties of V-space. The Tyneside V-space is an optimal distribution of speakers in an n-dimensional space, where n is the maximum number of criteria whose criterial states (variants) are relevant to the localized/non-localized area under consideration. Conditions for an optimal distribution are:

(a) (i) the number of single-member VCs, which will not increase in size regardless of sample increases, is a minimum;
     (ii) without contravening (i) above, the number of VCs is a maximum;
(b) each VC is well-represented[6] and has a relatively higher level of internal cohesion than would exist in clusters of a randomly distributed population;
(c) no VC has the same group mean profile on a high proportion of criteria as more than a very small number of other VCs.

Essentially we may say that all these conditions are related to the predictive qualities of hearers' judgements. That is, the assigning of a speaker to a group (even if it is unlabelled) is performable on the basis of the generality (a, i), the inclusiveness (a, ii), the discreteness (b), and the relative unambiguity (c) of the group defining properties previously encountered.

These conditions for an optimal V-space arise from the following considerations. Firstly, all the topics in the T.L.S. (see above, Sec. 0) seek to determine either distributions or the effects of changes. For instance, we wish to determine the relevance of (topographical) isoglosses to work on urban speech variation. We shall do this, in part, by determining the extent to which the range of varieties of all of a street's inhabitants is narrower (in an as yet undefinedly significant way) than the range of varieties we obtain from a random selection of the same number of speakers matched for age, sex, social attributes, and length of local residence. It seems relatively clear that such an investigation could be initiated as it stands, without depending on any prior research, but when one considers the 'significance' of the narrowness of the range of varieties in a whole street, one begins to see the general importance of the V-space as such and as a preliminary base. Consider these not unlikely hypothetical results from such an investigation.

VC(DP) number	1	2	3	4	5	6	7	8	9	
Representatives in whole street	0	11	1	7	6	0	16	1	0	(42)
Representatives in matched random sample	2	7	0	10	8	1	10	1	3	(42)
	(2)	(18)	(1)	(17)	(14)	(1)	(26)	(1)	(3)	

Now the application of statistical tests, utilizing the usual significance levels, is complicated by two factors in this particular instance:

(i)   we have no idea of the extent to which the VCs appearing in the table exhaust the total number of VCs in the population; and

(ii) we cannot assess the significance of the figures for VCs 1, 3, 6, and 9, unless we know the rarity or commonness of VCs across the whole population.

These problems relate to condition (a) for an optimal distribution in V-space.

Secondly, if the V-space has to serve as a basis for further topics of the T.L.S. (Pellowe, forthcoming b), then the VCs which it contains must be as stable as possible. Stability here refers to a measure of equivalence between properties of the data, and the underlying mathematical model of the classificatory method. The less this measure of equivalence is, the more the classificatory method will distort the data, and the more easily will the clusters break up under minute changes of method (e.g. alterations of criteria, different similarity coefficients, marginally different sample of informants etc.). Given that VCs can be made stable in this sense, another factor which will contribute to our confidence in them is that they are well represented. This, however, presents peculiar problems, related to the "rarity" mentioned above. Say that the adult population (over 21 years on a certain date) of the area being considered by the T.L.S. is 150,000 and estimate, rather generously, that 10,000 of those individuals habitually use non-localized varieties. Then in a theoretically perfect random sample of 150 informants, there will be 10 NL speakers. 'If on a given list of (relevant) criteria these 10 NL speakers are clustered into 5 non-coalescing groups, of 2 members each say, then we have a problem of poor representation. This problem highlights two strands of investigation of the T.L.S. which cause methodological difficulty. That is, we wish to make

(1) typological inferences from taxonomically adequate groupings, and
(2) predictive inferences from statistically adequate samples. The data provided by pursuing the second of these goals is not sufficient to fulfil the first. It may be that the kind of distribution which speech varieties have is the incomplete Gaussian curve of ecologists (Preston 1962), where there is a small number both of varieties which have very few representatives in the population, and of varieties which have very many representatives in the population. The curve would be something like this:

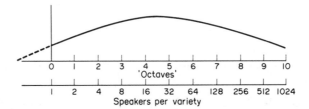

The only way of shifting the curve to the right to obtain these hidden varieties is by a massive increase of sample size. This is quite impractical for the T.L.S., so that I propose to use the estimation methods of Good (1953) and Good and Toulmin (1956), which yield (without making assumptions about the underlying population) the number of new species (sc. varieties) and the increase in population coverage to be expected on increasing the sample. In parallel with this estimation, I supplement a random sample with hand-picked speakers, known to have NL varieties. This handpicked addition to the sample is used for *classificatory purposes only*, not for statistical inferences to the population. These problems are the basis for the strong condition (b) in the specification of the optimal variety space.

Thirdly, since the model postulates an unambiguous mapping between the speaker's profile of variants and an array of non-linguistic values or "social meanings", we must try to ensure that the V-space does not contain too many cross-relations between VCs. This will, in part, be effected by a careful consideration of the relationship between criteria and informants. I have already said that the choice of criteria must be relevant to the nature of the informants, but it is perhaps even more important that the converse is fulfilled; namely that the choice of informants be exhaustive in terms of the range of the criteria. That is, if the VCs are seen as relatively denser swarms of points (speakers) in a multi-dimensional space, where each dimension is a criterion, and the scale of the dimension is the number of states of the criterion, then to approximate the best DPs from the available criteria, we want to determine the representation of the criteria in the statistical universe of informants. Aphoristically one might say that (in terms of the desired groupings) the selection of egregious criteria is more harmful to the classification than the selection of egregious informants.

I have indicated that even if it is relatively simple to establish a relevant classificatory model for the data, it is nevertheless exceedingly difficult to establish a method of sampling both criteria and informants, and to set up suitably subtle methods of statistical analysis and linguistic interpretation.

5.   The T.L.S. postulates that the hearer understands spoken utterances by decoding them under a set of complex hypotheses for which intermediate odds are deduced by means of empathic production. At the same time variants in the realization of the decoded elements, whose sum is equivalent to an undefined notion of perceptual strain, are discriminated (possibly in some other part of the brain) and used to derive non-linguistic information about the speaker. This state of affairs is taken as the point of departure for the T.L.S. methods of investigating urban speech varieties. The relatively non-ambiguous assignment of speakers to a particular group (by hearers) on the basis of apparently continuous differences, is taken to imply a form of classification which depends on neither necessary nor sufficient criteria for group membership (a polythetic classification). The notion of a variety space is developed as the methodologically most relevant generalization from this model of the individual hearer, conditions are specified for such a variety space to be an optimum, and certain problems of these conditions are discussed. The actual steps by means of which the optimal variety space is established are discussed in subsequent papers, where further theoretical problems and certain sociolinguistic generalities are also aired. The steps are simply:

(1) defining a list of linguistic elements;
(2) determining strings of variants associated with each element which are relevant to urban Tyneside;
(3) embodying slots in which these variants may be realized, in an interview schedule;
(4) sampling informants to whom the interview is to be administered;

(5) establishing for each informant a profile of variant realizations of elements;
(6) comparing every informant with every other on the basis of their profiles;
(7) establishing a measure of resemblance between every pair of informants;
(8) constructing groups of informants who are highly similar;
(9) deriving diagnostic profiles for these groups;
(10) examining these groups in terms of the social attributes of their members;
(11) testing the stability of the groups by varying the above procedures;
(12) testing the meaningfulness of the groups against hearer judgements.

(Pellowe, forthcoming *a*, *b*).

Notes

1. This paper was written whilst the author was in receipt of a DES Studentship. I am extremely grateful to Professor Barbara Strang for her patient reading of many drafts of this paper, and her invaluable suggestions. Remaining inadequacies are my own.
2. Sc. for right-handed persons and following.
3. For ease of reading, I refer to 'similarity between sets of variants' or "overall resemblance between Ss", rather than the more correct but cumbrous formulations "close intermediate odds (i. – odds) for the same hypothesis advanced on different occasions' and 'related configurations of final i. – odds for all hypotheses advanced on two separate occasions".
4. It is unfortunate that statisticians frequently fail to draw a distinction between partitioning a sample into an initially unknown number of groups with initially unknown properties (i.e. classification), and partitioning a sample amongst an initially known number of groups with initially known properties (i.e. discrimination in the sense of Fisher, 1936). This latter I shall call "allocation" to avoid confusion with perceptual discrimination.
5. 'Variety space' is not postulated as part of the hearer's perceptual equipment, although it does not conflict with the foregoing model; rather both it and later developments are methodological extensions and simplifications of the model.
6. An absolute definition of "well-representedness" of a (classified) group is not possible. It depends among other things, on the homogeneity of the items already in the group, the rarity of the group's members in the population, and the clustering method.

References

Beckner, M. (1959) *The Biological Way of Thought*. New York: Columbia University Press.
Bernstein, B. (1969) "A sociolinguistic approach to socialization". In Gumperz, J. J. and Hymes, D. H. (eds), *Directions in Sociolinguistics*, pp. 465–497. New York: Holt, Rinehart and Winston.
Cattell, R. B. (1966). Patterns of change. In Cattell, R. B. (ed.), *Handbook of Multivariate Experimental Psychology*, pp. 355 ff. Chicago: Rand McNally.
Cattell, R. B., Coulter, M. A. and Tsujioka, B. (1966) "The taxonometric recognition of types and functional emergents". In Cattell, R. B. (ed.), *Handbook of Multivariate Experimental Psychology*, pp. 228 ff. Chicago: Rand McNally.
Chomsky, N. (1964). *Current Issues in Linguistic Theory*. The Hague: Mouton. (Janua Linguarum: Series Minor 38).
Chomsky, N. and Miller, G. A. (1963) "Introduction to the formal analysis of natural languages. In Luce, R. D., Bush, R. R. and Galanter, E. (eds), *Handbook of Mathematical Psychology*, vol. 2, pp. 269 ff. New York: Wiley.

36   John Pellowe

Eisenson, J. (1962) "Language and intellectual modifications associated with right cerebral damage", *Language and Speech*, **5**, p. 49 ff.
Fisher, R. A. (1936) "The use of multiple measurements in taxonomic problems", *Annals of Eugenics*, **7**, 179 ff.
Good, I. J. (1953) "The population frequencies of species and the estimation of population parameters", *Biometrika*, **40**, 237 ff.
Good, I. J. (1965) *The Estimation of Probabilities*. Cambridge, Mass.: MIT Press.
Good, I. J. and Toulmin, G. H. (1956) "The number of new species and the increase in population coverage, when a sample is increased", *Biometrika*, **43**, 45 ff.
Labov, W. (1966) *The Social Stratification of English in New York City*. Washington D.C.: Center for Applied Linguistics.
Liberman, A. M., Cooper, F. S., Shankweiler, D. P. and Studdert-Kennedy, M. (1967) "Perception of the speech code", *Psychol. Rev.*, **74**, 431 ff.
Lieberman, P. (1967). *Intonation, Perception, and Language*. Cambridge, Mass.: MIT Press.
Pellowe, J. (1967). "Studies Towards a Classification of Varieties of Spoken English". Unpublished M.Litt. thesis, University of Newcastle upon Tyne.
Pellowe, J. (forthcoming *a*) "Establishing speech varieties of conurbations: II. Criteria and sampling.
Pellowe, J. (forthcoming *b*) "Establishing speech varieties of conurbations: III. Varieties and constructs".
Pellowe, J. (forthcoming *c*) "Linguistic variability and interviwer effectiveness".
Pellowe, J. (forthcoming *d*) "Establishing some prosodic criteria for a classification of speech varieties."
Pittenger, R. E., Hockett, C. F. and Danehy, J. J. (1960) *The First Five Minutes: a sample of microscopic interview analysis*. Ithaca, N.Y.: Martineau.
Postal, P. M. (1968) *Aspects of phonological theory*. New York: Harper and Row.
Preston, F. W. (1962) "The canonical distribution of commonness and rarity: I and II", *Ecology*, **43**, 185 ff, 410 ff.
Stevens, K. N. (1960) "Towards a model for speech recognition", *J. Ac. Soc. Am.*, **32**, 47 ff.
Strang, B. M. H. (1968) "The Tyneside Linguistic Survey", *Zeitschrift für Mundartforschung* (Heft 4), pp. 788 ff.
Wittgenstein, L. (1958) *Philosophical Investigations*. Oxford: Blackwell.

3

Aspects of the listener's role in speaker recognition

ROGER BROWN

Introduction

Speaker recognition may be defined as the ability to recognize the identity of a speaker from hearing a sample of his speech (Brown, 1982). The paradigm of speaker recognition experimentation is that the process involves a pattern-matching technique. A representation of the sample uttered by the voice to be recognized (the stimulus voice pattern) is compared with some form of internalized representation of voices previously heard by the listener (reference voice patterns). This exposure to reference voices may result from everyday contact or may be much shorter, as in some experimental tasks where the duration of the reference sample may be only a couple of seconds. A decision is then reached on the basis of the similarity between the stimulus and reference voice patterns.

Before discussing some of the listener-oriented aspects of the process, it is necessary briefly to describe the analytical framework within which the discussion is set. To summarize the main distinctions briefly (Brown, 1979, 1980, forthcoming), experimental speaker recognition tasks may be categorized by reference to two factors:

1. Whether the task involves the listener's long-term or short-term memory system. Long-term memory tasks involve reference voices which either are familiar to the listener through everyday business or social contact outside the experimental situation (e.g. Pollack et al., 1954; Abberton and Fourcin, 1978), or have been familiarized by means of a training session controlled by the experimenter (e.g. Williams, 1964; Stevens et al., 1968). Short-term memory tasks employ either a sequential presentation format, in which the reference and stimulus voices are presented one after the other (e.g. Shearme and Holmes, 1959; Doehring and Ross, 1972; Coleman, 1973), or simultaneous presentation, where the two voices are presented at the same time by double-tracking on a tape-recorder (Williamson, 1961; Brown, 1980) (see Figure 1).

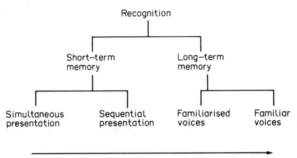

Length of time in storage of reference voice pattern

FIG. 1

2. The number of alternative reference voices available to the listener. The criterion is whether the task involves only one reference voice (single reference) or more than one (multiple reference). Evidence from Clarke *et al.* (1966) suggests that short-term memory multiple-reference tasks are impossible owing to the incompatibility of the two factors. The human short-term memory system appears incapable of reliably handling more than one stored (reference) voice pattern.

The terms in Table 1 are used to refer to the three remaining kinds of task, in accordance with the consensus of usage among writers in the field.

TABLE 1

	Single reference	Multiple reference
Short-term memory	Differentiation	
Long-term memory	Verification	Identification

Multiple reference (identification) tasks may be of two kinds:

1. The listener is informed that the stimulus voice will correspond to one of the reference voices (closed identification), or
2. the stimulus sample may have been uttered by a voice which is not one of the references (open identification).

Although the above discussion treats the categories as reasonably clear-cut distinctions, certain flexibility of interpretation and further explanation are necessary before such a categorical standpoint can be adopted, especially in respect of everyday, rather than experimental, situations. The major reservation relates to the listener's expectations.

Expectations for probable reference candidates

If the telephone rings in my office, I may expect the caller usually to be an acquaintance of mine. However, it is possible for the caller to be (literally) anyone in the world. It may be someone unexpected. Or indeed someone I have never spoken to before, in which case I will not have an appropriate stored reference voice pattern for that caller. Since this last possibility exists, the number of reference voices which need to be taken into account is equal to the total population of reference voices in my long-term memory, and I must also allow an extra category corresponding to "any other speaker". In other words, this situation corresponds to the experimental task of open identification described above.

It is unrealistic from a psychological point of view to suppose that the way in which I recognize the stimulus voice in the above situation is by comparing it individually with each voice pattern of my reference population. This process would involve a large amount of redundant psychological processing because it is improbable, or even impossible, for certain speakers in my total reference population to be telephoning me in my office. For example, we retain the reference voice patterns of many speakers who have died. The process would also take a great length of time to be performed – longer than identification in such a situation normally takes.

In identification tasks, the size of the reference speaker population to be taken into consideration may be large. Pollack *et al.* (1954) investigated the optimal size of experimental reference populations, using groups of up to 16 speakers uttering monosyllabic words. Since the limit of information transmitted was not reached, their data suggest that it is possible to use a greater number of speakers reliably in identification tasks. In contrast, Williams (1964) tested three listener groups with speaker populations of 4, 6 and 8 voices respectively. The drop in performance between the 6-speaker and 8-speaker tests was considerably larger than that between the 4-speaker and the 6-speaker, leading Williams to the conclusion that "considering such factors as training time, test time, amount of information, etc., it may well be that an ensemble of 5 or 6 speakers would be optimal for testing speaker identification" (Williams, 1964: 14). The opposing nature of these two conclusions suggests that what is important in experimental tasks may not be so much the size of the speaker group, but the homogeneity within the group.

In another part of Williams' (1964) study, he divided a speaker population of 12 randomly into two groups of 6 speakers (A and B). The discrepancy in the final test scores (50 per cent and 62 per cent correct respectively) indicates that "speaker identification depends not only on the individual characteristics of each of the speakers but also on the characteristics of the other speakers with whom he is being compared" (Williams, 1964: 22). In short, speaker group A was obviously more homogeneous than speaker group B.

The size of the total reference population for listeners in everyday situations may be very large, and the size and identity of the population will vary for each listener, depending on his social and business circles. Strategies based on expectations may therefore be adopted by listeners to reduce the very large total population to manageable proportions by the temporary discarding from consideration of reference voices with a low probability of corresponding to the stimulus, leaving a subset of more probable candidates. This might occur in two ways (or by a combination of these two).

Situational probabilities

If the telephone rings in my office, it is possible for the caller to be anyone in the world. However, it is more likely to be someone I know. Similarly, it is more likely to be someone in my town; more specifically, in the university; even more specifically, in my university department; and so on. In other words, the situation in which the speaker recognition process is called into operation allows the range of expected stimulus voices to be narrowed down (Ladefoged, 1978). The above example may therefore be expressed conveniently in Venn diagram terms (Figure 2).

If the telephone rings in my office, the most probable set of reference speakers is represented by the shaded area, corresponding to people in my university department (all of whom I know); the next most probable set is composed of the previous set plus those in the dotted area, corresponding in total to people I know in the university; the next most probable is that set plus those in the cross-hatched area, in all representing people I know in my town; and so on. It may then be hypothesized that the initial comparison of the stimulus voice is with the relatively small number of reference voices contained in the most probable set – in this case, the shaded area. If that

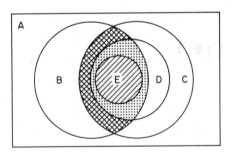

FIG. 2. Rectangle A = the universe (all people in the world)
Circle B = people I know
Circle C = people in my town
Circle D = people in the university
Circle E = people in my university department

analysis fails to produce a satisfactory correspondence between the stimulus voice and one of the references, the set of reference voices under consideration is enlarged to include the next most probable set (the dotted area in the diagram). The total set is now composed of the shaded area (people in my university department, all of whom I know) and the dotted area (people I know in the university, but outside my department), although the former will already have been considered and rejected. If an analysis of the latter set fails to produce a correspondence, the set is expanded again to include the cross-hatched area, and so on.

Parametric probabilities

The second approach to improving the efficiency of reference voice recall in identification tasks involving large populations of possible candidates employs a search procedure guided by features of the stimulus voice. The stimulus voice is analyzed parametrically, and only those reference voices which approximate closely in parametric features to the stimulus are called up initially for comparison. Thus, if a stimulus voice is analyzed as having a high mean pitch, low mean loudness and extremely breathy phonation, only those reference voices which are characterized by similar pitch, loudness and phonation values are called up. Again, a Venn diagram captures well this narrowing down of possibilities (Figure 3).

The most probable set of reference voices from the total population corresponds to the shaded area, and these reference voices are taken into consideration first. If the analysis finds that the set is empty (i.e. that there are no reference voices with high mean pitch, low mean loudness and

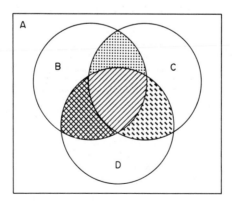

FIG. 3. Rectangle A = the universe (total population of reference voices in memory)
        Circle B = voices with high mean pitch value
        Circle C = voices with low mean loudness value
        Circle D = voices with extremely breathy phonation.

extremely breathy phonation), the set is enlarged by the inclusion of further voices which approximate closely to that set and are thus the next most probable – perhaps the dotted area in the diagram (voices with high mean pitch, low mean loudness, but not extremely breathy phonation), or the cross-hatched or broken-shaded areas, etc.

This process of narrowing down the range of probable reference voices is made all the more efficient if it can be shown that the stimulus voice contains an abnormal value in relation to a parameter, i.e. one deviating to a large degree from some physiologically and culturally determined norm. By virtue of the fact that it is an abnormal value, any such occurrence will cause the number of probable candidates to be reduced drastically. In terms of Figure 3 an abnormally high mean pitch value in the stimulus will produce a much smaller circle B. Since the probability of any reference voice falling within this (now much smaller) circle B is slight, it will be a strong characteristic of any reference voice if it does fall within it. Therefore, consideration of any parameter which does not have an abnormal value in the stimulus may be suspended while it is checked whether any reference voice pattern contains the abnormal parameter value. However, it may be that this reduction as a result of an abnormal value leads to an empty set (i.e. there are no reference voice patterns with similar abnormal parameter values). In this case the process will revert to the above procedure for non-abnormal parametric values, and the abnormal value in the stimulus is taken to have been caused by some nonce usage, paralinguistic function, transmission irregularity, etc. Separate consideration of abnormal parametric values is a feature incorporated in the model of the speaker recognition process in Brown (1980, forthcoming).

The attractive feature of these two processes (consideration of situational and parametric probabilities) is that analysis starts with a small set of very probable reference voices, which is enlarged only if recognition does not occur using that set. Each expansion of the set is likely to produce an increase in the number of new reference voices to be taken into consideration. Economies of psychological processing are therefore made by starting with a small number of very probable reference candidates before proceeding to any larger population.

Multiple task situations

In everyday life, the decision whether a given situation should be categorized as one kind of task (identification/differentiation/verification) rather than another, or whether the situation may indeed involve a combination of tasks, depends largely on the listener's expectations. The fact that expectations are involved, and that these are often covert and difficult to determine empirically, makes any categorical statement of this sort dubious. The difficulty in analyzing real-world speaker recognition tasks is illustrated by a hypothetical situation contained in the following plausible dialogue.

> John loves Mary. She works in an office with Julie, Susan and Anthea, all of whom John knows. She is senior to these people and therefore usually answers the phone, which is on her desk. John is trying to contact her by phone. He dials the office number.

Text	Analysis
1. Switchboard girl: "Good morning."	
2. John: "Extension 393, please."	
3. Switchboard girl: "One moment, please." (pause)	(D) (for John)
4. Susan (on extension 393): "Hello." (pause)	D/V/I (for John)
5. John: "Hello . . . Susan?"	I (for Susan)
6. Susan: "Yes. Hello, John."	(V) (for John)
7. John: "Hello. I was phoning to see if Mary was in."	(V) (for Susan)
8. Susan: "No. I'm afraid she's out at the moment."	(V) (for John)
etc.	(I = identification; D = differentiation; V = verification)

Let us first concentrate on the decision processes which John has to perform during the pause between utterances 4 and 5. He hears a female voice. The immediate task for him is to check that it is not the switchboard girl again, saying that she cannot get a reply on that extension. This is a short-term memory differentiation task (unless the switchboard girl's voice is already known to him). Having ascertained that the voice is not that of the switchboard girl, the next candidate, and an extremely probable one, is Mary; firstly, it is normally Mary who answers on that extension, and secondly, it is her that John wants to talk to. It is therefore a possible source of great economy of psychological processing if he first of all verifies whether it is Mary or not. The task is thus one of verification; there is only one reference voice under immediate consideration (and John has strong expectations that the stimulus voice will correspond to that reference) and it is stored in his long-term memory. However, having verified that it is not in fact Mary, John's next task is to decide who it is, and there are three very probable candidates – Julie, Susan and Anthea. The task thus becomes one of identification since there are more than one reference voice under consideration, and their patterns are all stored in his long-term memory (i.e. he already knows them all). He decides that the stimulus voice is Susan's, although he is not certain of this, as is shown by the questioning rise in intonation of his next utterance 5. The correctness of his decision is confirmed by Susan's utterance 6. Of course, the stimulus might not in fact have corresponded to one of these three references. However, they are by far the most probable in the particular situation.

He thus arrives at the correct recognition of the stimulus speaker of utterance 4. This decision may only take a second to be reached, but it is probable that it is the result of a sequentially ordered combination of more than one task, as described above – initially differentiation, then verification, and finally identification. The second process comes about as a result of a negative response to the first, and similarly the third is brought about by a failure to verify that the stimulus is Mary.

The differentiation task for John (utterance 3) is symbolized in parentheses because it is probably a less conscious process than those described above. It performs a confirmatory function, reassuring John that it is still the switchboard girl to whom he is talking, and that they have not been interrupted. It may well be that he has no good reason to doubt this. However, this confirmatory form of recognition must be assumed to take place, for otherwise one would have no means of explaining why John would react immediately to a different voice on the line. In other words, it is a continual process occurring at each utterance to confirm the very strong expectation that one is still talking with the same person. It is a differentiation task in the case of the switchboard girl, since hers is not a familiar voice for John, whereas in utterances 6, 7 and 8 it is verification since John and Susan are acquaintances.

Two more examples relating to the above dialogue will serve to illustrate further limitations on the analysis of everyday speaker recognition tasks. Firstly, the function, as far as speaker recognition is concerned, of Susan's utterances 6 and 8 is confirmatory, and has just been categorized as verification, since Susan's reference pattern is stored in John's long-term memory. However, this categorization assumes that the stored reference pattern of her voice plays a more important part in the speaker recognition process than any information added to that pattern, extracted from her utterances 6 and 8. That is, whether these confirmatory decisions are categorized as verifications or instead as differentiations depends upon whether the stored pattern is considered to be more important than the short-term information, or not. This taxonomic problem is more acute in certain circumstances. If the speaker has a temporary physiological condition such as a head-cold, the reference pattern for this confirmatory task will need to include this information as a fundamental feature. If the speaker is someone the listener has not spoken with for a long time, the reference pattern will be less distinct than that of someone he meets every day. The speaker's voice may have changed over the years and therefore the short-term information from contemporary utterances will play an important part in the decision. Even in normal situations it is intuitive to suppose that information derived from a speaker's most recent utterance does not play a totally insignificant part in the verification/differentiation of that speaker.

Secondly, in experimental formats, the reference voices in any one task have always been stored either all in short-term memory or all in long-term. In the real world, however, it is possible for a situation to arise where a mixture of these two is involved. For example, in the above dialogue situation, John may subsequently hear a voice on the line which is not Susan's. He decides this by the above verification/differentiation task. There are then three (or possibly four) very probable reference candidates: Julie and Anthea (and perhaps Mary), all of whose reference patterns are stored in John's long-term memory, and the switchboard girl again, whose pattern is in his short-term memory (assuming a not too long time-delay since he last heard her voice). Thus patterns in long-term and short-term memory are involved. The task must be categorized as identification since more than one reference pattern is taken into account, although this classification overlooks the fact that both memory systems are used.

Everyday occurrences of speaker recognition

The above discussion on the role of listener's expectations and multiple task situations illustrates the problems encountered in applying experimentally oriented categorizations to everyday situations. Further differences need to be taken into account in understanding everyday occurrences of speaker recognition.

The simultaneous presentation format is artificial in that it cannot exist in everyday situations while preserving the choice of "same"/"different" alternatives. That is, in everyday situations, two simultaneously heard voices must belong to different speakers.

The main characteristic of the distinction between familiar and familiarized reference voice patterns is that the choice of familiarized patterns to be used is under the total control of the experimenter. But since the control of the experimenter is precluded in everyday situations, this feature cannot be used as a defining characteristic. The distinction then rests on the time factor, and it becomes a matter of deciding the length of time in storage for patterns to be familiar rather than familiarized. Any decision of this kind would be arbitrary and therefore the category of voice patterns in long-term memory will not be subdivided.

It can be seen that it is odd to refer to instances of speaker recognition in everyday life as "tasks". Experimentally, a task generally requires the subject to produce a response based on a conscious decision. We have already seen that confirmatory instances of speaker recognition may not be overtly conscious decisions. Similarly, in everyday life, speaker recognition rarely has important consequences. At home, you are under little pressure to recognize a telephone caller correctly, except insofar as misrecognition momentarily impedes communication. As the listener, you may have differing feelings about your obligation to recognize the caller's voice, especially when external factors such as fatigue or boredom are considered. Restating this in experimental terms, the listener in an everyday speaker recognition task may feel little obligation to avoid reaching the equivalent of a "don't know" decision, and there may be few important consequences attached to an error response. For example, in the open initial identification of a telephone caller, there are three error possibilities. A listener may (i) identify the caller as one particular acquaintance when he in fact is a different acquaintance (false match identification), (ii) identify the caller as an acquaintance when he in fact is a stranger to the listener (false no-match identification), or (iii) fail to identify the caller although he is an acquaintance (false elimination). If you act on the basis of a false match or no-match identification, the caller will probably put you right in his next utterance. If you have falsely eliminated the caller, it is likely that he will declare himself in his next utterance. Knowing this, you may even feel justified in not concentrating on the speaker recognition task in the first place, relying instead on the habit of most callers revealing their identity in the first utterance.

All three kinds of task (identification, differentiation, verification) are possible in everyday situations. Verification in the real world usually takes place in courtroom situations, where the witness is required to recognize the voice of one specific suspect. If the suspect were required to produce an utterance in court, knowing that this might form the basis for his being convicted, it is likely either that he would try to subtly disguise his voice, or that any utterance he produced would not represent his normal articulation. For this reason, the suspect's voice is normally presented as a recording made when the suspect was not aware of it. Such use of a tape-recorder is experimental rather than everyday.

The use of verification in courtroom situations is an exception to the above observations that everyday speaker recognition need not be conscious and rarely has important consequences. The consequences of this speaker recognition decision are of obvious importance and the listener (witness) will therefore perform the task with conscious concentration. For this reason, this instance of verification is better treated as an experimental usage rather than as an everyday occurrence. The task involves the controlled selection of voices, pressure to produce a conscious response, initial rather than confirmatory recognition, the use of tape-recordings, all of which are typical features of experimental speaker recognition formats. Nowadays, however, the use of audio- and video-tape must also be considered as part of

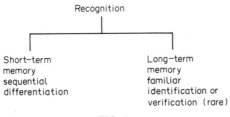

FIG. 4

everyday life, as well as such devices as the telephone, television and radio. Perhaps everyday situations are best defined as being characterized by a lack of such control.

Other forms of verification do occur, though less frequently, in everyday life. An example of this would be the situation where you telephone a friend and ask him to call back (for example, because you are using somebody else's phone and do not want to increase their bill). When the telephone next rings, you are therefore expecting your friend, and the immediate task is to verify the caller as your friend as against anyone else. Verification tasks are rare in everyday situations because they require that strong expectations be had as to the identity of the voice. If expectations are not strong, the task turns into one of identification because the population of probable speakers increases above one.

An example of everyday identification is the situation where you are in a room with a number of other people. Having turned your back, you hear somebody speak. The voice will therefore correspond to one of the people in the room. Naturally, in this case, speaker recognition will be helped by localization clues, but speaker recognition by voice alone will play an important part.

A common example of everyday differentiation is the situation presented above, where you telephone an office and are connected initially to the switchboard operator. Having asked to be put through to a certain extension, you then wait. The next voice to be heard may be either a different one (replying on the required extension) or the same one (the switchboard operator, to tell you that she cannot get a reply on that extension).

The categorization of experimental tasks given earlier may therefore be revised for everyday situations as shown in Figure 4.

References

Abberton, E. and Fourcin, A. J. (1978) "Intonation and speaker identification", *Language and Speech*, **21**, 305–318.
Brown, R. (1979) "Memory and decision in speaker recognition", *International Journal of Man-Machine Studies*, **11**, 729–742.

48   Roger Brown

Brown R (1980) "Auditory speaker recognition: a theoretical and experimental study". Unpublished Ph.D. thesis, University of Edinburgh.
Brown R. (1982) "What is speaker recognition?", *Journal of the International Phonetic Association*, **12**, 13–24.
Brown, R. (forthcoming) *Auditory Speaker Recognition*, to appear in Forum Phoneticum.
Clarke, F. R., Becker, R. W. and Nixon, J. C. (1966) "Characteristics that determine speaker recognition", *Report ESD-TR-66-636*, Electronics Systems Division, Air Force Systems Command, Hanscom Field.
Coleman, R. O. (1973) "Speaker identification in the absence of inter-subject differences in glottal source characteristics", *Journal of the Acoustical Society of America*, **53**, 1741–1743.
Doehring, D. G. and Ross, R. W. (1972) "Voice recognition by matching to sample", *Journal of Psycholinguistic Research*, **1**, 233–242.
Ladefoged, P. (1978) "Expectation affects identification by listening", *Language and Speech*, **21**, 373–374.
Pollack, I., Pickett, J. M. and Sumby, W. H. (1954) "On the identification of speakers by voice", *Journal of the Acoustical Society of America*, **26**, 403–406.
Shearme, J. N. and Holmes, J. N. (1959) "An experiment concerning the recognition of voices", *Language and Speech*, **2**, 123–131.
Stevens, K. N., Williams, C. E., Carbonell, J. R. and Woods, B. (1968) "Speaker authentication and identification: a comparison of spectrographic and auditory presentation of speech material", *Journal of the Acoustical Society of America*, **44**, 1596–1607.
Williams, C. E. (1964) "The effects of selected factors on the aural identification of speakers". Section III of *Report ESD-TDR-65-153*, Electronics Systems Division, Air Force Systems Command, Hanscom Field.
Williamson, J. A. (1961) "An investigation of several factors which affect the ability to identify voices as same or different". Unpublished diploma dissertation, University of Edinburgh.

4

Grammar for the hearer

CHARLES F. HOCKETT

C. F. Hockett, "Grammar for the Hearer". Author's introduction for the new appearance.

[In reviewing this 25-year-old article preparatory to its inclusion in the present collection, I was surprised at two things: on the one hand, the extent to which the meat of it foreshadows my current thinking; on the other, the remarkable irrelevance, as I now see it, of the more formal stage-setting passages. The latter reflect a fad which had me, as much as anyone, under its spell in the late 1950s. Only a few years later (as shown by *The State of the Art*[1*]) I became convinced that the then current mathematical model-building in grammar was at best futile, at worst dangerous, diverting our attention away from substantive problems to a preoccupation with trivial mathematics and bad linguistics. It does not seem appropriate to excise the outdated material for this reprinting. But I hope readers will join me in passing lightly over §§ 1 and 6–10, which are mostly pompous trivia, and concentrate instead on the parts which may actually afford a bit of insight into what listeners do in trying to comprehend what is said to them. The editor of this volume believes the latter is important for our scientific understanding of human language, and I fully agree. – C.F.H., April 1985.]

Introduction

This paper deals, in a preliminary way, with the problem of grammatical design from the vantage point of a hearer: that is, of a person who knows a language and who, for the moment, is silently listening to someone else speak.

Originally published in R. Jakobson, ed., *Structure of Language and its mathematical aspects* (Proceedings of Symposia in Applied Mathematics XII; New York: American Mathematical Society, 1961) pp. 220–236. Reprinted with the permission of the author and the American Mathematical Society.

* Superscript numbers refer to notes at end of chapter.

Perhaps this angle of approach should be called a "disadvantage point" rather than a vantage point. The grammarian can view a sentence as an enduring structure, to be scanned at leisure and repeatedly, and as easily from right to left or upside-down or inside-out as from left to right. He can do this because he deals not directly with a sentence, but only with a representation thereof, spread out before him like a cadaver on a marble slab, to be dissected at his convenience. The hearer has none of these advantages. He is exposed to an utterance just once, and is forced to register its ingredients in just the temporal sequence in which they reach him.

The hearer cannot know for sure, part way through a sentence, just what is going to be said next; he can at most have an array of expectations derived from earlier experience (that is, from his knowledge of the language) and from what has been said so far this time (that is, from his partial knowledge of the current sentence). For the hearer, then, a grammatical system must be viewed as a stochastic process.

The simplest stochastic model worthy of consideration is a finite Markov chain. Such a model, regarded as a "generative grammar," is called a finite state grammar, and it generates a finite state "language." Chomsky has shown that, if we accept certain very reasonable empirical assumptions about English, then English is not a finite state language.[2] He has also claimed that no finite state approximation to English can match the known facts of the language closely enough to be of any interest. This second point is, I believe, false. It will be shown later in this paper that it is in theory possible to match the facts of English as closely as we wish with a finite Markov chain.

1. Empirical assumptions

For the present investigation we shall make certain customary assumptions and two special ones.

The customary assumptions include the following three:

(A1) The vocabulary of a language is finite.

(A2) Grammar and semantics are separable.

(A3) We can validly confine our attention to spans of finite length called SENTENCES (though these need not coincide exactly with any traditional definition of "sentence").

The customary assumptions also include the following two, which are rarely stated explicitly:

(A4) We can distinguish between events in which a hearer is learning a language and those in which he is merely using it, and we can neglect events of the former sort.

(A5) The hearer always hears correctly: that is, he hears two words or sequences of words as different if and only if they are phonemically different.

Each of these five assumptions, save possibly the second, can be questioned on empirical grounds, but each can be imagined as ALMOST true, so that results based on the assumptions can constitute some reasonable approximation to the facts.

Our two special assumptions are as follows:

(A6) In order to understand what he hears, a hearer sometimes has to PARSE a sentence – that is, discover its grammatical organization – in much the same way a grammarian parses it.

(A7) Any fact about a sentence used by a hearer in parsing the sentence is itself a grammatical fact.

The point of assumption (A7) is to preclude the possibility that a hearer may sometimes first figure out what a sentence means and then, using that information about its meaning, infer its grammatical structure. In learning a language this must happen often. In merely using a language already known, we assume it does not, since the hearer's purpose is to understand what he hears; if he achieves this understanding without parsing the sentence in all detail, he no longer has any motivation for completing the parsing.

Assumption (A6) requires sharpening before we can use it. At one extreme, we might imagine that a hearer never parses a sentence until he has heard all of it. Apart from the fact that the subsequent parsing would have to be done very fast, this would put the hearer on a par with the grammarian, in the sense that the parsing done by either would be based on all the information the sentence contains: words received last would bear on the parsing of the first part of the sentence as much as vice versa. This version of the assumption is almost certainly false. Yet it is the sort of false-to-fact "stupidity assumption" often usefully made at certain stages in any field of investigation, and is, indeed, just the assumption that has underlain the procedures of marble-slab grammar from Dionysius Thrax and Panini to the present.

At the opposite extreme, we could pretend that a hearer does as much parsing as he can after he hears each successive linear ingredient of the sentence – after each new morph, let us say, or after each new word. This extreme vision is doubtless equally false. It is more likely that the actual frequency of hearer-parsing varies from occasion to occasion, as do, also, its completeness, its accuracy, and the degree to which the hearer is aware of the process. Some of the sentences we hear are long "idioms" for which no parsing at all is necessary. They have, it is true, an internal organization that can be dissected by a grammarian, but the hearer, once he recognizes that such-and-such an idiom is being uttered, can treat it as a single stored lexical unit. Other sentences are de novo creations of the speaker in most of their detail. For these, the hearer perhaps parses at a larger number of successive points.

But since we cannot know, in the majority of actual instances, just how frequently or completely a hearer parses, it makes a kind of sense to deal with hearer-parsing in terms of a stupidity-assumption that is the converse of the usual one. That is, we shall pretend that a hearer parses as best he can after receiving each successive word of a sentence. Thus the mesh of our net, though perhaps finer than absolutely necessary, is at least smaller than the fish we want to catch. The hearer can hardly do MORE successive parsing than is provided by our model.

2. Informal examples

Let us pretend that we are listening to a lecture, and that the first word we hear is *empathy*. We shall assume that this word is not accompanied by an "utterance-closing" intonation.

Now how can anyone, hearer or grammarian, parse a single unit? In one sense, he cannot. However, since the first word is not accompanied by an utterance-closing intonation, we expect more to follow, and we expect that whatever follows will stand in one or another grammatical relationship with the first word. It is therefore possible to tabulate the various grammatical relationships in which the first word could possibly stand with any continuation, as shown in Figure 1. The notation "*Na*" means that the word we heard is a noun of a certain subclass. The marks – borrowed from the typography, but in no sense from the semantics, of symbolic logic and mathematics – have the following meanings: ">" means that the next thing spoken might be something to which the part already spoken is an attribute, as in *empathy methods* or the like. "<" means that the next to come might be a postposed attribute modifying *empathy*, as in *empathy in psychotherapy*. "+" means that the next to come might stand in a coordinate construction with what has already been said: *empathy or intuition*, or *empathy and all similar magic*. "≡" means that the next to come might stand in apposition with *empathy*: *empathy, a method used in modern psychotherapy*. Finally, "ϵ" means that *empathy* might turn out to be all of a subject, the next element in the sentence beginning a predicate: *empathy is a powerful tool*.

This is a wide range of grammatical possibilities. Perhaps some further possibilities have inadvertently been omitted. But some grammatical relationships that function in English MUST be omitted: for example, it is entirely precluded that the next element should be the object of *empathy*, in

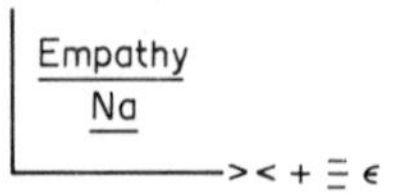

FIG. 1

the sense in which *you* is object of *for* in *for you* or of *see* in *see you*, since *empathy* is not the sort of word that can occupy the first position in any such construction.

Let us now assume that the next word we actually hear is *as*. The sequence *empathy* as yields, of course, a very different sort of diagram, as shown in Figure 2. Most of the possibilities left open by the uttering of *empathy* have

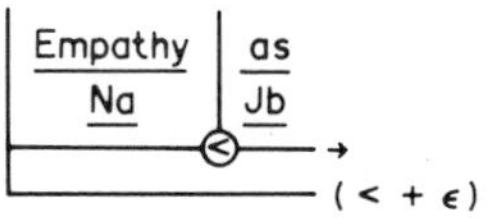

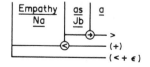

FIG. 2

now been eliminated. *As* begins a grammatical form that will stand as a postposed attribute to *empathy*.[3] This fixed fact is indicated by the mark "<" at the junction of the boxes in the diagram for *empathy* and for *as*. . . . *As* must itself be followed by something standing to it in the relation of object: this is the significance of the mark "→". The other three marks have the same meanings as before; they are put in parentheses because they do not indicate what can happen IMMEDIATELY next. The possibility of a further postposed attribute, or of something in apposition, or the like, is temporarily in abeyance, until the materials demanded by *as* have been spoken. However, though postposed, these possibilities have not been cancelled: they will come actively into play later.

Figures 1 and 2 are achieved by what we shall call OPEN-ENDED PARSING, and represent the GRAMMATICAL STATES established, respectively, but the first word and by the first two words heard. We can imagine that our idealized hearer does not register the incoming word *empathy* merely as a string of phonemes. Rather, the very act of perceiving the word generates in him all the information shown in Figure 1 – a bit of it determinate, the rest merely a PATTERN OF EXPECTATION. Since our idealized hearer is faultless, each successive word actually fits into the preceding pattern of expectation in one or another of the ways for which the pattern provides, and replaces that pattern of expectation by a new one, at the same time adding to what is determinate. That is, each new word replaces a grammatical state by a new grammatical state.

Figures 3 through 8 show the open-ended parsings of our target sentence after the receipt by the hearer of the third through the eighth words.

Empathy | as | a
Na | Jb

FIG. 3

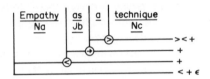

FIG. 4

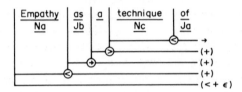

FIG. 5

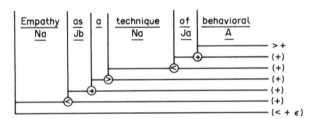

FIG. 6

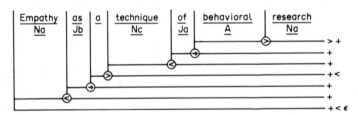

FIG. 7

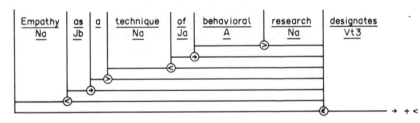

FIG. 8

Note that the receipt of *technique* (Figure 4) might be described as "opening up" certain of the possibilities that had been temporarily in abeyance. That is, while neither *empathy as* nor *empathy as a* could be followed by something that would be a postposed modifier of *empathy* or of some phrase centering on *empathy*, as soon as *technique* has been added this possibility is restored; hence the parentheses are deleted from around ">".

Note also the sharp difference between the situation after *research* and that after *designates* (Figures 7 and 8). After *research* the grammatical possibilities are numerous – if the diagramming is accurate, there are eleven. After *designates* they are far fewer; all but one of the eleven after *research* have been eliminated, since one has been converted into a certainty. It is finally established that everything spoken so far, except *designates* itself, constitutes a unit (i.e., the subject of the sentence), and that anything further in the sentence will relate to that whole composite unit, not to any of its individual components. But it should also be noted that it is not the receipt of the last word of the subject that signals to the hearer the completion of the subject; rather, it is the receipt of the first word AFTER the completion of the subject.

3. Residual indeterminacy

In our first test sentence, as an examination of Figures 1–8 will show, the indeterminacies after the first *n* words all concern the grammatical relationship which will hold between something already spoken and something not yet said. But it is also possible for the parsing of words already heard to remain partly indeterminate until crucial later material has been added.

Suppose, for example, that a speaker begins with

(1)   *The old men and women . . .*

Open-ended parsing of this initial fragment yields something like Figure 9. What can come next depends in part on whether *old* is construed with *men* or with *men and women*; but the hearer cannot tell which of these is the case

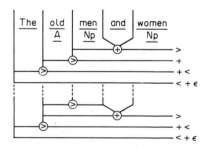

FIG. 9

until he has heard more. Even when the sentence has been completed, the ambiguity of parsing may remain: for example, if the rest of the sentence is

(2)   . . . *were all frightened*

In any such case, we shall speak of a RESIDUAL AMBIGUITY. Residual ambiguity is the structural basis for one kind of verbal joke: the pun.

On the other hand, suppose that the continuation of the sentence were one of the following:

(3)   . . . *stayed at home while the young folks went off to the dance.*
(4)   . . . *stayed at home while the young men went off to the war.*

There seems to be little SEMANTIC ambiguity about *old men and women* by the end of either of these sentences (1–3 or 1–4). But before we can conclude that there is also no residual ambiguity of parsing, we must recall assumption (A7). If the hearer resolves the ambiguity of parsing of (1) by virtue of information conveyed later in the sentence, the information so used must itself be grammatical, not merely semantic. Considering the high degree of parallelism between (3) and (4), we should have to conclude that *folks* and *men*, or *dance* and *war*, or both of these pairs of words, are grammatically different rather than merely lexically distinct members of single form-classes. Similar consideration of other sentences soon shows that, for a hearer, the vocabulary of a language must fall into a vastly larger number of grammatically distinct classes than most grammarians have wanted to deal with.[4]

I can see nothing wrong with such a conclusion, but there is an alternative possibility to be considered. We might decide to say that no continuation removes the ambiguity of parsing of (1). But if no context can remove the ambiguity, then it would be better to say that there is no GRAMMATICAL ambiguity about the phrase in the first place – any ambiguity is purely semantic. Our parsing machinery should then be revised in such a way as to provide the same grammatical description of *old men and women* regardless of the sentence context in which that phrase occurs. It is easy enough to do this: we merely recognize a four-part construction in which the first constituent must be a descriptive adjective, the second and fourth plural nouns, and the third the word *and*.

This second alternative might be attractive if we could carry it through so drastically as to achieve the following result: that at the end of a sentence there are never any residual ambiguities of parsing. I think it highly doubtful that any such result could be achieved, unless we were willing to transfer to the sphere of semantics an enormous number of distinctions that we have always thought were grammatical and without which our conception of grammar would be impoverished indeed. There are too many instances in which what strikes us intuitively as an indeterminacy of meaning seems to correlate with alternative interpretations of grammatical organization. We want to formalize the latter differences partly as a step towards the explication of the former. Therefore, whenever we seem to have some choice, we ought to accept a "richer" grammar rather than a poorer one. In the present connection, our empirical assumptions do not force either type of decision, but allow us to take our choice.[5] We shall choose a "richer" grammar – without necessarily implying that the particular examples displayed above must be among those for which the grammar provides, since they were meant merely to be suggestive. Our decision may be strengthened, perhaps, by a second example. Initial sequence (5) shows an ambiguity of parsing, unresolved by completion (6), resolved in one way – or at least pushed towards such resolution – by completion (7), and in a different way by (8):

(5)   *A man eating fish. . .*
(6)   *. . . has an unbalanced diet.*
(7)   *. . . called the piranha is found in the tropical waters of Brazil.*
(8)   *. . . on Friday is not necessarily a Catholic.*
Or, again (with credit to Noam Chomsky):
(9)   *Flying planes . . .*
(10)   *. . . can be dangerous.*
(11)   *. . . is dangerous.*
(12)   *. . . are dangerous.*

4. Garden-path jokes

Having concluded that an ambiguity of parsing can be removed by what follows the ambiguous phrase, we must now ask whether the reverse of this can happen. That is, can an unambiguous structure earlier in a sentence be rendered ambiguous by what comes later?

Something like this seems to happen in certain kinds of jokes. The jokester builds up in the hearer a conviction that a word or phrase is to be interpreted in a certain way, and then adds something that either renders the phrase ambiguous or forces a different unambiguous interpretation:

(13)   *He waxed wroth when I hit him, and Roth didn't like it a bit.* (Groucho Marx)
(14)   *We were going to take the plane to Chicago but it was too heavy.*
(15)   *Woman who cooks carrots and peas in same pot very unsanitary.* (Confucius)

However, in our model we are dealing with a faultless hearer who always does ALL the open-ended parsing he can after each successive word, regardless of the relative probabilities associated with the different possibilities. One residual fault of such a faultless hearer is that he can have no sense of humor. He cannot hear the difference between the adjective *wroth* and the surname *Roth* when he first hears the word, since they are homophones. Therefore his open-ended parsing of the initial sequence *He waxed wroth* must be ambiguous.

The impact on the hearer of a joke of this sort thus turns on the fact that real hearers are not faultless: they can be led up the garden path. They can be induced to neglect some of the grammatical possibilities and to expect others, and can thus be given a jolt by an unexpected though perfectly grammatical twist.

We conclude that, within our frame of reference, an initially unambiguous structure CANNOT be rendered ambiguous by what comes later. Whenever this seems to happen, the structure in question was actually ambiguous to start with.

5. End of sentence

We have been speaking freely of "end of sentence", but this, too, is a point about which a question must be asked: what signals "end of sentence" to a hearer?

Many of our co-workers on English would immediately say that end of sentence is signalled by the occurrence of a sentence-final intonation. There is doubtless a positive statistical correlation between so-called sentence-final intonations and grammatical ends of sentences, but the correlation is far from perfect. Thus someone might say (we use the Smith and Trager symbols for intonation):[6]

(16)   *I didn't want to go there at* $^3all^1\#$

Open-ended parsing shows that this CAN be a whole sentence (at least by our everyday definition of "sentence"). A hearer, registering this possibility, might proceed to say something in reply. Or, if this does not happen, the speaker might continue – perhaps after a considerable pause – with

(17) $^3yesterday^2\|$, $^2though\ to^3day^2\mid$ $^2I\ don't\ ^3mind\ so\ much^1\#$

Now (16) could be a whole sentence, as could also the sequence (16–17); but (17) alone could not. Therefore, if (16) is indeed followed by (17), it has turned out that (16) was not all of a sentence but only the beginning of one.

In general, the most that the hearer's open-ended parsing of an initial sequence can tell him – even if he takes into consideration, as he certainly does, the accompanying intonations – is whether or not that sequence CAN be a sentence. (16) is an instance of a sequence that can be; Figure 3 shows one that cannot be. If an initial sequence is fit to be a whole sentence, then the only reliable signal as to whether, in fact, it is one, is what is said next. If what is said next – by the same speaker or by some other, such as the erstwhile hearer – begins a new sentence, then the preceding sequence was a sentence; otherwise not.

This can be compared with the situation portrayed in Figures 7 and 8: *research* ends the subject, but the hearer cannot know this until he hears *designates*.

6. Constructional grammar

Our understanding of grammar for the hearer and our preference for one or another abstract "marble slab") grammatical model are necessarily inter-related. Before we can continue with our exploration of the former, we must turn briefly to the latter.

For this, the diagrams shown in Figures 1–9 supply a good point of departure. They provide symbolization for four different sorts of things: (1) words; (2) the form classes to which words belong; (3) hierarchical organization or IC (immediate constituent) structure; and (4) construction types.

A construction type is a set of constructions that have some formal property in common: for instance, *black cat* and *ran quickly* are both built by constructions of a so-called "attributive" type, in that one of the constituents resembles the whole more than does the other (*black cat* can be used much as *cat* can, but not as *black* can; *ran quickly* can be used much like *ran*, and not like *quickly*). In our diagrams, we symbolize construction types rather than individual constructions merely as a matter of convenience.

A CONSTRUCTION may be described as a way of putting forms together into larger forms – words into phrases, words and phrases into larger phrases. Abstractly, a construction is a relation: a class of ordered n-ads of forms, where n is always finite, usually small, often exactly 2, but never 1. A form "built by" a construction is necessarily COMPOSITE: that is, an atomic element (a word, in our current frame of reference) does not belong to a construction.

Two forms, simple or composite, belong to the same FORM CLASS if they have exactly identical privileges of occurrence: that is, if each occurs as the ith constituent in any construction in which the other occurs as the ith constituent. Two composite forms belong to the same construction if, for all relevant i, the ith constituent of each belongs to the same form class as the ith constituent of the other, and if the two composite forms belong to the same form-class. It follows that every member of a construction belongs to the same form class, but not necessarily vice versa.

The arrangement of constituents in a composite form is determined by the construction, and two constructions are different if the arrangement is different. Thus *John is here* and *Is John here?* both have ICs *John* and *is here*, put together by two different constructions of a single construction type: the first construction requires that *John* precede *is here*, while the second requires that *John* be inserted at a specifiable place within *is here*.

It is an empirical fact of English that in a great many instances the construction to which a composite form belongs is inferrable without residue from the identity of the constituents (and their arrangement). Thus *black cat* seems never to occur save in contexts in which the construction is a specific one of the type attribute-plus-noun-head. However, there are also ambiguous cases, and a great deal of the character of our abstract grammatical model depends on how we choose to deal with ambiguity.

Consider the two-word composite form *yellow clothes*. This can occur in sentence-contexts of either of the following varieties:

(18)   *Washing in strong soap will yellow clothes.*
(19)   *She likes to wear yellow clothes.*

In a CONSTRUCTIONAL GRAMMAR, we say that *yellow* is the same word in both, that *clothes* is the same word in both, but that the two words are put together by different constructions. The first construction is one of the type verb-plus-object, the second one of the type attribute-plus-noun-head. Along with this, we are able to say that two words are the same word if and only if they are phonemically identical (no homophones or zeros), and that no word belongs to more than one form class. Ambiguity is then handled wholly in terms either of constructions (*yellow clothes*) or of IC organization (*old men and women*).

An alternative method is to introduce inaudible differences among words in such a way that constructions are wholly eliminated as independent ingredients in the grammatical model. Thus, for example, we recognize two words, *yellow*$_1$ and *yellow*$_2$, the former belonging to some subclass of the class of verbs, the latter to some subclass of the class of adjectives. Sentence (18) contains the former, sentence (19) the latter. (Or, equally well, a single word *yellow* is assigned to two different form classes, and is said to be a member of one in the one context, of the other in the other.) This alternative deals with ambiguity in terms of homophony or of form classes (*yellow clothes*) and of IC organization (*old men and women*). It eliminates constructions by reducing them all to a single "construction" often called COLLOCATION. With certain further (optional) adjustments – for example, an insistence that forms in collocation must always be adjacent, never separated – this procedure yields what has been called a PHRASE GRAMMAR.[7]

Phrase grammar (as commonly understood) has a number of known weaknesses, the recognition of which has been the main motive behind the development of transform grammars. Constructional grammar does not share these weaknesses. In the first place, it is possible (as we shall see presently) for constructional grammar to handle quite simply those phenomena that any reasonably manipulable phrase grammar best leaves for a transformational overlay. In the second place, in constructional grammar it is possible to accept the intuitively desirable notion that some words, such as *and* or *or*, are not constituents at all but rather MARKERS OF CONSTRUCTIONS (if there are no constructions, then obviously there is nothing for these elements to mark). Finally, and specifically with reference to grammar for the hearer, the allocation of ambiguity to IC organization and to constructions, and the elimination of homophony at the word level, seem to yield a kind of realism that a phrase grammar, or a phrase-and-transform grammar, can deal with only in a more indirect and complex way.

However, in order to use a constructional grammar as the basis for our development of grammar for the hearer, it is apparently necessary to add one further assumption to those given in § 1.

(A8) The number of constructions in a language is finite.

This is empirically as realistic (or unrealistic) as our earlier assumptions. It has to be listed separately because it cannot be shown to follow from those already listed. Thus, if we were to consider only those constructions in which both (or all) of the constituents can be single words, then, because the vocabulary is finite by assumption (A1), we would clearly obtain at most a finite number of distinct constructions. However, there is nothing in the earlier assumptions to preclude any number of constructions in which the constituents are themselves always composite forms.

Assumption (A8) asserts that, for some finite n, any composite form longer than n words is built by a construction that also yields composite forms not longer than n words. This can also be paraphrased in terms of form classes: for some finite n, any composite form longer than n words belongs to a form class that also includes forms not longer than n words (hence the number of form classes in a language is itself (finite).

Finally, the implications of (A8) can be stated in terms of CYCLIC ENDOCENTRICITY. In the face of a finite number of constructions, if, as is obviously the case, there is no limit on the length of grammatical forms, then there must exist at least one finite set of constructions $C_1, C_2, \ldots C_n$ with the following property: for $1 \leq i < n$, C_i builds forms that can be used as constituents in forms built by C_{i+1}; and C_n builds forms that can be used as constituents in forms built by C_1. (If $n = 1$, then the one construction C_1 is endocentric in the traditional sense.)

7. Reducibility of transformations

A grammar that makes use both of constructions and of not more than a finite number of transformations can be converted into a pure constructional grammar.

It will suffice to deal with the English passive transformation as representative of all optional transformations.[8] Suppose that an inital sequence is

(20)   *The corpse of the seventh victim . . .*

LFH-F

Among the possibilities is that (20) will turn out to be all of a subject. Possible predicates would then include

(21)   . . . *was lying behind some bushes.*
(22)   . . . *was found by a troop of Boy Scouts.*

The open-ended parsing of (20) can provide for a distinction between these two types of possibility in the following way. We replace the single symbol "ϵ" by a pair, say "ϵ" to mean that what precedes may turn out to be a subject in an active clause, and "$\bar{\epsilon}$" to mean that what precedes, with what follows, may turn out to constitute a passive transform of an active clause in which what precedes would have been the object. As soon as the sentence has "grown" enough more to eliminate one of these possibilities, open-ended parsing will of course lack the symbol for that possibility.

We see, thus, that a constructional grammar provides for transformations by a proliferation of constructions. Since there are at most a finite number of distinct optional transformations, in addition to a finite number of constructions, this required proliferation will yield at most a finite number of constructions.

Conversion in the opposite direction is obviously also possible, provided that some of the constructions in a pure constructional grammar prove to be related in an appropriate way. For many purposes a mixed constructional and transform grammar has the advantage of compactness and the merit of highlighting certain relationships that might otherwise be missed. For grammar for the hearer, a pure constructional grammar seems somewhat preferable.

8. Reducibility of constructions

To reinterpret transformations as constructions achieves a more "homogeneous" abstract grammar, in that there is a smaller variety of seemingly different kinds of things. A constructional grammar can, in turn, be rendered more homogeneous if we redefine constructions not as relations between constituents but as themselves constituents. A comparison of Figure 10 with Figure 8 shows how this can be done. In Figure 8, where constructions are regarded as relations, the construction in which two constituents stand is indicated roughly (via a symbol for construction type) at the point of junction of the boxes for those constituents. In Figure 10, the same symbols are put in line with the words; the boxes now show nothing but the IC structure. (The latter fact is underscored even more by the redrawing in Figure 11, where the IC structure is represented by a "tree" in the way currently more popular). The conversion involves a general recognition of composite forms with three rather than two immediate constituents, but this is clearly trivial.

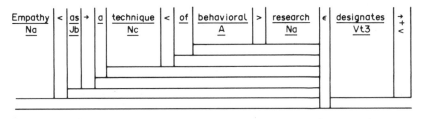

FIG. 10

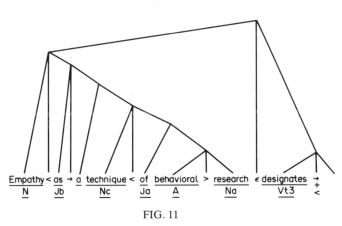

FIG. 11

Seemingly less trivial is that the change forces a recognition of two kinds of basic elements in the vocabulary: elements that the hearer can hear (words), and those (constructions) that the hearer cannot hear but can only infer. For abstract grammar this does not matter – as long as the required inferences are of the sort that can be made, and this is a topic that has already been discussed. In any case, the dichotomy is not an entirely clearcut one. In our earlier view, certain "words" were taken not as constituents but as markers of constructions. By the earlier view, *men and women* would be diagrammed as shown in the upper half of Figure 9: here *and* and the sign "+" actually give the same information. By the new view, the diagram would be as shown in Figure 12, where the redundant sign "+" is omitted. The logical status of the audible form *and* is the same as that of the inaudible elements written on the line in Figures 10 and 11. Similarly, the handling of *a* and of *of* in Figures 10 and 11 is based on the notion that some CONSTITUENTS may stand in one-to-one correlation with certain constructions, so that both need not be recognized.

We see, thus that a constructional grammar can be converted to a phrase grammar; in the light of § 7, it also follows that a transform grammar can be converted to a phrase grammar. However, this reducibility entails a (finite) expansion of the basic vocabulary. If we insist that the basic vocabulary must

FIG. 12

be invariant from one tentative abstract grammar to another, the reductions are not possible.

In the sections that follow, it will be more convenient to speak of constructions as relations, but what will be said will apply with equal validity to the sort of phrase grammar achieved by the reduction described above.

9. The formal respectability of grammatical states

We have imagined a faultless hearer who always does all the open-ended parsing he can. But just how much does this amount to? If the powers ascribed to the ideal hearer differ too drastically from those of real hearers – and of grammarians – then the paradigm is of no help to us.

Now the grammarian, in seeking to discover and describe the grammatical state established by an initial sequence of words, proceeds by testing various continuations of the sequence and determining how each possible continuation would fit grammatically into the initial sequence. Unless he goes about this systematically, he can easily miss some of the possibilities. Even if he proceeds systematically, he will still miss some of the possibilities unless they can all be discovered by a FINITE number of trial-and-error operations. This would seem to be a fitting limitation to impose on the powers of our ideal hearer.

It is immediately obvious that the grammatical state established by a given initial sequence cannot be tied to the whole class of sentences that might begin with the initial sequence, since in the typical case that class of sentences is infinite. We should still have an infinite class to deal with were we to consider only one out of each set of grammatically identical sentences of the whole class, since two sentences are necessarily grammatically distinct if they are of different lengths, and there is no theoretical limit to the length of a sentence.

What we have to demonstrate, then, seems to be along the following lines: The sentences that begin with a given initial sequence fall into families. Two sentences belong to the same family if all constructions (unambiguous or ambiguous) within the initial sequence are the same for both, and if all constructions (unambiguous or ambiguous) across the boundary between sequence and continuation are the same for both. Many, perhaps all, of the families include an infinite number of sentences, but there is a finite number of families. If this last is true, then the grammatical state at the end of the initial sequence can be discovered by a finite number of trial-and-error operations, since one need consider only one sentence of each family.

But in this form the assumption is clearly true. Assume that we know nothing about an initial sequence except that it consists of n words. Each of the n words is a grammatical form. Each pair of words, adjacent or not, might turn out to be a grammatical form; likewise each triad, each tetrad, and so on up to the whole sequence. Therefore the actual number of grammatical forms in the initial sequence cannot exceed

$$\sum_{i=1}^{n} {}_nC_i,$$

which is obviously finite. Now any of these grammatical forms either stands in construction only with other grammatical forms within the initial sequence, or else with grammatical forms in the continuation. Therefore there can be only a finite number of grammatical forms with constituents on both sides of the boundary between initial sequence and continuation. Further, by assumption (A8) each one of these latter can stand only in one or another of a finite number of constructions. This proves that there is only a finite number of families. The infinite membership of any one family stems from the absence of any limit on the length of grammatical forms in possible continuations.

As a limiting case, consider the degenerate initial "sequence" of no words at all. All possible "continuations" yield sentences of a single family.

10. Stochastic representation

The total number of grammatical states provided for by a language is not finite. A glance at Figure 7 shows why. There is no limit to the number of additional postposed modifiers that could be added after *Empathy as a technique of behavioral research*, indefinitely postponing the beginning of the predicate. Each would complicate the diagram by one more horizontal line pointing to the right; therefore each would yield a new grammatical state, not a repetition of one already passed through.

A given grammatical state, however, can be immediately followed only by one of a finite number of grammatical states. This follows from assumption (A1): a given initial sequence can be extended by one additional word only in a finite number of ways.

These two facts about states suggest that grammar for the hearer might be treated as an infinite-state Markov process. To construct the matrix, we order the infinite set of states as follows: First comes that which pertains when nothing has been said; then all those (a finite number) that can be established by an initial sequence of one word. After that, we order the rest in such a way that, for some finite n, and for all $m > n$, the ABSOLUTE probability (or frequency of occurrence) of the $(m + 1)$th state is not greater than that of the mth state.

Row sums of transition probabilities are unity because the probability that a grammatical state will be followed by SOME next grammatical state is unity. In any row, there will be some finite n such that all entries after the nth are zero. The non-zero entries will appear only in two loci: in a strip of columns on the extreme left, and in a strip of diagonals. The first locus for non-zero entries is because there are some relatively common states (those established by no word or by a single initial word) that can occur after a great many different states. The second locus is because any really rare state has a chance to occur only after some state that is almost as rare.

It follows from this stochastic representation that the grammar of a language can be APPROXIMATED AS ACCURATELY AS ONE WISHES by a finite state Markov process: from the infinite matrix for the infinite state process we delete all rows and colums after the nth, for some suitability large n, and make arbitrary small adjustments in the non-zero entries to preserve row sums.

11. Grammar for hearer and for speaker

There is a large and important class of phenomena in the actual use of English for which no existing abstract grammatical theory – nor, indeed, this grammar for the hearer – makes provision. Any honest examination of running conversational English shows that the neat, complete, "grammatical" sentence is something of a rarity (and this seems to be true regardless of our choice of definition of "sentence," unless we select a definition so weak as to be useless). We do find some, of course; but we also find a high incidence of false starts, of parenthetical insertions, of ungrammatical pseudo-sentences, and so on. Grammarians have for decades almost studiously ignored these phenomena. But speakers and hearers do not ignore them – they carry a sizeable share of the communicative load.

This suggests that we may have to reexamine our basic premises, and perhaps overhaul them rather completely and make a new start. Before we undertake any such drastic move, however, we should consider certain ways in which we might be able to make empirically profitable use of the results of abstract grammatical theory.

It can be argued that grammar for the hearer, as discussed in this paper, has a certain kind of priority over grammar for the speaker. A speaker sometimes knows what he is going to say next; a hearer cannot know for sure until he has heard it. Yet the contrast between the terms "hearer" and "speaker" is misleading. One may at moments function purely as a hearer. The alternative to this is not to function purely as a speaker, but to function as BOTH speaker and hearer – since anyone hears his own speech. The planning-ahead, in which a speaker obviously indulges sometimes, can be viewed as a rapid scanning of the alternatives allowed grammatically by what he has said up to a given point, and a selecting of one of them. These alternatives are public property, as available to the audience as to the speaker himself. Hearing thus involves no operations not involved in speaking; but speaking involves all the operations involved in hearing, plus the logistic operation of scanning ahead and making choices.

The logistics of speaking is something like that of playing very amateurish chess, in which one is allowed to take moves back and in which one may overlook part of the situation on the board (even to failing to notice that a king is in check!). However, taking moves back does not erase the sound waves that were produced: the audience has heard them and has drawn its own conclusions. Thus:

(23)   *I felt like kiss – like shaking his hand.*

A direction of development can be abandoned because of changes in the external circumstances:

(24)   *I felt like – Get out of here, Joe!*

An abandonment may be temporary (and its resumption may or may not entail recapitulation):

(25)   *I felt like – Get out of here, Joe! – like shaking his hand.*

A speaker may "lose the thread," and produce an "imparsible" sentence that is nevertheless understood in its context:

(26)   *Empathy as a technique of behavioral research developed originally in psychiatry, but later taken over by anthropologists, and some of the latter have put it to work in ways the psychiatrists never dreamed of.*

Along such lines as these, we can perhaps begin to understand the difference between a language as an abstract system and the way real human beings use the system.

One common phenomenon, however resists this approach: the blend. I once intended to say *people born and raised in a culture* but came out with *people braised in a culture*. Everyone understood both the actuality and the intention. I do not know how to parse this phrase in a way that gives overt recognition to the blend. Until we can, our grammatical theories are and will remain inadequate.

Notes

1. The Hague: Mouton (1968).
2. The proof is given informally in Chomsky, 1957 [2, chapter 3]; formally in Chomsky, 1956 [1].
3. The possibility of something like *Empathy, as you all know*, . . . is precluded by the assumed intonation.
4. Harris, 1946 [3], works with only about 18 form classes of words, and Harris, 1957 [4], with only 7; but in both cases the classes are *not* pairwise disjunct, as we require.
5. A third alternative, of course, is to suspend Assumption (A7). But this would seem to threaten the highly-prized fundamental postulate of the separability of grammar and semantics (our assumption A2).
6. Only relevant parts of the intonation are marked. Pitch levels run from bottom to top, /¹/ through /⁴/;/|/, /||/, and /#/ represent terminals.
7. See Chomsky, 1956, 1957 [1; 2]. We shall not here constrain the term "phrase grammar" to those in which constituents must be adjacent.
8. Obligatory transformations are a matter of morphophonemics and hence of no interest to us here.

References

1. Noam Chomsky, Three models for the description of language, *IRE Transactions on Information Theory*, vol. IT-2 (1956), pp. 113–124.
2. ——, *Syntactic Structures*. Mouton & Co.: 's-Gravenhage, 1957.
3. Zellig Harris, From morpheme to utterance, *Language* 22 (1946), pp. 161–183.
4. ——, Co-occurrence and transformation in linguistic structure, *Language*, **33** (1957), pp. 283–340.

5

The importance and irreducibility of the comprehension/production dialectic

H. STEPHEN STRAIGHT

Statement of intent

Language ability, like many other complex human skills, is divisible into two distinct but interacting realms: perception and action. The evidence for a split between comprehension[1]* and production, which can even be seen in the posterior (receptive) versus anterior (expressive) representation of language functions in the brain, is wide-ranging and unarguable (Straight, 1976). Virtually all previous and most ongoing work on the topic of language – descriptive, applied, historical, critical, sociological, and typological, as well as psychological – is thrown into a new interpretive perspective in light of this fundamental dichotomy.

Yet most language scholars – literati, language teachers, linguists, psychologists, philosophers – appear to remain unconvinced that this comprehension/production distinction has radical implications for the content and conduct of all research and theory relating to language. They do accept the conclusion that the psychological processes that are responsible for language performance are divisible in some respects into processes that are specific to language comprehension versus processes that are specific to language production. But they insist (without anything but *a priori* "evidence") that the vital ("grammatical") core of processes is common to the two realms. They therefore reject the contention that the processual bifurcatedness of language performance undermines the hallowed non-bifurcated conception of the "competence" that makes both comprehension and production possible.

* Superscript numbers refer to notes at end of chapter.

69

The present essay brings together and elaborates upon ideas opposed to this dominant unicameral view of language. My hope is that presentation of a dialectical–processual[2] theory of language will prove valuable in addressing the problem of "Language for Hearers".

Antecedents

In a nutshell, the dialectical–processual view of language holds that the processes of language comprehension and the processes of language production are not in any respects reducible to "linguistic processes" (or, worse yet, to items of "structural knowledge") that are neutral (or even bidirectional) with respect to the comprehension/production duality. Because of this, an understanding of the psychological bases of language is possible only in the framework of a theory in which this fundamental dichotomy is made explicit and unbending. Such a theory must have separate components pertaining to the psychological processes that result in language comprehension and to the psychological processes that result in language production, plus an account of how these dialectically opposed processes interact with each other in acts of understanding and saying.

Such a move toward dialectically opposed sets of processes – and away from processually neutral structures – as the focus of linguistic theory may at first blush appear to be a drastic departure from most previous linguistic scholarship. The dominant view for most of the present century has been that linguistic theory should focus on linguistic structures abstracted away from their psychological–processual context. The two most prominent American theorists exemplify this point well. After giving up his youthful attachment to Wundtian psychology as a basis for linguistic theory (Bloomfield, 1914), Leonard Bloomfield (1933: vii) asserted "that we can pursue the study of language without reference to any one psychological doctrine, and that to do so safeguards our results and makes them more significant to workers in related fields". Noam Chomsky (1965), on the other hand, brought linguistics solidly back into contact with "psychological doctrine", but the doctrine was his own: Because a theory of performance (the processes of language comprehension and production) must "incorporate" a theory of competence (linguistic knowledge), linguistics must seek first and foremost to provide a description of this supposedly process-neutral competence. To insist, as does the dialectical–processual approach, that comprehension and production processes themselves must be the focus of linguistic theory does, by these lights, look rather revolutionary.

"Every revolution is in part a revival." Ironically, the widely acknowledged founder of modern structural linguistics, Ferdinand de Saussure (1916[1959]: 11–15) explicitly identified language as a set of conversion mechanisms (the "speaking circuit") within the individual human brain, and he detailed the contrast between the mechanisms of audition, perception, and association and those of formulation, construction, and articulation. He identified the former (receptive) processes as *langue*, which he believed to be the proper object of linguistic investigation. The remainder, the "executive" portion of the speaking circuit, he referred to as *parole*, which he believed to be too variable from person to person and too much an accident of circumstance to be amenable to meaningful investigation.

In his actual descriptive practice, however, Saussure, like all other linguists before and after him, presented a view of language that largely ignored processual issues, but which exhibited, if anything, an implicit bias toward variables more relevant to speaking than to listening. His phonology focused almost exclusively on the articulatory basis of speech sounds, and the remainder of his grammar neglected such things as how a listener might go about recognizing and understanding words, phrases, sentences, and so forth. He thus not only flouted his own dictum that *langue* resides in comprehension processes, but also implicitly disproved his own claim that the processes of production, or *parole*, could not be scientifically studied.

In the end, then, Saussure's work is rightly called "structural": Despite his initial reference to linguistic signs as the events that occur when "auditory images" become associated with "concepts" in the receptive portion of the speaking circuit, he describes language in terms that have no specifiable connection to events that might occur in a neuropsychological model of language performance. Language, according to this approach, is not a set of neural events but rather a set of "signs", each consisting of a fused pair of "mutually implicative" elements. One element of each pair is a superficial (producible–interpretable) linguistic form, an overt and transcribable "signifier" (*signifiant*). The other element is a deep (intendable–intelligible) linguistic meaning, a covert but inferrable "signified" (*signifié*). A structural "grammar" specifies the nature of, and the similarities, differences, and combinatorial possibilities among, these fused, bipartite signs. One or another variant of this structural approach has characterized all of the schools of linguistics in this century.[3]

The persistent focus on structure as something abstractable away from process, and the bias toward features of production over features of comprehension, appear to result in part from historical and practical factors. The linguists who preceded (and instructed) Saussure had developed non-processual and production-oriented categories and variables for describing speech sounds and parts of speech. These descriptive devices had proven serviceable for a wide variety of data-collection and analytic tasks, and since the kinds of psychoacoustic and other perceptual measures that would be required for a comprehension-oriented approach to language had not been developed, Saussure simply adopted the tools that were available, despite their profound incompatibility with his own perception-oriented precepts.

With the rise of acoustics and cognitive psychology, the speaker bias of linguistic research has attenuated somewhat, as more has become known about human perception. Yet this new knowledge has not led to a revival of Saussure's strong arguments for a strict separation between accounts of language comprehension and accounts of language production. This has been blocked by the established non-processual assumptions of structural–linguistic theory. Therefore, new perception-oriented insights have either been incorporated into linguistic models as additional characteristics of the structures of language (for example, the "simultaneously articulatory–acoustic" features of linguistic phonetics), or else relegated to a status external to the grammar (for example, the "perceptual strategies" that render some "grammatical" utterances incomprehensible and some "ungrammatical" utterances comprehensible).

Confession

The longstanding and ubiquitous neglect of the fundamental conflict between comprehension-based and production-based description of language is one of the most lamentable features of modern linguistic theory, because it has kept linguists from exploiting the explanatory value of a theory of interaction between these two realms of ability. Many of the most intractable theoretical and descriptive problems of linguistics derive from the belief that linguists can (or even must) study language structure independently from language processes. The dialectical–processual approach focuses on processes, consistently separates the processes of comprehension from the processes of production, and shows how they work together in language understanding and saying. This approach not only leads in the direction of solutions to old problems but also opens up large and promising new areas of linguistic investigation.

Some fairly recent developments (about which I will have more to say in the present essay) encourage me to think that evidence for the comprehension/production dialectic has led some researchers to temper their allegiance to non-dialectical, non-processual assumptions about the nature of language ability, but the overall pattern of rejection (or polite acknowledgement followed by neglect) of this sort of evidence over the years has given me pause for thought. It's possible, I imagine, that what strikes me (and a few others) as a clear and compelling truth about the nature of language is wrong in some embarrassing way that no one can bring themselves to say, but it may also be that the dialectical–processual alternative to received structuralist theory demands a shift of perspective so great that few are willing to accept it, despite the evidence for it. A (possibly grandiose) analogy may be instructive.

The dialectical–processual view of language bears much the same relation to the dominant structural view of language that Copernican (heliocentric) astronomy bore to Ptolemaic (geocentric) astronomy in the late Middle Ages (cf. Boorstin, 1983: 294–304). This holds for ontology (What is real?), epistemology (How can we be sure?), and phenomenology (How does the world relate to our subjective experience?). The dialectical alternative in linguistic theory is just as abstract, just as difficult to prove, and just as contrary to common sense as the Sun-centred view of celestial objects. And structuralist assumptions about language are just as commonsensical and just as wrong as Earth-centred conceptions of the heavens.

The parallel extends even to the nature of the bulk of the available "evidence", which, because of the sophistication, diligence, and prejudice of the adherents to the dominant view, actually appears to be better explained by that view than by the newer, opposing view. Ptolemy and the myriad geocentric observers and theorists that preceded and followed him had the evidence of common sense on their side: The one thing that we can tell before we have even set up our instruments or begun jotting down our observations is that the Earth is immobile while the Sun, Moon, and stars move above it. That it is the Sun that moves, not the Earth, is clear, isn't it? Copernicus and his at first scattered and meagre followers were bucking not merely the powerful academic–religious establishments of their times but also the evidence of everyday experience. How could they believe that the Earth moved while the Sun stood still? This idea was not simply heretical but outright mad.

And if the evidence of everyone's senses were not enough to refute the heliocentric heresy, there was abundant scientific evidence. The detailed geocentric charts of the heavens, with all those beautifully gyrating stars and planets, and the carefully calculated tables of astronomical predictions based on geocentric models, were excellent predictors of the movements of the stars in the sky. Heliocentric charts and tables were at first far inferior to these as astronomical guides. And when the geocentric system did show its weaknesses,

Astronomers were adept at explaining away what seemed only minor problems by a variety of complicated epicycles, deferents, equants, and eccentrics, which gave them a heavy vested interest in the whole scheme. The more copious this peripheral literature became, the more difficult it became to retreat to fundamentals. If the central scheme was not correct, surely so many learned men would not have bothered to offer their many subtle corrections (Boorstin, 1983: 295–296).

Similarly, common sense and the extensive work of generations of grammarians attest to the validity of a unitary (not dialectical), structural (not processual) view of language ability. How can you say that all we need to have in order to comprehend and produce language is "know-how"? Isn't it clear that we have knowledge about our language, some of it conscious but most of it apparently unconscious, that guides both our interpretation of others' speech and our formulation of ideas in language? Would you have us believe that what linguists have been doing is fundamentally misguided? The common linguistic–theoretical presumption that highly abstract propositions about language (grammatical rules) are unconsciously known to all language users may be hard for some to swallow, but to argue that language ability depends on mental processes that are not only unconscious but dialectical, and that there is no necessary body of unitary and propositional knowledge we need to possess in order to comprehend and produce language, strikes the common mind as unparsimonious, insubstantial, and even nonsensical.

On the positive side, though, I am comforted, perhaps even emboldened, by the idea that once the dialectical–processual view takes hold (as it is sure to, I imagine), its precepts will be just as integral to our common knowledge about the processes of language and mind as the Copernican view is integral to our common thinking about the solar system. Linguistics is after all a very young science, and also it may take some time for the general intellectual climate to become hospitable to the view of mind and of language that is embodied in dialectical–processual theory.

Know-that versus know-how: propositions versus processes

The distinction between knowledge and ability (or between know-that and know-how, or between propositions and processes) has become increasingly complex in recent work on language. For example, in a trenchant critique of structural linguistic theory, G. P. Baker and P. M. S. Hacker (1984) have shown (among other things) that the linguist's employment of "rules" in describing language "knowledge" fails to cohere with any of the intelligible meanings of the terms "rule" and "knowledge". They insist that the conscious normative rules that people cite when correcting errors or accounting for linguistic behaviour constitute a compelling explanatory basis for language theory: there is no need for the linguist's host of unconscious and abstruse "rules". They are not only unintelligible but also unnecessary.

The conclusion is only half right. Postulation of myriad unconscious propositions about languages has not resulted in a viable theory of the workings of language, but substitution of conscious propositions won't be any better. What little propositional knowledge language users have of their language is flawed, fragmentary, and largely irrelevant to fluent language comprehension and production. Baker and Hacker's attachment to the normative (prescriptive) force of such knowledge reveals that they have a rather outmoded faith in the importance of school grammar. My own experience as a university-level linguistics instructor has shown me that the correlation between a person's ability to articulate grammatical rules and the ability to speak effectively and listen comprehendingly is insufficient to use the former ability to explain the latter. To the extent that language users do appeal to rules in accounting for linguistic behaviour, these appeals are at best insightful but rather ad hoc rationalizations and at worst rote-learned and absurdly doctrinaire admonitions. And in either case, if we use these overt formulations of rules as explanations of certain things people say, what will we use as a basis for explaining the rule statements themselves? There appears to be an infinite regress here.

On the other hand, Baker and Hacker appear to have rather different ends in mind than those espoused by the linguists they criticize. In particular, the rules that linguists devise do not purport to be justifications for what people say, but rather causes. On this widely held view, linguistic rules are not normative, as Baker and Hacker assume they must be, but rather constitutive. That is, linguistic rules describe not how you *should*, but rather how you *do*, comprehend and produce language. The psychological version of this view holds that linguistic rules are causally related to acts of speaking and hearing in much the same way that movements of pistons, gears, and shafts are causally related to automotive locomotion. The grammar describes the internal manipulation of linguistic units in a way that directly corresponds to the psychological processes that occur during language comprehension and production. The more cautious (and orthodox Chomskyan) version of this view holds that linguistic rules are not the efficient but rather the formal causes of language performance, rather like an engineer's instructions to the factory regarding materials, measurements, and tolerances for a new automobile: the grammar is a list of specifications to which psycholinguistic processes must conform in order for language performance to occur.

It is understandable that Baker and Hacker implicitly reject both of these possible presumptions regarding the status of rules of grammar (see Cooper, 1975 and Matthews, 1979 for explicit and thorough debunkings of the "unconscious rules" of recent linguistic theory), but they end up speaking at cross-purposes with those who are seeking to devise a theory of language ability. It is for this reason that I have consistently avoided using the term "knowledge" to describe the focus of dialectical–processual theory. Baker and Hacker are correct in claiming that the conscious normative rules people know concerning their language constitute the only language "knowledge" we can study, but they are also correct in noting that an account of language "ability" will require something quite different from this. They say nothing at all about this second problem, which many linguists have thought was the central problem for linguistics. What Baker and Hacker are saying to such linguists, more by implication than by assertion, is that this problem is not in fact being addressed in current linguistic research.

Let's look, then, at the gap between what many linguists seem to want to achieve and the things that have actually been produced in the course of linguistic research. Virtually all previous and current theories of language have assumed that to know a language is to have in one's head something (or some set of things) that contains approximately what published dictionary and a published reference grammar of that language contain: to know a language is to know the pronunciations and meanings of a number of phrases, words, and word-parts and a number of principles concerning how these building blocks can be arranged. It is now commonplace to see linguists describe such unconscious propositional knowledge about language as a complex and variegated set of "rules": lexical rules for words, syntactic rules for phrases, phonological rules for pronunciations, semantic rules for meanings, etc. An infinite set of words, phrases, sentences, and discourses of indefinite complexity is in this way supposedly made "accessible" to the language user. Different theorists make different assumptions and construct competing hypotheses about what elements of sound, meaning, and symbolic structure must be posited as the phonetic, semantic, and categorial contents of one's internal grammar, and no-one claims that a complete grammar for any language has yet been created, but linguists are widely agreed that this goal is the one to which they are all directed.

But let's consider this goal in relation to the descriptive work that linguists actually do. Right off, the idea that we might be able to speak and understand on the basis of the information contained in a dictionary or grammar is wildly false if we look at published (as opposed to hypothetical) dictionaries or grammars (or fragments of grammars). Consider dictionaries: far from being "processually neutral", their entries are organized so as to be accessible on a phonetic, alphabetical or other non-semantic basis; these modes of access appear to resemble the modes of access that we have to the words of our language during language comprehension. However, wonderful as dictionaries are for looking up words you've heard or read (or thought of using yourself) so as to determine their (likely) meaning, they are notoriously frustrating as tools for the speaker or writer who cannot think of a word to express an idea.

Indeed, semantically organized listings of related words arose precisely to fill the needs of language composers as opposed to language perceivers: Recall that the full title of Peter Mark Roget's 1852 compendium was *Thesaurus of English Words and Phrases Classified and Arranged so as to Facilitate the Expression of Ideas and Assist in Literary Composition* (Roget, 1977: ii). A thesaurus can help you hunt down that perfect word even if you have only the vaguest and most general idea of what conceptual domain it resides in. This valuable aid to language composition presents information quite distinct from the information universally found in regular dictionaries, and this information is, moreover, arranged in an entirely non-alphabetic manner (though accompanied by an alphabetical index so that you can use the categorized list more efficiently when you are able to think of a word close to the one you need).

No-one would claim that a thesaurus is a plausible approximation to what would presumably be needed to explain how a complex of conceptual "stuff" gets verbalized by a person's brain, but the tip-of-the-tongue synonymizing that we observe in actual word-finding behaviour does suggest that some such cross-referencing network of semantically related words is involved. Dictionaries, if we include thesaurus-type classification schemes as well as standard word lists, thus do not provide the sort of process-neutral picture of word-sized elements that are assumed in linguistic theory; instead, they appear to be either comprehension-oriented or production-oriented, but never neutral or ambi-functional.

Published descriptions of the non-lexical aspects of language, on the other hand, go too far in the opposite direction. Descriptions of the phonology, morphology, syntax, semantics, pragmatics (etc.) of languages, whether of the traditional "reference grammar" variety or of the more modern descriptive or generative varieties, are scarcely "usable" at all. For example, although they may occasionally offer advice on how to process syntactic input to arrive at interpretations (when particular constructions are seen to pose difficulties for users), they do not organize these instructions in a way that would be efficacious for ongoing syntactic processing. They also contain no instructions as to how to process thoughts to construct linguistic output.

In short, published grammatical descriptions do not exhibit any mechanisms whereby the utterances that are possible in a language can be made accessible to a language user when they are needed, whether for comprehension or for production. The descriptions presented in these handbooks, sketches, and research papers do not provide information that could be used for any aspect of language performance other than *post facto* editorial revisions of actual utterances, to make them adhere to the explicit or implicit prescriptions espoused by the describers. Their use appears to be limited to the presentation of information about "language structure" for people who may wonder, for reasons of uncertainty or curiosity, what that structure "is", even though such knowledge is largely irrelevant and clearly unnecessary for the fluent language user. Linguistic theory promises to be a (subpart of a) theory of mind, but descriptive linguistic practices do not made good on this promise.

The dialectical–processual theory of language proposes to resolve this discrepancy between the goals and the methods of linguistics. To phrase the solution in the terms of the preceding discussion, the dialectical–processual theory of language assumes that to know a language is to have in one's head not one dictionary/grammar but two. One of these is arranged for the purpose of making sense out of what one hears or reads, and the other is set up for the purpose of constructing sensible speech and writing. Just as in the case of dictionaries versus thesauruses, these two stores of input or output processes are accessed in different manners and contain different information. They are not "known" in any ordinary sense, not even "tacitly" or "implicitly". Although they can be presented as sentences, such as "Upon encountering the word *the*, expect next a noun referring to a contextually establishing or assumable entity" (see Clark and Clark, 1977: 57–79), they are not propositions that you know in the way that you might know that "an English noun phrase can begin with the definite article *the*". Instead, they are sets of processes that are triggered by input of a specific kind, to yield output that serves in turn as triggering input to other sets of processes.

The processual non-neutrality of linguistic representations

A corollary of the belief that language ability can be explained on the basis of non-processual knowledge is the long-standing assumption that the products of language production and the percepts of language perception are, if not absolutely identical, at least completely isomorphic. The speaker articulates something and the listener hears that thing; the thing articulated is the thing perceived. This belief may in fact lie at the root of the non-processual approach to language. It is a commonsensical assent to the testimony of our consciousness to believe that the object of our linguistic perception and the object resulting from an act of linguistic production are identical. This belief encourages us to treat utterances as objects to be collected, classified, and dissected, and then to devise a deductive scheme that uses the analytic categories we have devised for observed utterances to enumerate the infinite set of potential objects that would "count" as utterances. Such a scheme is the guiding aim of modern linguistic research.

If, on the contrary, utterances are seen not as objects but rather as events, events with causes and effects, then the focus of investigation shifts: Instead of asking What is the structure of this object?, seeing it as something external to and independent of language users, we ask What are the causes and effects of this event? What leads a speaker to produce such an event? What effects does the event have on listeners? The implication to be avoided here, of course, is that the dialectical–processual approach might revive the long-discredited stimulus-response approach to language behaviour and perception. But this can be avoided if a continuing insistence upon a processual approach is maintained: Even the most overt "stimuli" and "responses" that sometimes appear in the causal chains in which language performance occurs are not describable in terms external to the sensory and motor processes of perceivers and behavers, and most of the links are not overt but rather consist of events internal to language users. These events are in turn caused by various processes of cognition and intention that must be inferred on the basis of a wide variety of indirect evidence. Seen in this light, utterances suddenly take on a new aura. A processually neutral description of them cannot hope to capture the possibilities for discrepancies between the causes that impelled the production of an utterance and the effects that that utterance had in comprehension.

It is of course generally acknowledged that mismatches between what a speaker says and what a listener understands do arise in language use, but most such mismatches are attributed to non-linguistic factors that "interfere" with the "performance" of speakers and listeners, rather than affecting their "competence". And even when noise and other error-inducing factors have been eliminated, the fact that the intention of the speaker in uttering a particular linguistic "structure" may not always be reflected fully and accurately in the interpretation that the listener puts on that structure is attributed not to something inherent in the structures themselves, but rather to differences in structural knowledge between particular speakers and listeners. This individual and group variability may complicate efforts to discover the structure of language, admittedly, but it has not been allowed to compromise the assumption that language structure is neutral with respect to the processes of language comprehension and language production.

There is much to recommend this "processual neutrality" assumption about the nature of language. Obviously, it would seem, the data of linguistic investigation – the recordable utterances themselves – are simultaneously the output from speakers and the input to listeners. How unproblematic it seems, then, to describe the physical form of utterances in terms that supposedly merge the auditory and articulatory aspects of listening and speaking into "phonetic" descriptions. And how reasonable it seems to describe the "higher-level" aspects of linguistic structure in terms that neutralize (or, more often, ignore) whatever differences there may be between structures as objects of word-recognizing or syntactic parsing and structures as products of word-finding or syntactic phrasing.

Viewed processually, however, recordings of utterances are not the true data base for linguistics. We cannot describe the objects of comprehension and the products of production without first specifying our point of view toward these events. At the most superficial level of analysis, an utterance can be seen either as a sequence of sensory patterns or as a sequence of muscle commands. The recordings upon which linguistic analysis is based present neither of these. Even the most faithful and complete electronic registration of the acoustic effects of a spoken utterance tells you only what pattern of sound waves struck the listener's ear drum; it does not tell you what pattern of neural activity might be provoked by the transmission of this physical energy into the inner ear. And even an X-ray motion picture will depict only the movements made by a speaker in producing an utterance, not the neural commands that are responsible for those movements.

At the deepest, non-audible, non-articulatable level of analysis, linguistic events also fall into two types: interpretations and intentions. Like sounds, meanings differ in their neural origins (sensory–cognitive versus motor–intentional). Unlike sounds, though, it may be that interpreted and intended meanings possess a great deal of commonality in neural content. The on-the-spot distinction between the act of *understanding* x (or interpreting input I to mean x) and the act of *meaning* x (or executing output 0 with the intention of having it understood as x) is not fuzzy. Listeners don't typically mistake their interpretation of a received linguistic input for an idea that has just come into their heads on its own. But this distinction does often fade over time, which suggests that at some point at least the memorable contents of linguistic interpretations and linguistic intentions become neuro-psychologically equivalent. During the interpretive/formulative phases of central interest of linguistics, however, these two types of representation are vividly distinct.

The comprehension/production dialectic in children's lexical development

There are many sources of evidence for the comprehension/production dialectic (Straight, 1976), ranging from historical linguistics to neuroanatomy, and from semantics to phonetics. Of course, most re-searchers present this evidence in the context of a non-processual, non-dualistic theory of language and are therefore forced to treat observed discrepancies between comprehension and production, if they are noticed at all, as facts to be described separately from the "grammar". Often these items of evidence are found almost by accident, seldom being the focus of the research in which they arise. It is therefore often difficult to ferret these facts out, and to disentangle them from the usually hostile theoretical environ-ment in which they have been discovered. The present section of this essay deals with the contrast between comprehension versus production vocabu-laries in young children. This discussion highlights the complexity and pervasiveness of the comprehension/production dialectic in lexical develop-ment and sets the stage for the last section of the essay, which deals with the repercussions of the comprehension/production dialectic in adult language, where its manifestations are subtler but probably no less important than in child language.[4]

The literature on the discrepancy between comprehension and production in child language has grown steadily in the two decades since Colin Fraser, Ursula Bellugi, and Roger Brown published their classic study of the child's "[c]ontrol of grammar in imitation, comprehension, and production" (1963). Their initial (and not very surprising) conclusions were that the ability to imitate a heard form is not sufficient to have that form appear in a child's spontaneous speech production, and that emergence of a new item of intelligible non-imitative speech production by a child probably depends on the prior emergence of that item in the child's speech comprehension. Since then, a large number of empirical studies have been addressed to this comprehension/production issue.

One decade after the Fraser, Bellugi, and Brown study, Ruth Clark, Sandy Hutcheson, and Paul Van Buren (1974) concluded that the differences between comprehension and production were greater than had been realized previously, but – distinguishing between "comprehension of verbal messages as such and comprehension based on exploitation of cues which are not verbal in this special sense" – they "attributed the superiority comprehension might show to production to comprehension in the [second] broader sense, rather than taking the view that a different grammar might underlie each of the two processes, comprehension and production" (Clark et al., 1974: 51–52). They and others have in this way attributed the comprehension/production differences to general principles of human development and cognition, rather than to properties intrinsic to "language knowledge" itself. Candidates for such extralinguistic or "performance" factors are the lag between sensory development and motor development, the greater difficulty people generally have in recall as opposed to recognition, and the availability of various non-linguistic and pragmatic/semantic strategies for the comprehension of utterances containing words and constructions that are not understood (see Huttenlocher, 1974; Bloom, 1974; Bloom and Lahey, 1978: 237–265).

Appeals to general principles of physical development and memory are, however, question-begging, since nobody knows why auditory and articulatory development or recognition and recall differ in the ways they do, either. More is known about the nature of various comprehension strategies, but the fact that an utterance containing a given word *can* be understood without understanding one of its parts is no proof that the superfluous word is *not* understood. Nevertheless, the dominant non-dialectical view of adult language has led most researchers to explain observed asymmetries between comprehension and production on the basis of an *a priori* metatheoretical principle that the two processes have differential access to a shared linguistic system; a principle that is assumed rather than systematically verified.

There is, fortunately, one very notable exception to this general pattern of non-processual approaches to child language: a recent article by Eve Clark and Barbara Frant Hecht in the *Annual Review of Psychology* (1983). Clark and Hecht build gradually to a decidedly dialectical–processual conclusion, though they don't call it that. They begin with the observation that "Language . . . use demands that two distinct processes – production and comprehension – be coordinated . . . And this in turn suggests that one part of acquisition consists of coordinating what one can produce with what one can understand" (1983: 326). Clark and Hecht then observe that the distinction and coordination between these processes has gone largely unexplored in developmental psycholinguistic research because of "the tendency of most investigators in the field to focus on the *product* – the language itself – rather than on the processes language-users rely on"

(p. 327). After an extensive review of the literature (which has averaged, according to their references, about five articles a year since 1972), they conclude that language users, both children and adults, "might draw on at least two sets of memory representations, one for understanding and one for producing it" (pp. 343-344), and that, given such an assumption, "a more abstract, single set of representations analagous to the kind of linguistic competence postulated by Chomsky (1965, 1976) . . . would appear both redundant and unparsimonious" (p. 344).

Although she does not claim this honour in her recent review article, Eve Clark may actually have been the first prominent developmental psycholinguist to speculate in print that, instead of a single shared lexical system, children may be developing two different systems – one for comprehension and one for production. This speculation occurred in one of her many contributions to the literature on early vocabulary growth (Clark, 1979), in a one-paragraph discussion of Thomson and Chapman's (1975) finding that, for example, a child may call cows, sheep, zebras, horses, and some other large four-legged animals *horsie* even though that same child points only to horses when asked to point to a *horsie*, and points correctly to cows, sheep, zebras, and others when their names are called out.

Clark concludes from this evidence that "children may continue to overextend certain words in production *after* they have worked out the adult meaning just because they do not yet have enough words to talk about all the things they want to" (Clark, 1979: 153). Two points should be noted about this conclusion. First, Clark has put her point a bit clumsily. The phrase "do not yet have enough words" implies that to "have" a linguistic structure is to be able to use it in production, which reflects the very bias toward production that she is challenging. This habit of speaking is a pervasive and subtle deterrent to a process-oriented approach to language and language acquisition; it is to be avoided.

Second, mismatches between comprehension and production vocabulary have been the most frequently noted items of evidence for a comprehension/ production "problem" in child language, and more intensive study of such mismatches has shown them to be rather more complex than Clark's 1979 remark indicates. Most strikingly, comprehension and production vocabularies differ not only in how words are used but even in the number and type of words that occur in each: comprehension vocabularies (words that a child responds to in some consistent and intelligible manner) are invariably larger than production vocabularies, and the relative proportions of words in various semantic–syntactic categories in the two also appear to differ (see Benedict, 1979, a study not cited by Clark and Hecht, for an exceptionally extensive empirical study of the quantitative and qualitative developmental contrast between comprehension vocabulary and production vocabulary).

The difference between comprehension and production vocabularies is most obvious in cases where children understand words they don't produce (as in the Thomson and Chapman study cited by Clark), but the reverse – producing words they don't understand – also occurs, and much more frequently than is usually recognized. Clark and Hecht (pp. 332–334) correctly argue that most cases of production without comprehension are rather cases of production without full comprehension: children often use some words or phrases in situationally appropriate ways before they exhibit understanding of the adult meaning and morphological or constituent internal structure of these forms. However, they also use words in senses that they do not understand those "same" words to mean when they hear them. Lois Bloom's Allison, for example, produced what Bloom (1973: 72, not cited by Clark and Hecht) transcribes as *"car"* when cars moved by on the street below her window, but did not produce it as a label for cars under other circumstances, even though her ability to point or orient to cars when adults mentioned them was presumably not affected by this underextension in production. In this sense, then, we find production occurring in the absence of (exact) comprehension. Lois Bloom would understand a recording of Allison saying *car* to mean "car moving by on the street below", but it is doubtful that anyone else would, including Allison!

The most commonly noted lexical mismatch, however, is not due to relative underextension in production but rather overextension. Children frequently use a word to label objects that are only perceptually similar to the objects that they are willing to point to in response to that "same" word. In this case too we find that production is occurring in the absence of comprehension, for the child does not, for example, understand *doggie* to mean "medium-sized furry quadruped", but rather "dog", even though the broader category is the one that seems to be referred to in the child's own speech.

Such asymmetrical overextension of word use occurs not only in production, but also in comprehension.[5] Deborah Kay and Jeremy Anglin (1982), in an experimental study not cited by Clark and Hecht, have shown that in a yes/no measure of word comprehension ("Is this a(n) TARGET WORD?") 2-year-olds would answer yes when presented with pictures of objects perceptually similar to the picture used in training them to recognize and use a new word, even though a labelling measure of word production ("What is this?") revealed little tendency to extend its use beyond the word/object relation established by the experimenter's training. It would be important to find out whether such situationally induced overextensions in comprehension have lasting effects on children's comprehension of words, or whether, for example, in a selection measure of comprehension ("Point to all of the TARGET WORDS.") the original (training) interpretation would reassert itself. In any case, this too is a case of production without accurate comprehension, in that the childen in Kay and Anglin's study did not limit the reference of heard words to just those meanings that underlay their speaking of them.

In some cases, moreover, production without any comprehension whatever occurs. For example, children sometimes produce baby-talk or other idiosyncratic pronunciations of words and show no or little comprehension of these pronunciations (Dodd, 1975, cited by Clark and Hecht). Marlys Macken (1980, cited by Clark and Hecht) has shown that the differences between the production and comprehension forms of auditorily and articulatorily similar words can lead to very complex mismatches. Using the same data as Macken (namely Smith, 1973), we may well ask: When Amahl Smith produces what we transcribe as *puggle* for *puddle*, and *puddle* for *puzzle*, how are the heard words *puggle, puddle, and puzzle* interpreted by the child? It might be argued that these strictly phonological mismatches are beside the point, but when we consider that children's use of words is often at variance with adults' use (and children's understanding) of those "same" words (as discussed above), then we can see that the intersection of these two possibilities would, if only in rare instances, result in a word that a child could use consistently and (to the adult) intelligibly, but that had no corresponding comprehension form for the child.[6]

But even if exactly this pattern is not found, consider the example provided by Melissa Bowerman's (1976: 136) Christy, who used what Bowerman transcribes as "*hi*" both as a social greeting and has a description of things that were on her hands or feet (presumably because this word had been uttered by her mother while she was wearing a finger puppet). But did Christy ever show any signs of understanding this word in these two senses as well? Bowerman, in keeping with the usual non-dialectical assumptions, apparently didn't check; in any case, she doesn't say. Presumably Christy understood *hi* in its greeting sense, but is it likely that – after that one occasion in which she thought her mother was talking about rather than for the puppet – Christy would have understood anything an adult could say, or even a recording of herself saying *hi*, to mean "something that is on someone's hands or feet"? As usual, this implausible conclusion is never stated and, therefore, never explored or discussed. In the absence of disconfirming evidence, then, we can tentatively identify Christy's *hi* in the sense of hand/foot covering as an example of production without comprehension.

A child's productions are almost invariably attempts to imitate something they have heard, and those heard things will only be imitated when some interpretation or other has been put on them by the child. For these reasons, it is unlikely that a child will produce a word for which there is no adult model that the child will "comprehend". In this strictest sense, production without comprehension, although scarcely the "logical" impossibility that Clark and Hecht seem to think it is (p. 331), is rare to the point of negligibility. But anyone who thinks that this fact strengthens the case for a non-dialectical theory of language abilities, or a non-processual theory of language knowledge, wherein what one is able to say and what one is able to understand are inferrable from a single body of processually neutral language knowledge (e.g. Chomsky, 1976; Fremgen and Fay, 1980), is dreadfully mistaken.

The functionality of the comprehension/production dialectic

If language ability is not based on any body of processually neutral knowledge, but rather on processually specific skills, then when I understand something that someone has said to me it is *not* because I share with that person particular items of knowledge about the words that were uttered and about the order and manner in which they were uttered. When I am engaged in listening, the processes whereby I recognize and understand (or misunderstand) an utterance need not make any contact with (nor be in any way correlative with) the processes that might enable me to speak that or any other utterance, and vice versa.

Thus, to cite an example of considerable poignancy in current American social relations, my vigilant attentiveness to the use of *he* as the unmarked animate pronoun is very effective in comprehension; in the late 1960s I became acutely aware of the fact this masculine pronoun coerces listeners into believing that the set (or the typical exemplar in the set) being referred to is male. This is the meaning of *he* for me as a comprehension item, and I frequently (though not invariably, for fear of appearing demagogic) interrupt speakers who use this word to ask them to clarify their intent. Fortunately for the preservation of my own humility, however, my vigilance concerning this word was very acute indeed: I used to catch myself using it when I shouldn't. The only contact that was made between my production and comprehension processes thus often occurred after the (processual) fact, as a result of auditory feedback. On occasion I would catch myself before it was too late, before I had actually articulated the offending pronoun, but even in these cases, I had (alas) yet again formulated an utterance whose comprehension effects would not match my (liberated) intentions.

This dissociation between comprehension and production skills reveals itself clearly in cases of immature development (as shown in the previous section of this essay) or acquired impairment (Brown, 1972), but its existence in normal adult language users turns out to be an important premise even if evidence for it is rare (cf. note 6). Your understanding of a word or phrase or sentence constitutes no guarantee that you can produce it, and even if you do produce it, there is no guarantee that you mean the same thing by it as you would understand it to mean if you heard it. There is an irreducible dialectic between the processes evoked by the reception of linguistic input and the processes invoked in the emission of linguistic output.

This dialectic between perception and action is attenuated only by the constant interaction between interpretive and formulative processes in the course of speaking and listening: speakers monitor their actual and their anticipated output and listeners anticipate forthcoming input on the basis of previous input. But the ephemerality, redundancy, vagueness, and automaticity of communicative interaction are such that this ongoing interaction never succeeds in eliminating the discrepancies between how you interpret input and how you formulate output. True, you may succeed in eliminating the bulk of your child-like discrepancies between comprehension and production, but this equilibrium is constantly threatened. It is threatened, for one thing, by the addition of new words and constructions, most of which become part of your comprehension skill without becoming producible. More importantly, it is threatened by the vagaries of subsequent contexts in which you comprehend input, which may lead you to understand an old word in a new way (without affecting your use of it), and of subsequent contexts in which you may try to express some new idea, which may lead you to use an old word in a new way (without forcing you to think very hard or very long about how difficult it might be to understand this new meaning in some changed circumstance).

There is no way to overstate the absoluteness of the dichotomy between these two different realms of language ability, but there is also no way to overstate the creative value of their dynamic interplay. The apparently bewildering and challenging consequences of this comprehension/production split are great: you can't really know what you mean by what you're saying any better than someone else can; you can't hope to build your production skills by simply comprehending more and more – you have to do a lot of talking (even if it's only the tacit talking called thinking) in order to learn how to talk effectively. But there are compensatory benefits:

1. You don't need to have established the ability to use a form meaningfully in order to find that form fully and readily intelligible when someone else says it. This ability is of inestimable value not only in the process of language acquisition, wherein the interpretability of input is necessarily prior to the formulability of intelligible output, but also in the transmission of information from highly skilled "experts" to their merely "educated" audiences (though various dangers of misinterpretation also arise in both cases, of course).

2. You don't need to have established exactly the "right" way to say something you are trying to say: you are free to bend the productive resources of your formulating ability to try to meet your need. The measure of whether such bending is successful is, above all, your communicative success (however that might be ascertained), but you can also gauge this success through self-monitoring. Recognition of such failure

can trigger rethinking and reformulating to make yourself clear. (Failure to recognize such failure, on the other hand, is an important source of mismatch between interpretative and formulative processes, as you come to formulate ideas in ways that neither you nor anyone else can interpret correctly.)

3. Self-monitoring also makes it possible for you to tailor your output to meet the demands of a listener whose background knowledge or interpretive abilities may not be identical to yours. Your measure of what will be necessary in order to get your ideas across to someone else will be their verbal and non-verbal responses to what you have said to them (or others "like" them) in the past. By means of this experience, plus experience in hearing how they express themselves, you can develop a number of qualitatively different comprehension and production potentials. The stuff I call *soda* when I'm talking to a New Yorker, I will call *pop* when talking to a Michigander, and *carbonated beverage* to a Britisher.

4. This same self-monitoring ability has the further value of giving you the chance to benefit from your own output: rather than simply making sure that the most plausible interpretation of what you have said, according to your own comprehension processes or the processes you impute to your addressee, is an interpretation that you find satisfactory (the usual goal of self-monitoring), you can also subject that output-become-input to continuing exploratory interpretation (What might that mean?) to come up with new interpretive and expressive possibilities. The hermeneutic potential of this "formulation–interpretation circuit" (Straight, 1982) is, with respect to human-evolutionary adaptive value, by far the most important benefit of the comprehension/production dialectic in language ability.

Notes

1. The term "comprehension" appears frequently in this essay (even in the title!), but it is not the precisely correct word to use, because "comprehension" implies *correct* interpretation of input, while what I mean by it is rather whatever interpretation a language perceiver puts on input, correct or not. I haven't yet found a fully satisfactory solution to this terminological problem. (1) "Listening vs. Speaking" is too auditory–vocal; most of what I have to say on the contrast between the processes that result in language perception and the processes that result in language action holds for reading and writing, or watching and signing, as strongly as for speech. Moreover, it is possible to "listen" so hard to some superficial aspect of heard input (Does this speaker have a cold?) as to be oblivious to the results of Interpreting. Also, you can listen to utterances in an unfamiliar language without being able to make out anything at all. However, it has not been shown that you can avoid Interpreting if you are Receiving something that you can interpret, nor Receiving if you are hearing. (2) "Reception vs. Emission" is too information-theoretic; it implies the same old message- or form-centred bias I am trying to avoid. (3) "Input vs. Output" is too computeristic, and I would like to be able to use these terms to refer to what is acted upon versus what is constructed by each of the various processing components involved in language perception and action, regardless of whether they are "Comprehension" components or "Production" components. (4) "Perception vs. Production"

repeats one of the two terms, perception and action, that I would like to say that comprehension and production, respectively, are special cases of. (5) "Construing vs. Saying" is perhaps the best solution intellectually, but it has the unfortunate ring of near-neologism: Readers should not have to contend with new terms for familiar ideas when familiar terms are available.

Therefore, let me stipulate that, unless I specifically state that I am talking about a language perceiver's *correct* apprehension of the idea that led a given language composer to produce a given output, the term "comprehend" (and its synonyms and derivatives) should in this essay be understood to refer to workings and products of the fallible processes whereby we arrive at interpretations of linguistic events, whether these be stimulations of our external senses or figments of our internal imaginings. This use of the term "comprehension", despite its departure from ordinary usage (and all of the dictionary definitions I have been able to find to date), is virtually universal among linguists and psycholinguists, though not (alas) among philosophers of language.

2. I use the term dialectical in its least tendentious meaning: "marked by a dynamic tension, conflict, and interconnectedness of its parts or elements" (Webster's Third), but with the understanding that this interconnectedness is achieved only through ongoing interaction between elements rather than by means of some overarching intermediary or "synthesis". The dialectic between language comprehension and language production is not that of a Hegelian or Marxian thesis moving through an antithesis and struggling to resolve the conflict between these by achieving a synthesis, but rather "the dialectical tension or opposition between two interacting forces or elements" (Webster's Third). This all-pervasive linguistic dialectic is the creative polarity between how we interpret what we hear and how we formulate what we speak. Interestingly, though, I do see a provocative intimation of the sort of dialectic I have in mind in the first of Karl Marx's *Theses on Feuerbach*: "The chief defect of all previous materialism (including that of Feuerbach) is that things, reality, the sensible world, are conceived only in the form of *objects of observation*, but not as *human sense activity*, not as *practical activity*, not subjectively. Hence, in opposition to materialism, the *active* side was developed abstractly by idealism, which of course does not know real sense activity as such." My aim is to bring these two strands of theorizing, the idealistic and the materialistic, together by means of a dialectic that makes full and separate recognition of both sensory and motor processes.

3. To avoid possible misunderstanding here, I should stress that although generative and other post-Bloomfieldian schools of linguistics have opposed their views to those of what they call "structuralism", they have in no case challenged the anti-dialectical assumptions of pre-Chomskyan linguists, and their "processes" (or generative rules, or relational strata, or whatever) have in only tangential ways touched upon the question of how speakers and listeners go about the task of language comprehension and production. The "structuralism" to which they sometimes oppose themselves, then, is simply one variant of what I would call structural linguistics, and I would include both pre-Chomskyan and post-Bloomfieldian views in this larger category.

4. As a bibliographical aside, let me note that my previous work on the comprehension/production dialectic has been primarily general and theoretical (e.g. Straight, 1971, 1976, 1979, 1980c, 1982). I have written specifically about its developmental aspects on a couple of occasions (1985 on second language acquisition, 1980a on phonology), but my only previous opportunity to focus on general issues in first language acquisition came in the form of a multiple book review (1980b) in which I included just a few remarks concerning the dialectical–processual aspects of "Cognitive development and communicative interaction as determinants of the emerging language abilities of children."

5. I add the modifier "asymmetrical" here because overextension or underextension of a word's use in the same way in both comprehension and production, although interesting evidence for the question of how children's vocabularies differ from adults', does not in itself bear on the issue of comprehension/production mismatch. Note, however, that such symmetrical misextensions are likely to give way to some sort of asymmetrical pattern, as the child's comprehension and production experiences with a word accumulate.

6. Just as in particle physics, some of the most important theoretical insights into the nature of language development may derive from the analysis of "rare events".

References

Baker, G. P. and Hacker, P. M. S. (1984) *Language, Sense and Nonsense: a critical investigation into modern theories of language*. Blackwell, Oxford.

Benedict, H. (1979) "Early lexical development: comprehension and production", *Journal of Child Language*, **6**, 183–200.

Bloom, L. M. (1973) *One Word at a Time: the use of single word utterances before syntax*. Mouton, The Hague.

Bloom, L. M. (1974) "Talking, understanding, and thinking". In Schiefelbusch, R. L. and Lloyd, L. L. (eds), *Language Perspectives – acquisition, retardation and intervention*, pp. 285–312. University Park Press, Baltimore.

Bloom, L. M. and Lahey, M. (1978) *Language and Language Disorders*. Wiley, New York.

Bloomfield, L. (1914). *An Introduction to the Study of Language*. Henry Holt, New York.

Bloomfield, L. (1933) *Language*. Henry Holt, New York.

Boorstin, D. J. (1983) *The Discoverers*. Random House, New York.

Bowerman, M. (1976) "Semantic factors in the acquisition of rules for word use and sentence construction". In Morehead, D. M. and Morehead, A. E. (eds), *Normal and Deficient Child Language*, pp. 99–179. University Park Press, Baltimore.

Brown, J. (1972). *Aphasia, Apraxia*, and *Agnosia: clinical and theoretical aspects*. Charles C. Thomas, Springfield, IL.

Chomsky, A. N. (1965) *Aspects of the Theory of Syntax*. MIT Press, Cambridge, MA.

Chomsky, A. N. (1976) *Reflections on Language*. Random House, New York.

Clark, E. V. (1979) "Building a vocabulary: words for objects, actions, and relations". In Fletcher, P. and Garman, M. (eds), *Language Acquisition: studies in first language development*, pp. 149–160. Cambridge University Press, Cambridge.

Clark, E. V. and Hecht, B. F. (1983) Comprehension, production, and language acquisition. *Annual Review of Psychology*, **34**, 325–349.

Clark, H. H. and Clark, E. V. (1977) *Psychology and Language: an introduction to psycholinguistics*. Harcourt Brace Jovanovich, New York.

Clark, R., Hutcheson, S. and van Buren, P. (1974) "Comprehension and production in language acquisition", *Journal of Linguistics*, **10**, 39–54.

Cooper, D. E. (1975) *Knowledge of Language*. Prism Press, London; Humanities Press, New York.

Dodd, B. (1975) "Children's understanding of their own phonological forms", *Quarterly Journal of Experimental Psychology*, **27** 165–172.

Fraser, C., Bellugi, U. and Brown, R. (1963) "Control of grammar in imitation, comprehension, and production", *Journal of Verbal Learning and Verbal Behavior*, **2**, 121–135.

Fremgen, A. and Fay, D. (1980) "Overextensions in production and comprehension: a methodological clarification", *Journal of Child Language*, **7**, 205–211.

Huttenlocher, J. (1974) "The origins of language comprehension". In Solso, R. L. (ed.), *Theories in Cognitive Psychology*, pp. 331–368. Lawrence Erlbaum, Potomac, MD.

Kay, D. A., and Anglin, J. (1982) "Overextension and underextension in the child's expressive and receptive speech," *Journal of Child Language*, **9**, 83–98.

Macken, M. A. (1980) "The child's lexical representation: the "puzzle–puddle–pickle" evidence", *Journal of Linguistics*, **16**, 1–17.

Matthews, P. H. (1979) *Generative Grammar and Linguistic Competence*. Allen and Unwin, Winchester, MA.

Roget, P. M. (1977) *Roget's International Thesaurus*, 4th edn., revised by Robert L. Chapman. Harper and Row, New York.

Saussure, F. de (1916[1959]) *Course in General Linguistics*, translated by Wade Baskin. McGraw-Hill, New York.

Smith, N. V. (1973) *The Acquisition of Phonology: a case study*. Cambridge University Press, Cambridge.

Straight, H. S. (1971) "On representing the encoding/decoding dichotomy in a theory of idealized linguistic performance". In *Papers from the Seventh Regional Meeting*, pp. 535–542. Chicago Linguistic Society, Chicago.

Straight, H. S. (1976) "Comprehension versus production in linguistic theory", *Foundations of Language*, **14**, 525–540.

Straight, H. S. (1979) "A redefinition of the relationship between psycholinguistics and linguistics? (Quo Vadis Psycholinguistics?)", *International Journal of Psycholinguistics*, **6**, 57–60.

Straight, H. S. (1980a) "Auditory versus articulatory phonological processes and their development in children". In Yeni-Komshian, G. H., Kavanagh, J. F. and Ferguson, C. A. (eds), *Child Phonology*, vol. 1: *Production*, pp. 43–71. Academic Press, New York.

Straight, H. S. (1980b) "Cognitive development and communicative interaction as determinants of the emerging language abilities of children (review article)", *International Journal of Psycholinguistics*, **7**, 143–167.

Straight, H. S. (1980c) "Structural commonalities between comprehension and production", *Revue de Phonetique Appliquée*, **55/56**, 313–316. [Reprinted with subtitle, "products of monitoring and anticipation", in Lowenthal, F., Vandamme, F. and Cordier, J. (eds), *Language and Language Acquisition*, pp. 177–180. Plenum Press, New York.]

Straight, H. S. (1982) "The formulation–interpretation circuit: a linguistic motor for the creation of meaning", *Quaderni di Semantica*, **3**, 123–128.

Straight, H. S. (1985) "Communicative proficiency through comprehension". In Ramirez, A. G. (ed.), *Teaching Languages in College: communicative proficiency and cross-cultural issues*, pp. 19–43. Center for Languages, Literacy and Cultures Education, SUNY at Albany, Albany, NY.

Thomson, J. R. and Chapman, R. S. (1975) "Who is 'Daddy'? The status of two-year-olds' over-extended words in use and comprehension", *Papers and Reports on Child Language Development* (Stanford University) 10.59–68. [Reprinted in 1977, *Journal of Child Language*, **8**, 359–375.]

6

Do you understand? Criteria of understanding in verbal interaction

TALBOT J. TAYLOR

Perhaps the most important, and surely the most perplexing, concept associated with the role of the hearer in verbal interaction is that of understanding. Indeed, it might be argued that how theorists conceptualize what it is for a hearer to understand an utterance constitutes one of the fundamental pillars supporting the edifice of modern linguistic thought. For on the concept of understanding depend the related notions of communication and language; and it is these notions which serve a foundational role in determining the goals and methods of modern language study. Consequently, if we are to search for the foundations of modern thinking about language, about communication, or about the role of the hearer in verbal interaction, and if we are to pursue this search with the purpose of examining the strength of those foundations, we could hardly do better than to begin by examining modern assumptions about the nature of understanding.

In what has arguably been the most influential work in the history of linguistic thought, John Locke's *An Essay Concerning Human Understanding*, verbal communication is represented as a form of telementation: i.e. as the transmission of thoughts from the mind of the speaker to that of the hearer (Locke, 1689: III, 1, 2). Understanding a speaker's utterance, then, is viewed as a mental event occurring when the hearer derives from the utterance the thought which the speaker intended to convey by it.

> To make words serviceable to the end of Communication, it is necessary that they excite, in the Hearer, exactly the same *Idea*, they stand for in the mind of the Speaker. Without this, Men fill one another's Heads with noise and sounds; but convey not thereby their Thoughts, and lay not before one another their *Ideas*, which is the end of Discourse and Language (Locke, 1689: III, 9, 6).

This telementational conception of the nature of communication and understanding has cast an enduring spell on the development of Western linguistic thought (cf. Harris, 1981; Taylor, 1981, 1985, and forthcoming); however, it was certainly not original to Locke. Indeed, it can be found lurking in the linguistic reflections of Aristotle, St Augustine, the Modistae, the Port Royal grammarians, Hobbes and many others. But what does appear to be original to Locke's reflections on telementation, and has since become a central factor in his influence on linguistic thought, is his concern with what he called the "imperfection of words". We can never know, Locke argues, if the ideas we signify by certain words are the same as our hearers signify by the very same words. Consequently, we can never be certain that our hearers receive the thoughts we intend by our utterances to convey. That is, the "imperfection of words" consists in the fact that, because the understanding of words is a private, mental event, they do not provide speakers with a means of knowing whether their words are being correctly understood.

Locke's concern with the imperfection of words focuses on what we may call the question of the "intersubjectivity of understanding". Since, under Locke's telementational view of communication, understanding is a private, mental event, my understanding of a word or utterance is not observable by you or anyone else. Consequently, the speaker cannot be sure if the hearer's understanding of utterances is what the speaker intends them to be.

It was never Locke's concern in the *Essay* to do more than draw attention to the threat that the imperfection of words poses to the intersubjectivity of understanding; he did not attempt to trace the implications of that threat for the study of language and communication (although he did suggest that such a study, called "semiotic" or "the doctrine of signs", should form a fundamental part of the new sciences: Locke, 1689: IV, 21). Instead, his overriding concern was to suggest how, for the purposes of understanding in the sciences, the imperfections of language could be remedied. This intention conforms with what appears to have been the primary purpose of the *Essay*, viz. to perform the conceptual ground-clearing required for the laying of solid, empirical foundations to the investigations of the Royal Society (cf. Aarsleff, 1982: 24 ff). Locke argued that communicational intersubjectivity could be assured in scientific discourse if speakers clearly defined all complex ideas in terms of the simple ideas of which they are composed. The intersubjectivity of our understanding of words signifying simple ideas was assured; so, if all words signifying complex ideas were defined in terms of their component simple ideas the threat posed by the ordinary imperfection of words could be averted. On these grounds, and in response to this view of language and understanding, Locke built his scientific method.

The implications of Locke's remarks on the imperfection of words were left to those that followed him to consider. In the eighteenth century, theorists of the origin of language, such as Condillac, Monboddo, and Tooke, endeavoured to explain how intersubjectivity of understanding was achievable by the ordinary use of language, in spite of the imperfection of words. They argued that in the natural origins of sign-using lay the required guarantee of the mutual understanding of signs. A rediscovery of the natural sources of our common heritage as language-users, they argued, would provide us with a notion of language free from Locke's doubts about intersubjectivity. In the twentieth century, Saussure countered this naturalist response to Locke with a conventionalist account of how ordinary language guarantees the intersubjectivity of understanding. From Saussure's conventionalist point of view we may be certain that all speakers of the same language link the same *signifiés* with the same *significants* because that connection is arbitrarily imposed on them by the conventions of language. Saussure's reply to Locke's worries about the intersubjectivity of the connection between words and ideas was to argue, in effect, that speakers and hearers do not possess any ideas other than those given to them by the signs of their language. Two speakers of the same language must then, by definition, mean and understand the same things by the same words, for meaning and understanding are language-given properties of the mind. This conventionalist solution to Locke's worries about understanding has endured until the present day, although now and again (and with increasing force in recent years: cf. Andresen, forthcoming), it has been complemented by naturalist arguments reminiscent of the reasoning of the eighteenth-century Lockeans.

It is important to see that both eighteenth-century naturalism and Saussurian conventionalism have adopted the same strategy in attempting to remedy the problem raised by Locke's doubts about the intersubjectivity of understanding. This strategy aims to formulate a picture of the essence of language that makes it clear how, by the use of language, ordinary speakers can safely convey their thoughts to hearers. For naturalism, the essense of language lay in its genetic roots in natural signs; for conventionalism, that essence was to be found in its arbitrary and supra-individual form as a socially imposed norm. Consequently, since the eighteenth century it is the concept of language which, one way or another, has been assumed to hold the key to Locke's puzzle about intersubjectivity. The Lockean tradition, has, to the present day, taken it for granted that a proper conception of the nature of language, once formulated, would simply make the puzzle of the intersubjectivity of understanding disappear. Therefore, it is on the enduring drive to preserve Locke's telementational concept of understanding and to protect it from his doubts about its intersubjectivity that we should today focus our attention if we hope to explain the source and inspiration of modern theories of language, and if we seek to understand why modern linguistic theory should neglect the role of the hearer in verbal communication.

However, while post-Lockean linguistics has endeavoured to explain what language must be for it to be a vehicle capable of conveying an individual's thoughts, it has neglected a related issue. Although Locke was

LFH–H

the first to face theoretical dilemmas regarding the intersubjectivity of understanding, ordinary speakers are faced every day with the need to be understood and to know that they have been understood. And yet ordinary speakers do not appear to be stymied by the theoretical complexities surrounding the notion of understanding. Indeed, they will sometimes complain that they have been misunderstood, while at other times they will claim that they have been correctly understood. Yet linguistics – in spite of its concern with the intersubjectivity of understanding – has neglected to investigate the basis for speakers' knowledge of their hearers' understanding of their utterances. By what criterion do speakers judge their hearers' understanding? This should be the first question asked, for the ordinary layman apparently has always had the practical solution to the Lockean puzzle that has troubled linguistics and determined the course of its theoretical development for nearly 300 years.

Although naturalism and conventionalism offer explanations of how telementational success can be achieved, their explanations have no bearing on the ordinary communicator's practical need for and reliance on means for determining communicational success. For ordinary communicators are not aware of the theories of naturalism and conventionalism. Furthermore, if, in order to find out if he had been correctly understood, a speaker had to determine if his hearer had received the thought he had intended to convey, then no speaker could ever by certain that he had been correctly understood. But it would be absurd to claim that no speaker ever knew if his utterances were understood. It is not the case that, as speakers, we are constantly puzzled about whether our hearers understand us. And not only would it be absurd to insist that, because of a lack of determining evidence, speakers never know if they are being correctly understood; it also would render obscure ordinary communication practice. Speakers do occasionally claim that they have or have not been understood, in spite of Locke's worries about the theoretical incoherence of such claims.

In this case it should be of great interest to the student of language to investigate the grounds on which ordinary communicators make such claims. Given that, as speakers, we often find ourselves of the opinion that we have, or have not, been understood by our hearer(s), as professional students of language we ought to make it a primary concern to discover the criteria applied in forming such opinions. We need to investigate the reasons speakers will provide in support of such assertions as "he (you) did not understand me when I said . . ."

It is worth emphasizing the importance of this question. A modest claim for its importance would point out, at the very least, that it is essential to the study of conversational structure to investigate the criteria conversationalists invoke in justifying claims that they have been understood. A fundamental premise of conversation studies is that speakers ordinarily try to be understood. Indeed, it is not hard to find instances of speakers complaining if they feel they have been misunderstood. So, if speakers do care whether they are understood, and if their own behaviour in conversational interaction is in some part responsive to their perception of their communicational success, then it should be important to analysts of conversational structure to examine the reasons conversationalists provide for taking a hearer to have understood or to have misunderstood.

At least one of the burgeoning schools of conversation analysis has recognized the importance of investigating when and why conversationalists believe themselves to be understood (or misunderstood), the reasons given for those beliefs, and their interactional consequences, Ethnomethodological analysis of conversation recognizes the role that lay accounts of understanding play in conversational structure, and this may be taken as at least one source of their interest in repair, in formulations, in understanding checks, in securing agreement, and in reference specificity (cf. for instance, Atkinson and Heritage, 1984).

A much less modest claim for the importance of investigating criteria of understanding might take its cue from Wittgenstein's dictum, "An 'inner process' stands in need of outward criteria" (Wittgenstein, 1953, section 580). That is, it might be argued that the ordinary concept of understanding, and the criteria which determine the application of that concept, should provide the foundation for its theoretical formulation. Furthermore, the ordinary concept of understanding is manifested in what we do, specifically in how we use "understanding" and other related terms. If we are to construct a solid theoretical account of understanding, and on those foundations build a theory of language, we should, by this reasoning, first turn our attention to the commonplace use of "understanding", e.g. in the justifications speakers provide of claims that their hearers did or did not understand their utterance.

Such a methodological reversal would turn on its head the priority which the Lockean tradition confers on the theoretical explanation of understanding. But this reversal would be warranted by the fact that the dilemmas encountered by the theoretical explanation of the concept of understanding are manifestly not encountered by the ordinary speaker's practical use of that concept. And, in turn, this might result in demonstrating that Locke's worries about the intersubjectivity of understanding are groundless, arising from the theoretical preconception of communication as a form of thought-transfer. In the end a revised notion of understanding, based on the investigation of ordinary communicational practice, might allow us to form a radically original, yet nonetheless empirical, account of the function of language in communicational interaction. (An example of the philosophical interest in criteria of understanding may be found in recent work in the Wittgensteinian tradition, cf. especially Baker, 1974 and Richardson, 1976.)

In order to begin this investigation, we might first ask ourselves: what sorts of reasons do speakers provide when they support a claim that a hearer (H) understood or failed to understand them? On reflection it would seem that they come up with a wide variety of reasons, invoking many different kinds of evidence in criterial support of their claims. (In the following, the original utterance will be abbreviated by "U"; "S" will be the speaker of that utterance and will take a masculine pronoun; "H", referred to by a feminine pronoun, will be the hearer of U whose understanding has been queried; "E" will be the reason(s) S provides in support of his claim that H understood U; "Q" will be the person asking S why he feels that H understood U.)

We might imagine S providing the following type of justification:

(i) I told her to close the door, and she got right up and did it; so of course she understood what I said.

Here, as E, S refers to H's behaviour following U. This might be expected to be a very typical sort of justification of an understanding-claim. At the same time, however, we should note that, in some contexts, H's lack of behaviour could be taken as evidence of her understanding.

(ii) I told her to leave the door open; and, since she didn't go ahead and close it, she must have understood me.

So, it would seem possible both for particular behavioural acts, as well as the absence of such acts, to be used as evidence in support of an understanding-claim. Related to the latter type, we might imagine a typical sort of justification in which S points out that, since H made no sign of misunderstanding, she must have understood.

For many (perhaps all) U, there do not appear to be any fixed limits as to the sorts of behaviour by H a speaker can invoke as evidence of H's understanding. For instance, we might imagine a situation in which S said:

(iii) Since she left the room when I told her to close the door, she must have understood me. She always objects when I treat her as a subordinate.

In fact, it would seem that there will always be some possible context for any sort of E to be invoked in support of a claim that H understood U. The type of E chosen will thus be dependent on the situational context. Consider:

(iv) I know she understood me because, when I told her to close the door, she took out her handkerchief and blew her nose. She always feigns indifference to even the smallest of my requests.

At the same time we should note that, depending on the context-of-utterance, it is not hard to image types of E that could be invoked either in support of a claim that H understood U, or as evidence against it. Consider again the evidence provided in (i) and (iv).

(v) She must not have understood me when I told her to close the door because she got right up and did it; yet she always makes a point of ignoring me when I tell her to do something.

(vi) Since she blew her nose when I told her to close the door, she obviously hadn't understood me.

These examples indicate what might be called the "practical ambiguity" of an E invoked in support of an understanding-claim. No E provides independently conclusive proof that H understood U since, given the appropriate situational context, the same E could be used to support a claim that H had *not* understood U. At the same time it is always possible, given the appropriate situation, to respond to S's use of E in support of an understanding-claim: "But what makes you think *that* shows she understood?"

Of course, a very common reason which speakers provide in support of understanding-claims involves reference to H's verbal behaviour following U. This might be taken as a subcategory of the behaviour-invoking justifications already discussed.

(vii) Since she replied to me that *she* wasn't the one who left the door open, she must have understood my complaint that Fido had escaped from the kennel again.

Again, it is possible to imagine a situation in which S invoked the same E in defence of a claim that H had not understood U.

(viii) She must have misunderstood me as accusing her of being the cause of Fido's escape since she immediately replied that *she* wasn't the one who left the door open.

Two particular types of verbal response by H should be mentioned as commonly cited evidence of understanding. We might imagine S citing H's production of what he takes to be an acceptable paraphrase of U as indicative of her understanding.

(ix) She must have understood me when I said Reagan was unpredictable because she replied correctly that I really meant he was a hypocrite.

Again we could easily imagine the same evidence being used to argue that H had not in fact understood U. The second type of verbal response often citable as evidence of H's understanding is the reply "Yes" to S's query "Do you understand?" Speakers will often support their claims that H had understood by pointing out that, when asked if she did, she had replied affirmatively. But, at the same time, given the appropriate context, it is possible to imagine S taking H's simple reply of "Yes" as evidence that she had not really understood.

Many other types of evidence which a speaker might offer in support of an understanding-claim could be imagined. For present purposes, it is only necessary to mention one more.

(x) Of course she understood what I said. I've known H for fifteen years and her English is as good as or better than mine.

In this invented example, S does not refer to H's behaviour in supporting his claim that she understood U; rather he refers to his familiarity with H and with her command of the language in which U was spoken. We might also imagine S indicating that H had been listening attentively, or that the room was perfectly quiet, or that he knew her hearing was fine, or that she was quite familiar with the topic, as well as many other examples of E where neither H's verbal nor non-verbal behaviour is invoked to support the claim that she understood U. Indeed, the evidence invocable as criterial support of an understanding-claim is far from being restricted to H's behaviour in response to U. It might well seem an impossible task to limit it at all.

There is no point in pretending that the imagined examples just discussed constitute satisfactory evidence for the investigation of criteria of understanding. Not only ought we to widen the survey of examples to include explanations of the meaning of utterances, objections to understandings, and more, but – above all – we ought to direct our attention not to invented but to naturally occurring examples.

For instance, the use of an invented example makes us rely on decontextualized acceptability judgements, i.e. when we decide intuitively whether a proposed act would or would not be a way a speaker might justify the understanding of U. Imagined examples of justifications of understanding claims are far from being acceptable substitutes for the real thing. Indeed, there is every reason to suspect that empirical samples of conversational data will reveal even greater variability, ambiguity, and indeterminacy than imaginary data; although, on the other hand, in the empirical study of justifications of understanding-claims, problems will arise as to how to determine what should count as an instance of the category sought. It is all too easy, as an armchair linguist, to imagine that what people actually do with language conforms to our theoretical preconceptions. If the study of criteria of understanding is as important to discourse analysis and linguistics as has been argued above, then those criteria should be the subject of empirical, not just speculative, investigation.

On the other hand, I would maintain that some important benefits may be gained through reflection on artificial data. At the very least we may begin to deal with the sorts of questions that will be raised concerning how the data should be interpreted. That is, we have the opportunity now of forestalling future attempts to force the data into inappropriate theoretical moulds. In the remainder of this essay I will discuss and argue against two interpretations of criteria of understanding that will inevitably be raised.

In the empirical investigation of criteria of understanding, we might conceive of ourselves as looking for the conditions which competent speakers know must be satisfied for it to be appropriately asserted of a hearer that she understands U. This quest may be dissolved into two main assumptions:

1. For any S, H, E, and U, the connection between
   (a) the assertion of E, and ·
   (b) the assertion that H understood U
   is a rule-governed connection, given in the language.

In support of this assumption, one might invoke the general Wittgensteinian maxim that the criteria justifying an assertion of an utterance, i.e. its "assertion-conditions", are given in "grammar". The communicational competence of the speaker of (e.g.) English would then include knowledge of the assertion-conditions, for any English U, of "she understood U".

2. Knowledge of the rule-governed relationship between (a) and (b) is tacitly applied by any S in judging his hearers' comprehension of utterances.

That is, when producing U, S unconsciously applies his knowledge of the assertion-conditions of "H understands U" to his perception of H's response to his utterance. This latter assumption might be taken to explain why it is that speakers are not perpetually in doubt whether their hearers understand them. Tacit application of language-given assertion-conditions would thus supply speakers with an intersubjective criterion of communicational success, a criterion which Locke's discussion of the imperfection of words had seemed to banish forever.

Given these two assumptions, the empirical investigation of criteria of understanding might be taken to hold the promise of providing a "window" on the mind of ordinary speakers. An empirical instance of a speaker justifying an understanding-claim would be interpreted as an explicit version of a rule-governed process performed implicitly by all speakers, during the course of every verbal interaction: i.e. the use of language-given criteria to judge whether their hearers understand what they are saying.

At the same time these assumptions would bring the study of criteria of understanding into line with what some take as given in the study of ascriptions of pain and other "private" phenomena. The assertion-conditions of an utterance like "Y is in pain" are taken to be a rule-governed feature of the language, knowledge of which (a) is tacitly shared by all its speakers and (b) informs their implicit judgements regarding Y's ordinary behaviour. So by studying the evidence people invoke in support of pain ascriptions, we might think ourselves to be discovering the tacit criteria all speakers of our language unconsciously apply in judging whether someone is or is not in pain.

It is tempting to think that, given the two foundational assumptions of the grammar-given determinacy of, and the tacit use of, assertion-conditions for understanding-claims, a new theory of conversational structure, and indeed of communicational interaction, could be constructed. However, although it is doubtless true that, for some, what we might call this "utopian" picture of criteria of understanding has a definite attraction, a consideration merely of our invented data quickly reveals that the real world of verbal interaction is far from being organized on utopian principles.

For what is immediately apparent is that the ways in which speakers justify claims that their utterances have been understood are heavily dependent both on the contexts in which those utterances were produced and on the contexts in which their justifications are produced. Although the utopian view may leave some room for the assertion-conditions of English sentences to vary according to the contexts in which those sentences are uttered, it could not permit the assertion-conditions to vary according to the contexts in which they themselves are invoked. And yet even our brief glance at the types of justifications speakers produce indicates that the nature of those justifications depends on:

1. S's interpretation of the context of U (call this UC)
2. S's interpretation of the context in which he is asked for E (call this context QC)
3. What S knows about H
4. What S knows about the person who asked for a justification (Q)
5. Why S thinks, in QC, he is being asked for a justification, by Q, of his claim that H understood U
6. What interactional objectives S thinks he can accomplish in his response to Q
7. What S thinks Q knows about H, U, and UC
8. What S thinks Q knows about S
9. What S thinks Q's interpretation of QC is
10. How much S wants to convince Q of H's understanding of U.

It would not be difficult to expand on this list. What becomes increasingly apparent is that what S will invoke as E is not independently decidable or limitable simply by reference to U and to H's behaviour in response to U. Instead, the justification of an understanding-claim is an organic feature of the context in which it occurs (and of S's interpretation of that context). Consequently it is illegitimate to make assumption 1 above: the assertion-conditions for "H understood U" are not "given in grammar"; they are not determinable independently of the context in which the justification of "H understood U" is supplied.

It might help at this point to return to the analogy with justifications of pain-ascriptions, where X says Y is in pain and Q asks him how he knows. It seems unreasonable to suppose that, in response to Q, X pays no attention to what he knows about Q, to why he thinks Q is asking him this question, to the circumstances in which the question is asked, to what he, X, knows about Y ("I've known her for thirty years, and she couldn't fake pain if her life depended on it"), to what X thinks Q knows about Y (Oh come on! Why pretend she's in pain? You know she could never do that"), to the circumstances in which the question is asked (Y is writhing on the floor during the production of a play; X says she's really in pain; Y asks how he knows that's the case and not that she's just acting), and so on.

Furthermore, we must not forget that many justifications of understanding-claims (like those of pain-ascriptions) are potentially ambiguous. They might just as easily be used to justify a claim that H had not understood U (cf. invented examples i, iv, v, and vi above). And in no case do they provide incontrovertible proof that H understood U. Instead they are best viewed simply as instances of what S feels will accomplish the task requested of him in the situation given. How S views that task will depend on the individual S, on the context in which it is requested, on who requests it of him, and on the particular utterance, hearer, and utterance context to which it refers.

It would seem then that the assertion-conditions for "H understands U" are neither fixed nor determinate. Instead, it seems more plausible to assume that, in justifying an understanding-claim S does not follow any rule but acts creatively according to his interpretation of the interactional context.

Given the argument against taking criteria of understanding as governed by language-given rules, it is clear that assumption 2 should also be rejected. There is no possibility of speakers tacitly applying language-given criteria if those criteria cannot exist. Yet for many there will still be an attraction to the notion of speakers constantly assessing their hearers' behaviour to determine if it indicates understanding or misunderstanding. "After all", they will say, "why would speakers ever complain that their hearers misunderstood what they had said if they had not, at least unconsciously, been assessing their hearers' responses to their utterances?" While the force of this argument may be admitted, it should, however, be pointed out that a speaker's assessment of his hearer's understanding will be dependent on the context (UC) in which that utterance and its response occurs. At the same time we must recognize that that context is not identical with the context (QC) in which the speaker is asked to justify his claim that H understood U. Thus we may not infer the characteristics of the context-dependent, unconscious assessment of H's behaviour, an assessment performed ("on-line") in the context UC, from the characteristics of the context-dependent justification performed in the context QC. Similarly, we have no grounds for assuming that, for any utterance U, the criteria according to which one speaker will unconsciously assess a hearer's understanding of U are the same as those another speaker would employ in assessing the same hearer's understanding of U. Indeed, speculation about the criteria unconsciously employed in private assessments of understanding can only lead us straight back to Lockean worries about the intersubjectivity of mental phenomena to which we, as observers, have no access.

What we both as observers and as interactants, do have access to are the justifications of understanding-claims that speakers and others produce as a functioning part of particular interactions. It is important that, as students of language, we turn our attention to their study, as well as to the study of explanations of, objections to and corrections of particular, situated uses of the concept of understanding. It is equally important that we, like the interactants themselves, take what we observe at face value, and not simply as surface images of "hidden" internal processes.

To conclude: the telementational picture of communication, passed down to us from Locke, takes the understanding of an utterance to be an unobservable, private, mental event. According to this picture, then, we can never know if our hearers understand what we say to them. Yet this is manifestly not the case: speakers do often object that they have been understood, and they will occasionally produce justifications for their objections. I have argued that it is important for students of language and understanding to focus greater attention on the reasons speakers (and others) will provide for their assertions that a hearer understands an utterance. For these reasons constitute the lay, common-sense theory of understanding which holds the answer to Locke's telementational picture of communication and the sceptical doubts to which it leads.

We should, however, be wary of interpreting the empirical instances of these justifications in a way that only leads back to Lockean scepticism. We would risk that danger were we to interpret actual examples of justifications of understanding-claims as explicit illustrations of implicit reasoning mentally performed by speakers during every interaction. In doing so we would be replacing the Lockean notion of understanding as a private, mental event with a new picture of criteria of understanding as private and mental. And a similar sceptical problem would arise: do all speakers, even of the same language, use the same criteria in judging the understanding of the same utterance?

Such a turn of events would only show that we had not learned the lesson of the failure of the Lockean notion of understanding. If understanding and/or criteria of understanding are private, mental phenomena then we have no way of dispelling doubt whether different individuals possess identical versions of those phenomena. But ordinary speakers and hearers do not share these doubts. What this should teach us is that the communality of understanding, and indeed of criteria of understanding, is established in public, observable practice. The intersubjectivity which is the essence of communication is a part of communicational interaction itself and not a phenomenon to be explained by the identity of the private, mental events of different individuals. It is because the intersubjectivity of understanding and of criteria of understanding is a public, interactional phenomenon that speakers do not regularly question its existence. Consequently, we must learn not to study the public face of verbal interaction simply for the value it supposedly has as a window on the private events of the mind, where the "real" and essential activity is occurring. Communication is not a private, internal process; it is a public, co-operative activity.

References

Aarsleff, H. (1982) *From Locke to Saussure*. Athlone Press, London.
Andresen, J. (forthcoming) "Some observationss on a current issue in American linguistics." In *Proceedings of ICHoLS III* (ed. L. Kelly). J. Benjamins, Philadelphia and Amsterdam.
Atkinson, M. and Heritage, J. (1984) *Structures of Social Action*. Cambridge University Press, Cambridge.
Baker, G. P. (1974) "Criteria: a new foundation for semantics", *Ratio*, **xvi**, 2.
Harris, R. (1981) *The Language Myth*. Duckworth, London.
Locke, J. (1689) *An Essay Concerning Human Understanding*. Oxford University Press, Oxford (1975).
Richardson, J. (1976) *The Grammar of Justification*. Sussex University Press, London.
Taylor, T. J. (1981) *Linguistic Theory and Structural Stylistics*. Pergamon Press, Oxford.
Taylor, T. J. (1985) "Linguistic origins: Bruner and Condillac on learning to talk", *Language and Communication*, **4** (3).
Taylor, T. J. (forthcoming) "The place of Charles Bally in the Lockean tradition". *Proceedings of ICHoLS III* (ed. L. Kelly). J. Benjamins, Philadelphia and Amsterdam.
Wittgenstein, L. (1953) *Philosophical Investigations*. Blackwell, Oxford.

7

Make, make do and mend: the role of the hearer in misunderstandings[1]*

CLAIRE HUMPHREYS-JONES

Introduction

One of the foremost preoccupations of our age is communication. We are all becoming increasingly aware that the processes of expressing ourselves to others and of being understood correctly by them can be immensely difficult. Problems in communication are often cited as contributory factors in marital, educational and numerous other social disharmonies. There is no easy way to alleviate these problems because the root cause is the fact that each of us is an individual with a unique range of beliefs, intentions, wishes, assumptions and so on, which are primarily expressed through the medium of language. Thus for anything to be communicated, one person has to produce an utterance and another has to try to understand what is meant by that utterance. The success of the communication depends on the ability of language-users to use language, in terms of both production and understanding. Each language-user, however, can only communicate from his own perspective and it is often the case that gaps between language-users' perspectives are not satisfactorily breached by language.

Linguists have gradually been shifting their focus of interest from language as an entity in itself to language as a medium used by actual speaker-hearers (Moore and Carling, 1982 offer a particularly radical argument relating to this point). Communication is thus becoming a central concern of linguists; communication, that is, in the sense of *how* language-users communicate rather than *what* communication *is* (cf. development from Shannon and Weaver, 1949 to McGregor, 1984). Nevertheless, a number of linguists remain chary of becoming involved in consideration of what language-users are doing when they communicate and how they are affected by the process.

* Superscript numbers refer to notes at end of chapter.

All too often, concentration is on the substance of communication – utterances – with speakers and hearers being treated as catalysts responsible for the existence of these utterances (e.g. much of the work of discourse analysts and ethnomethodologists) rather than participants who create, respond and react to utterances.

A major problem in studies relating to communication is the failure to heed the distinction between speakers and hearers. It is generally assumed in linguistics that a language-user who produces an utterance is a "speaker" while another language-user who listens to that utterance and duly processes it is a "hearer". The apparent dichotomy between the two is by no means straightforward because the roles are reversed when the initial hearer produces an utterance in response to the initial speaker's utterance; the initial speaker then becomes a hearer while the initial hearer becomes a speaker. Because language-users fulfil both roles, sometimes at the same time, it is common to refer to them as "speaker–hearers".

Unfortunately, in references to speaker–hearers focus is frequently placed on the role of the speaker rather than on that of the hearer. The tendency to discuss language primarily in terms of the speaker and to pay only lip-service to the hearer has been pervasive in linguistics until recently (Grimshaw, 1980). Phonologists, for example, concentrate on the range of sounds produced by speakers, although their transcriptions and descriptions of these sounds are dependent on their ability to hear, and could vary because of the auditory processes of each phonologist, in addition to variation between sounds and between the vocal processes of speakers; this is particularly true in respect of non-segmental phonological features (see Pellowe, 1980; Pellowe and Jones, 1978).

Similarly, grammars, be they transformational–generative, systemic or case, are based on the production of sentences and ignore the understanding of them. This approach gives rise to the assumption that the competence of the ideal hearer is simply the converse of the competence of the ideal speaker; no evidence has yet been advanced to support this assumption.

It is easy to present speakers as the positive creators of language, and hearers as passive receptors, arguing that what a speaker says constitutes the substance of conversation while the hearer only becomes positive and creative when it is his turn to be speaker. Certainly the utterances produced by speakers do create the substance of conversation but this does not preclude the hearer from playing an important and influential role at the same time as the speaker. The way in which the hearer orients himself to the speaker and the nature of the relationship between them can affect the utterance produced by the speaker. The hearer, in endeavouring to understand the utterance correctly, is engaged in a highly complex cognitive process which has crucially important linguistic, social and psychological consequences for the development of the conversation.

The hearer may not understand the utterance as expressing what the speaker intended it to express, and therefore that utterance conveys different meanings for the two participants, irrespective of the meaning which could be attributed to it were it a context-free sentence. The production and understanding of subsequent utterances could then be affected. The hearer's understanding of the utterance also affects his social and psychological responses to it, particularly if he has misunderstood it without being aware of having done so (Gumperz and Tannen, 1979 and Milroy, 1984 discuss the hostility experienced by speaker–hearers involved in certain misunderstandings). Since the hearer does not necessarily respond to the utterance with an utterance of his own, thereby becoming a speaker, these linguistic, social and psychological consequences occur while he is ostensibly in his passive role. The idea of the hearer's role being passive would thus appear to be a misleading fallacy.

Linguists have distinguished between different types of hearers. Goffman (1976: 260), for example, distinguishes between hearers who "overhear", hearers who "are ratified participants but . . . are not specifically addressed" and hearers who "are ratified participants who *are* addressed". Goodwin (1981: 5) comments that "hearer" can refer to "the complementary position to 'speaker' ", "the addressee of an act by a speaker" or "a party performing acts in his own right relevant to the position of hearer." Irrespective of the types of hearer which can be identified, every hearer tries to understand correctly the utterance which he hears, chances to hear or contrives to hear. The process of understanding is carried out regardless of the relationships between speaker and different hearers, although the degree of correct understanding achieved by hearers is affected by these relationships.

Clark and Carlson (1982: 343) isolate the roles of "speaker", "addressees", "side participants" and "overhearers". Ostensibly their concern is with hearers but they do not credit hearers with much positiveness in conversation:

These four roles are defined by the speaker . . . He makes these role assignments by the way he designs his utterance, and by the way he positions himself with respect to the audience . . . On any occasion, the speaker may not succeed in getting his hearers to recognize the roles to which they are being assigned, despite a flawless performance on his part; hearers do make mistakes.

This view sustains the idea of the speaker's positiveness and the hearer's passivity. It is surely impossible for the speaker to assign roles; he is not a dramatist dealing out characters (though cf. Pirandello's *Six Characters in Search of an Author*). The speaker produces an utterance and assumes that his hearers will adopt particular roles but he cannot control whether or not they do so in accordance with his assumptions. A hearer can elect to adopt a different role and this is not necessarily a mistake; it can be intentional. Thus each participant defines his own role and makes assumptions about the roles of others, rather than any one participant defining the roles for the others.

The attention which has been paid to how the speaker can communicate successfully has tended to minimize the hearer's communicative effort. Chafe (1976: 28), for example, gives the impression that the success of the hearer's understanding is to a large extent dependent on the speaker:

It is only . . . when the speaker adjusts what he says to what he assumes the addressee is thinking of at the moment that his message will be readily assimilated by the addressee.

This implies that the hearer can do little on his own behalf. In fact, hearers often readily assimilate messages irrespective of the speaker's assumptions; children, for example, are remarkably adept at assimilating messages which have been adjusted with the express purpose of concealment from them.

In general, then, the hearer has not been given enough credit for his role in communication. It is easy to see why the speaker has been accorded the dominant role: he produces tangible utterances whereas the processes by which the hearer deals with these utterances, before becoming speaker himself, are not accessible for direct investigation. Instances in which communication fails to be successfully achieved, however, such as misunderstandings, offer a means by which the processes undertaken by the hearer may be studied (Humphreys-Jones, 1986). A misunderstanding is "made" by a hearer; subsequent utterances reveal the ways in which speakers and hearers "make do" with that misunderstanding, that is, conceal it, tailor the conversation to accommodate it or fail to be aware of its occurrence, or "mend" it, that is, resolve it so that the hearer ultimately understands the misunderstood utterance correctly.

This chapter discusses the phenomenon of misunderstandings. All examples are taken from a corpus of data collected chiefly by the "diary method" (a precedent set by Fromkin, 1971 and Milroy, 1984) from actual conversations in unmarked settings (see Humphreys-Jones, 1986). A description of how misunderstandings are structured is given, and then the implications for the role of the hearer are discussed in the light of what hearers apparently do during the course of misunderstandings.

Misunderstandings

What is a misunderstanding? The word "misunderstanding" can be applied to a range of phenomena which involve the failure to understand correctly: one can misunderstand a gesture, a situation, a painting, an advertisement, a book, an utterance and so on. In all instances of misunderstanding, the common factor is the incorrect understanding by one person of the intention underlying the output of another. When language is involved, this intention can be in respect of speech or writing and of a single utterance or sentence, or of multiple utterances or sentences comprising conversations or texts.

In this chapter a misunderstanding is limited to a particular phenomenon:

a misunderstanding occurs when a hearer (H) fails to understand correctly the proposition (p) which a speaker (S) expresses in an utterance (x); furthermore, H must subsequently produce an utterance which is based on or in some way derives from his incorrect understanding of p. Without this proviso, there is no evidence that any misunderstanding has occurred. S and H are native speakers of the same language so that inter-language difficulties are not involved; dialectal variation is also excluded.[2]

"Proposition" is not used here in the strict sense in which logicians use it; it is not restricted to being declarative and it is not subject to truth valuation. When a speaker produces an utterance he has assembled particular semantic, syntactic and phonological components in order to express "something", be it a question, request, statement, command, phatic greeting or whatever. Proposition is here taken to be the "something" which S intends to express through the medium of language, specifically in an utterance. A number of propositions may relate to one "topic", which is here taken to be the subject-matter of a conversation or part of conversation.

When H hears an utterance it is not necessarily the exact x which S has produced. The utterance which H believes to have been produced is determined by the sounds which he hears and the way in which he processes these sounds. Exactly how this processing is undertaken has not yet been determined, although various hypotheses have been put forward (see e.g. Clark and Clark, 1977; Matthei and Roeper, 1983). The utterance which H receives, that is, hears and processes, is deemed x^r.

Similarly, the proposition which H understands to have been expressed by S in x is not necessarily the exact p which S has intended to communicate. The proposition which H receives, that is, understands, is deemed p^r.

Exact replication between x and x^r and between p and p^r is probably impossible, given that S and H are distinct individuals who have seemingly unique cognitive systems and separate auditory and vocal mechanisms, and who communicate through a medium beset by interferences. x^r is therefore an approximation of x, and p^r an approximation of p. Close approximation counts as equivalence; when $x^r = x$ the utterance is correctly heard and processed, and when $p^r = p$ the proposition is correctly understood. When $x^r \neq x$, that is, when they are not equivalent, a mishearing or incorrect processing of the components of the utterance occurs. When $p^r \neq p$ a misunderstanding occurs. The various combinations of x^r and p^r in relation to x and p thus detail the possible outcomes of communication. When, for example, $x^r \neq x$ and $p^r = p$ the utterance has been misheard or incorrectly processed but the proposition which it expresses has been correctly understood. In addition to equivalence and non-equivalence, a final possible outcome is $\emptyset$. When $x^r = \emptyset$ no utterance is received and when $p^r = \emptyset$ no proposition is received; when no proposition is received the outcome is non-understanding.

It is important to distinguish between misunderstanding and non-understanding. In non-understanding H fails to receive any proposition at all, whereas in misunderstanding H *has* received a proposition and *does* understand the utterance, but incorrectly. The consequence of this for conversation is crucial because when a misunderstanding occurs, H, initially at any rate, believes he has understood the utterance correctly, whereas when he fails to understand the utterance he is immediately aware of the problem and can solicit help from the speaker or can take steps to conceal his lack of understanding.

Specification of how x^r and p^r relate to x and p results in the communicative outcome of any one utterance. Conversations consist of more than single utterances and the outcome of a misunderstanding may be the consequence of a series of utterances exchanged by S, H and any other participants, O^1, O^2, O^n. In order to determine how the communicative outcome may develop from $p^r \neq p$ to $p^r = p$, it is necessary to consider the structure of a misunderstanding, which can be extremely complex.

A misunderstanding is composed of primary and secondary components which have a variable order dependent on the participants. A misunderstanding *originates* in one utterance, is *manifested* in another and is developed through other utterances, the contents of which depend on whether participants *realize*, that is, are aware that the misunderstanding has occurred.

The primary components are (i) x, the utterance by S which is misunderstood by H, termed the *origin*; (ii) the utterance by H which is a product of H's incorrect p^r, that is, misunderstanding of the origin, termed the *manifestation*; and (iii) the awareness which S, H and O have of whether or not the misunderstanding has occurred, termed their *states of realization*. These three components are essential to every misunderstanding.

The states of realization can differ for each participant. Initially, after the origin, each participant's state of realization is " − real." but subsequently their states may change.[3] Thus, if S on hearing the manifestation *realizes* that H has misunderstood the origin, his state of realization becomes "+ S real." and if H fails to realize, his state of realization remains "− H real.". An observer or analyst cannot always be certain of participants' states of realization and therefore when they are assumed but not known "? + real." or "? − real." are deemed to obtain and when they cannot be assumed "? real." is deemed to obtain.

Identification of the states of realization which obtain usefully indicates the understandings which participants have of the origin and of the subsequent conversation. In a misunderstanding in which "+ S real. − H real." obtains S and H have different understandings of the origin; S knows what p he intended to express and he suspects what p^r H believes to have been expressed whereas H has only his p^r which he assumes, incorrectly, is the correct and only understanding of the utterance.[4] Unless S resolves the misunderstanding H will continue the conversation under this incorrect assumption.

Evidence for the states of realization which obtain is provided by the utterances subsequent to the manifestation, as illustrated by the following example, (a), in which H is describing morris-dancing, a pursuit which he does:

(a) (1)   ORIGIN   S: Where do you do this?
     (2)   MANIFESTATION   H: To make the crops grow
                                  ——— + S, O real.
     (3)   S, O: [laugh]
     (4)   O: (S) said *where* do you do it
                                  ——— + H real.
     (5.1)   H: [laugh]
     (5.2)   :   In a tin hut in Greeba

H does not hear the origin, (1), correctly and believes S to have asked "Why do you do this?". He replies to this question with the manifestation, (2), explaining why he morris-dances. S and the additional participant, O, immediately realize that H has misunderstood (1) because of the inappropriacy of (2). The fact that they both laugh and that O explains what S actually said in (1) indicates that " + S real. + O real." obtains. In the light of the explanation in (4) H realizes that the misunderstanding has occurred. He acknowledges it by laughter in (5.1) and correctly answers the origin question in (5.2); the fact that he does these things indicates that his state of realization has become "+ H real.".

Utterances such as (3), (4), (5.1) and (5.2) constitute the secondary components of a misunderstanding. Secondary components are mostly utterances which relate to the origin, such as (4), or to the manifestation, which relate to the occurrence of the misunderstanding or to a problem caused by its occurrence, or which develop the topics raised in the origin or the manifestation, as in (5.2). Secondary components can also be paralinguistic features, such as the laughter in (3) and (5.1) which serves to signal and acknowledge the misunderstanding respectively, or extralinguistic features such as a positional movement which influences the development of the misunderstanding in some way, such as enabling a participant to identify a referent correctly. The secondary components constitute the various ways in which participants develop, resolve or fail to resolve misunderstandings and are termed *devices*.

Devices are divided into four groups. The first group comprises devices which relate to the production and reception of the origin and to the intention behind and understanding of the proposition expressed therein, that is, to x, what is uttered; to x^r, what utterance is received; to p, what S intends to express; and to p^r, what proposition is received by H. x can be completed, repeated, emphasized, amplified (that is, expanded), explained or queried. x^r, p and p^r can be explained, refuted or queried. In (a) x is explained and emphasized in (4); two devices are combined in one utterance: the explanation of x and the emphasis of a part of it.

The second group of devices relate to the misunderstanding and to the awareness of a problem or error in the conversation. These devices signal and acknowledge either misunderstandings or errors in H's p^r. In (a), (3) signals a misunderstanding and (5.1) acknowledges one.

Devices in the third group (i) relate to the manifestation by repeating all or part of it or (ii) express new propositions. Every utterance is an x and every proposition expressed therein is a p, but in this discussion of misunderstandings x is limited to the origin and p to the proposition expressed in that origin. An utterance which expresses a new proposition, developing the topic of either the origin or the manifestation or introducing a new topic, but without being related to x, p, x^r or p^r by explaining them, refuting them or whatever, is deemed "y" if it precedes realization and "z" if it is subsequent to realization.[5] In (a) the utterance (5.2) is a "z" utterance; subsequent to the resolution of the misunderstanding it answers the question posed in the origin.

The final group of devices relate to extralinguistic activity, such as the device "action".

By using any of these devices separately, in combination in one utterance, or sequentially in a series of utterances, participants have the facility to alert one another to misunderstandings and to resolve them. There is no constraint on which devices participants use, nor on which order they should be used in, although if the misunderstanding is caused by a mishearing devices are likely to relate to x and x^r rather than p and p^r, as in (a). Once x^r is established as being equivalent to x, H is usually able to determine the correct p^r.

The sequencing of both primary and secondary components can vary enormously. The only fixed component is the origin, which must precede the others; all other components are a consequence of the origin. The manifestation is often but not invariably adjacent to the origin. Realization can be effected in any order for participants, although "+ S real." is more likely to precede "+ H real." because S knows what p he intended to express and also has some indication of what H's p^r might be, in the light of H's manifestation, whereas H only has his p^r until further utterances by S or O cause him to re-assess that p^r.

The structural sequence of a misunderstanding is dependent on its participants. Example (a) above exhibits the following structural sequence:
ORIGIN → MANIFESTATION → + S, O real. → S, O device (misunderstanding

signal) $\rightarrow$ O device (x explained & x emphasized) $\rightarrow$ + H real. $\rightarrow$ H devices (misunderstanding acknowledgement, z). The sequence is developed by the participants, whose interaction depends on their understandings of each utterance.

It is apparent from this brief account of misunderstandings that both S and H play creative roles which influence and develop their conversations. The particular role played by the hearer is now considered.

The role of the hearer

Initially in a misunderstanding H's role is to misunderstand the proposition which S has endeavoured to express in his origin utterance. Exactly how H misunderstands remains a mystery, in the same way that the process of understanding, a "cognitive act" (Lyons, 1977: 731), cannot be described. Psycholinguists have undertaken various experiments designed to investigate the effects on understanding of particular language constructions, such as transformations, of particular interferences, such as the simultaneous transmission of two messages, and so on (see e.g. reports of experiments in Greene, 1972; Clark and Clark, 1977). These experiments have enabled hypotheses to be put forward in respect of how hearers might conceivably set about understanding utterances, but the fact that conflicting hypotheses are often equally well supported by the results of the various experiments suggests that linguists are scarcely nearer to specifying what the process of understanding entails.

Consequently, no claims can yet be made about how hearers misunderstand utterances. It is, however, possible to consider why they do so. H hears an utterance, processes its constituents and determines what proposition S intended it to express. H can make an error or encounter a problem at any or all of these stages and a misunderstanding often ensues.

H can fail to hear the utterance correctly, as in (a) above. He can also interrupt it so that the utterance which he hears is not the complete utterance which S intended to produce.

The constitution of the origin utterance offers numerous potential problems for H. Syntactic and lexical ambiguities, homophones, ellipsis and insufficiently specified referents can all result in misunderstandings. On many occasions H is able to disambiguate utterances, to interpret homophones correctly, to supply elliptical items correctly and to identify referents correctly. Correct understanding predominates in conversation. However, there are numerous occasions when misunderstandings occur because H has failed to disambiguate an utterance, correctly amend ellipsis and so on.

In the following example, (b), H incorrectly identifies the referent of "It's". S is about to dose herself with cough medicine; she is suffering from a chest infection and is consequently taking things easy while O is having to face a hectic week:[6]

(b) (1)   O: I wouldn't mind being ill
     (2)   ORIGIN   S: It's not very nice
     (3.1) MANIFESTATION   H: That's a very nice one
     (3.2) y : I had it when I was ill
                                  ——— + S real.
     (4) p^r exp. incmp.   O: Oh I thought you meant
     (5) p exp. prtl.   S: Yes I did
                                  ——— + O real.

H attributes the pronoun "It" in (2) to the cough medicine rather than to the state of being ill, which is the referent intended by S. Attributing the referent incorrectly can be identified as the cause of the misunderstanding but is it the only cause? O has no difficulty in attributing the referent correctly and therefore it is not the case that the utterance is constructed in such a way that the correct referent cannot be recovered. O does not misunderstand (2) although she believes she must have done after she hears the manifestation and the following "y" utterance, which suggest an understanding of (2) other than the one she has made.

Because H misunderstands (2) and O correctly understands it, it cannot be claimed that the cause of misunderstanding is absolute. If it were, all participants other than S would misunderstand origin utterances. In fact, O understands correctly more often than he shares H's misunderstanding.[7] Why should H misunderstand and O correctly understand the same utterance? The answer which suggests itself is that each participant's perspective or "line of thought" predisposes him to understand an utterance in a particular way; in H's case this happens to be an incorrect understanding.

This hypothesis is supported by the following example, (c), in which there is no obviously discernible reason for H's misunderstanding of the origin. S and H are two women who have just moved into a high-ceilinged flat and whose landlord lives in the flat below them:

(c) (1.1)   S: I don't know how we change the bulb
     (1.2) ORIGIN   :   Hope he's got a ladder
     (2) p^r err. sig.   H: What?
     (3) y S: For when the bulb goes
     (4)   MANIFESTATION   H: It's got a little hole at the top
     (5) p^r err. sig.   S: What?
     (6) y H: To change the bulb
                                  ——— + S real.
     (7) p exp.   S: I mean a ladder to get up to the bulb
                                  ——— + H real.

(8)	mus. ack.	H:	Oh
(9)	mus. ack.	S, H:	[laugh]
(10)	p' qued.	S:	What on earth did you think I meant by ladder?
(11.1)	p' exp.	H:	Well, like a ladder in tights
(11.2)	p' exp.	:	I thought you meant pull it apart

It is most unlikely that anyone, linguist or lay speaker–hearer, would predict from (1.1) and (1.2) that H would associate "ladder" with the sort of running hole to be found in a pair of tights and would further associate this hole with the hole which provides access to a lightbulb fitting, rather than associate "ladder" with an implement which enables one to reach above one's own height, thereby gaining access to a lightbulb fitting. The fact that H makes such bizarre associations appears to be due to her "line of thought" being at variance with S's rather than to any obvious linguistic reasons, such as S's construction of (1.1) and (1.2).

The contention that linguists should heed such an imprecise, mentalistic concept as "line of thought" is not compatible with a discipline which demands, though often does not display, a rigorous and precise methodology, the results of which should be capable of being tested empirically. Nevertheless, the fact remains that each language-user is an individual whose understanding of utterances is not always in accordance with what specifiable language conventions would lead one to expect. Since other participants do not invariably experience the problems which H has in correctly understanding origin utterances, the causes of misunderstandings cannot be attributed solely to the ways in which speakers construct and produce utterances; therefore one has to conclude that H is sometimes predisposed to misunderstand particular utterances which do not appear to be linguistically problematical.

This conclusion is particularly important because it raises questions about the wisdom of emphasizing the speaker's role. A common assumption is that speakers carefully organise the "information-content" of their utterances, making allowances for the needs of hearers in terms of shared knowledge, cohesive links and so on (e.g. Chafe, 1976). It is difficult, however, to explain how speakers can make allowances for hearers' idiosyncratic thought processes. In order to be more certain of being understood correctly in (c), S could have organized the information-content of her utterances more carefully by saying "I wonder how we *get up to* change the bulb", which ought to have alerted H to the fact that the problem was one of access to the fitting because of its height rather than its mechanics. However, the reference to "ladder", one would have thought, should have supported the "height" interpretation rather than the "mechanics" interpretation. The speaker can only do so much; understanding ultimately depends entirely on the hearer. To dismiss examples such as (c) as exceptions brought about by particularly inept hearers, and therefore atypical examples of conversation, is to pass the buck on the whole question of how communication is successfully achieved. Communication is a highly complex undertaking which requires a great deal of both speakers and hearers, particularly when they have to contend with a problem such as a misunderstanding.

The assumption that a speaker takes care in the production of his utterance so that it will be understood correctly is not supported by evidence from misunderstandings. It is too idealistic to claim, as Prince (1981: 224) does, for example, that care is taken by speakers:

the crucial factor appears to be the tailoring of an utterance by a sender to meet the particular assumed needs of the intended receiver. That is, information-packaging in natural language reflects the speaker's hypotheses about the receiver's assumptions and beliefs and strategies.

While careful "information-packaging" probably does take place in certain marked communication (e.g. lawyers to clients, politicians to interviewers, teachers to pupils, and often vice versa) it does not appear to take place in other types of communication, such as casual or intimate conversations. The origin utterance in the following example, (d), offers little guidance for the hearer. S and H are listening to a record while watching television on vision only; "Focus" are a pop group:

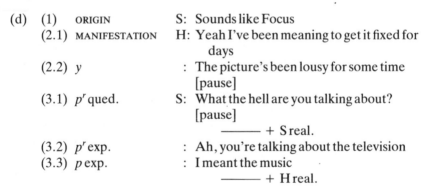

(d)   (1)   ORIGIN   S: Sounds like Focus
        (2.1) MANIFESTATION   H: Yeah I've been meaning to get it fixed for
                                 days
        (2.2) y   : The picture's been lousy for some time
                                 [pause]
        (3.1) p^r qued.   S: What the hell are you talking about?
                                 [pause]
                                 ——— + S real.
        (3.2) p^r exp.   : Ah, you're talking about the television
        (3.3) p exp.   : I meant the music
                                 ——— + H real.

The origin, (1), is not tailored to meet H's needs. It contradicts the assumption that an utterance at the start of a conversation does not fail to identify its referent, an assumption which tends to limit problems of referent identification to subsequent utterances, as Chafe's (1976: 32) discussion of the extent of givenness suggests:

The speaker's treatment of an item as given, therefore, should cease when he judges that item to have left his addressee's consciousness. Such a judgement may be difficult to make, and that is an area in which speakers are especially prone to err, saying "he", for example, when the addressee is no longer thinking about the referent in question.

In (d) S treats the item as given right from the start of the conversation simply because he knows what he is intending and it does not occur to him that H might not also know this. If S had undertaken "information-packaging" and had hypothesized about H's "assumptions and beliefs and strategies" and about what was in H's consciousness, he would not have expressed his proposition in an elliptical utterance which contained the homonym "Focus" but which did not offer any indication as to how "Focus" should be interpreted. For S, the referent of the utterance is the music, which sounds like music played by the group, "Focus"; for H, the referent of the utterance is the television, which has a faulty picture which could be due to a problem with the focus adjustment on the set.

S has not given any consideration to H's needs but this lack of care in the production of (1) does not cause H any problems. H has no difficulty in understanding (1), albeit, unbeknown to him, incorrectly; he understands the elliptical utterance to be a suggestion as to what could be wrong with the television: "(It) Sounds (to me) like (the problem might be the) Focus (adjustment)". His "line of thought" has led him to associate "Focus" with the television and he is not aware that this association is incorrect and will cause S problems in understanding.

In this discussion of misunderstandings, "H" is limited to the participant who misunderstands the origin; the role of the hearer, however, is not limited to H. Having misunderstood the origin, H becomes a speaker and produces a manifestation. The role of the hearer then passes to S, who hears the manifestation and has to try to understand it. Again the assumption that the speaker takes care with his utterance is not borne out. Because H has misunderstood the origin his response, in (d) a manifestation and a "y" utterance, cannot easily be understood correctly by S although H has no idea that his utterances will be problematical. Speakers believe that their utterances will be understood correctly and hearers believe that they have understood utterances correctly until they receive evidence to the contrary.

In (d) S has to appreciate that the referent of the manifestation differs from that of his origin. His question in (3.1), "What the hell are you talking about?", indicates the problem he has in reconciling H's manifestation and subsequent "y" utterance with his origin. In order to understand (2.1) and (2.2) S has to realize that H has misunderstood the origin and is talking about a different topic. The inappropriacy of (2.1) and (2.2) as responses to (1) makes S aware that the conversation is not proceeding coherently. (2.1) and (2.2) cannot refer to the music and therefore S considers what their referent might be. He successfully identifies the television as the referent of H's utterances and thus manages to understand H's manifestation and "y" utterance correctly.

Understanding an utterance correctly is not necessarily easy, and the task of being a hearer is made more difficult when the utterance which that hearer is trying to understand is a manifestation. S assumes that H's manifestation is a response to the p expressed in his origin, whereas in fact it is a response to the p' which H believes to have been expressed. S must therefore detect that p' is not equivalent to p; that is, realize that a misunderstanding has occurred.

An important resource which enables S to detect non-equivalence between p and p' is the recognition that the manifestation is an inappropriate response to the origin. There is no absolute criterion for appropriacy. A response is appropriate if it accords in some way with linguistic and pragmatic conventions and with a speaker's expectations. Expectations range from the general to the particular. To the utterance "Sounds like Focus", S could accept as appropriate any response which refers to the music or to the group Focus, but not "Yeah I've been meaning to get it fixed for days". For a teacher, on the other hand, who asks a pupil how much two plus two equals, the response "Four" would be appropriate and correct while the response "Five" would be appropriate though incorrect. An appropriate response would be a number close to four; an inappropriate response would be "Thirty-seven" or "Blue" or "Yesterday I went to the zoo".

A manifestation can be inappropriate in a number of ways. It is pragmatically inappropriate if it does not accord with the circumstances pertaining to the spatio-temporal location of the conversation or to relevant background information. It is socially inappropriate if it conflicts with the social norms which are pertinent when it is produced; social norms are in respect of the role and status of participants and the conventions governing the spatio-temporal location of the conversation. A manifestation is linguistically inappropriate if it is incohesive with the origin. A manifestation is cognitively inappropriate if it is not what S expects, in general terms.

The manifestation in the following example, (e), is both linguistically and cognitively inappropriate. S has admired H's jumper:

(e) (1)   ORIGIN   S: Is it wool?
     (2)   MANIFESTATION   H: Very
                               ——— + S real.
     (3) x exp. & x' ref.   S: I said wool not warm
                               ——— + H real.
     (4.1) mus. ack.   H: Oh
     (4.2) z : Yes I think so

Because "Very" is an intensifier, in accordance with grammatical conventions, it should be applied to something which does not admit degree; it is therefore linguistically inappropriate to apply it to "wool". "Very" is cognitively inappropriate because S expects "Yes" or "No" in response to her polar question, perhaps supplemented by a more detailed description of the material. S detects the inappropriacy of (2) and this enables her to realize that H has misunderstood (1). S, in the role of hearer, then demonstrates her skill as a language-user; although H has not said "warm" S correctly understands that this is what H heard, x^r. Thus she realizes that H has misunderstood her utterance and knows exactly why the misunderstanding occurred.

The ability to understand a manifestation, to recognize its inappropriacy and to use such recognition to realize a misunderstanding has occurred indicates how complex the work of a hearer can be. The hearer who achieves these things then becomes a speaker again and can draw on his new knowledge about the conversation. In (e) S uses two devices to ensure that H also realizes that she has misunderstood the origin and that she knows how it should have been understood: she explains x, what she said, and she refutes x^r, what H heard. The successful use of devices in effecting realization is wholly dependent on the participants. The participant who uses devices does so in the light of his understanding of the conversation, his awareness of x, x^r, p and p^r. The participant who hears the devices must endeavour to understand them correctly, as with any utterance. In (e) S is explicit and successfully effects realization. Similarly, in (a) and (d) S is explicit and successfully effects "+ H real." by using "x explained & x emphasized" and "p^r queried, p^r explained, p explained" respectively.

A number of devices are used in (c). H, aware of having difficulty in understanding the origin, seeks to clarify it by asking "What?", which signals an error in her p^r. S's response, a "y" utterance which gives additional information, "For when the bulb goes", does not resolve the potential misunderstanding and leads to H's manifestation, which in turn prompts S's signal of p^r error, "What?" and H's "y" utterance giving additional information, "To change the bulb". These devices and the subsequent devices – explanations, queries and acknowledgements – enable both S and H to realize the misunderstanding and to know exactly what both p and p^r were and why they were non-equivalent.

In (b) "− H real." is preserved while "+ O real." is effected:

(b) (4) p^r exp. incmp.   O: Oh I thought you meant
     (5) p exp. prtl.   S: Yes I did
                           ———— + O real.

O believes she has misunderstood the origin after she hears the manifestation which gives evidence that H's p^r differs from her own p^r. She begins to explain her p^r but S interrupts her. S agrees that O's p^r is what she intended the origin to express, even though O's p^r has not been explained. (4) and (5) demonstrate the remarkable ability of hearers to understand correctly utterances which are incomplete and are highly elliptical, utterances which one might predict would cause problems in understanding. This ability reinforces the argument that the process of understanding is dependent on participants rather than on their utterances. Much is left "unsaid" in (4) while the agreement with (4) which is expressed in (5) is an agreement with all that is "unsaid". S understands (4) correctly, O understands (5) correctly and thus "+ O real." is effected even though the devices used are not at all explicit. H, on the other hand, continues to fail to realize that she has misunderstood the origin and it is quite possible that she does not understand (4) or (5), utterances to which she appears to pay no attention and to which she does not respond.

The responsibility for successful communication lies with both speakers and hearers, and the ways in which they are able to achieve successful communication can involve complex negotiation. In examples such as (c) this negotiation is easily apparent to both participants and analyst. In the following example, (f), much of the negotiation is covert; S is apparently unaware of it. S, Bob and James are all friends known to H, who is S's sister. The expression "doing a foreigner" is Manx idiom for "moonlighting", that is, performing one's trade in one's own time and for one's own gain rather than as part of one's job. Bob, a builder, has been married twice. "Surby" is a local village and "the Jane" is the local maternity home:

(f)	(1.1)	ORIGIN	S:	Bob's doing a foreigner in Surby for somebody
	(1.2)	y	:	The brother-in-law came over and he doesn't speak any English so Bob was in a mess
	(1.3)	y	:	He got him to the pub but the guy kept talking German
	(1.4)	y	:	James knows a bit so they managed
	(2)	MANIFESTATION	H:	How's his marriage?
	(3)	y	S:	Which one?
	(4)	y	H:	The second
	(5)	y	S:	She's going into the Jane in a couple of days' time
	(6)	2nd MANIFESTATION	H:	Well what about the one in Surby?
	(7)	y	S:	No it's only a foreigner
	(8)	p' err. sig.	H:	But . . . oh God
				———— + H real.

S, in (1.1) to (1.4), describes an amusing inter-language problem concerning a building job. H, however, understands "doing a foreigner" as "having an affair with a foreign girl" and consequently believes (1.1) to (1.4) to be a flippant description of an inter-language problem concerning unsavoury licentiousness, made even more sordid by the fact that the affair was being carried out "for somebody", with overtones of pimping. S and H are both native Manx and both know what "doing a foreigner" means. On this occasion, however, H misunderstands the expression. Her misunderstanding is supported by S's "*y*" utterances – the fact that the woman's brother-in-law was German and that Bob "was in a mess" when having to deal with this man – and by H's knowledge of Bob's occasional transgressions in the past.

Rather than openly comment on Bob's behaviour, H chooses to elicit comment from S on the affair. The manifestation in (2) is an *indirect* manifestation – that is, one which is an apparently appropriate response to an origin and which does not provide evidence that the misunderstanding has occurred.[8] H's inquiry after the state of Bob's marriage is an oblique response to S's utterances and is intended as a conversational implicature (Grice, 1975) in that although it does not appear to relate directly to the utterances to which it is a response H actually intends S to understand it to have a meaning other than its literal one.

S, however, in his role of hearer, understands (2) in its literal sense and treats it as a shift in topic from an incident concerning Bob to Bob's personal life, accepting that H has taken up the subject of his utterances, Bob, and has chosen not to respond to the narration which those utterances express. S fails to perceive that H is performing a conversational implicature and is attempting to elicit comment on the morality of Bob's action. Since S has not said anything pertaining to Bob's personal life and therefore to his morality, he cannot perceive H's implicature and consequently fails to realize that a misunderstanding has occurred.

Conversational implicature is dependent on a participant's ability to understand correctly. Indeed, the "Cooperative Principle" suggested by Grice (1975: 45) depends on mutual understanding, the very thing it is assumed to facilitate:

Make your conversational contribution such as is required, at the stage at which it occurs, by the accepted purpose or direction of the talk exchange in which you are engaged.

The problem with this Principle lies in the determination of "the accepted purpose or direction of the talk exchange". In many conversations this is neither absolutely determined by one participant nor consciously agreed upon by two or more participants. Grice himself points out that the direction of a conversation may be "fixed" or may "evolve" and may be "definite" or "indefinite"; his contention is that certain conversational moves are "unsuitable". Such a contention, together with the Cooperative Principle, is based on the assumption that the conversational contribution is that of a speaker. The hearer's role is once again neglected. The direction in which a conversation proceeds depends on how utterances are understood as well as on what utterances are produced. Consequently, in (f), as in (d) initially, the conversation proceeds in different directions because H has misunderstood an utterance of S's. Neither S nor H is aware that the conversation is proceeding in different directions, and this lack of awareness indicates a further problem with the Cooperative Principle and with Grice's attendant proposals for how the conversational implicatures are performed and perceived; if participants believe that the Cooperative Principle is being followed or that conversational implicatures are being performed they will not be able to realize that a misunderstanding has occurred because they will attempt to understand a manifestation and to establish its coherence in the conversation on the assumption that its inappropriacy is intentional and that it is a valid response rather than the product of a misunderstanding.

S's response to the indirect manifestation is therefore to seek a clarification of which marriage H is referring to, rather than to query why H asks the question. H provides in (4) the clarification which S seeks and then S performs a conversational implicature, informing H that Bob's wife is "going into the Jane in a couple of days time". This utterance indirectly expresses the proposition that Bob's wife is about to have a baby and by implicature it informs H that the marriage is a happy one. H perceives the implicature, correctly understanding that the imminently productive marriage is a happy one. Unfortunately for H, correctly understanding (5) causes more problems because she finds it difficult to reconcile her understanding of Bob's behaviour with S's unconcerned attitude towards it, particularly in view of the forthcoming baby. In a further attempt to draw S's comments on the situation H produces a second manifestation which refers back to the Surby woman.

S, in his role of hearer, cannot possibly understand (6) correctly since to understand this second manifestation correctly he needs to realize that it is the product of a misunderstanding of (1.1). Failure to realize that a misunderstanding has occurred thus leads to *compounding* of that misunderstanding. S appreciates that the question relates to Bob's connection with the woman in Surby but because there is no personal connection between the two he cannot understand why H should ask the question. He explains in (7) that there is no connection by pointing out that "it's only a foreigner": Bob is only doing a foreigner, that is, a building job, for the woman in Surby.

At this stage H is in turmoil. She cannot believe that S is as chauvinistic as (7) suggests, yet he must be in the light of her understanding of (7); this understanding is that the affair with the woman in Surby is of no consequence because she is "only a foreigner". Further compounding of the initial misunderstanding occurs since H's understanding of utterances subsequent to the origin is based on the unrealized misunderstanding of that origin. It is therefore impossible for H to understand (7) correctly. This impossibility, however, is constructive because H becomes aware that she cannot be understanding (7) correctly and this awareness prompts her to re-consider the conversation and to re-interpret "doing a foreigner". She signals the error in her p^r by uttering "But . . . oh God" and then, aware that the problem which she has with the conversation is not apparently shared by S, she remembers what "doing a foreigner" means and thus realizes the misunderstanding. H does not effect "+ S real."; S never realizes the misunderstanding and consequently never understands H's utterances correctly.

(f) illustrates the complex problems which can beset hearers. Both S and H have difficulty in understanding each other's utterances, though S appears to be unaware of such a difficulty. Apart from H's "p^r error signal" in (8) the only device to be used is "y", an utterance which develops or changes the topics introduced in the origin or the manifestation. In other words, neither S nor H raise any queries about their understandings or offer any explanations of their intentions. Even though H has doubts about what she believes S is expressing she does not make any direct attempt to clear these doubts. The inability to be direct augments the communication problem which has derived from the participants' failure to realize that the misunderstanding has occurred. Monitoring of the conversation can thus be an important factor in its success. Such monitoring need not be as detailed and intrusive as, for example, that of the assignments reported by Garfinkel (1964) in which hearers demanded precise clarification of what speakers meant by their utterances. The unspecific "p^r error signal" "What?", for example, is often sufficient to elicit assistance in the understanding of an utterance; whether it is understood as a request for a repeat or an explanation it makes the speaker aware that the hearer is having difficulty with his utterance. As the two signals in (c) show, however, there is no guarantee of success: the first prompts an utterance which leads to the manifestation and therefore provides no constructive assistance to the hearer whereas the second signal prompts an utterance which enables "+ S real." to be effected. Nothing in language-use can be taken as absolute; there are no guarantees in communication.

The conviction that one understands correctly and is being understood correctly is deep-rooted and can threaten successful communication. It is apparent that when misunderstandings occur, belief by participants that the Cooperative Principle is being observed is counter-productive. They exchange utterances without questioning whether or not these utterances are being understood as intended and they assume the conversation is coherent. The process of understanding and of being understood can thus be more complex than the Gricean "blueprint" for conversation might suggest. Grice's "Maxims" (1975: 45–7) focus on the utterance produced, crediting the speaker with an active role while the hearer passively assimilates the utterance, assuming it to be in compliance with the appropriate maxims or to be a flouting of a particular maxim for a specific purpose. This approach ignores the fact that a hearer is not a replica of a speaker. What is informative, true, relevant and perspicacious for one is not necessarily so for another. Each is a distinct individual who communicates from his own perspective.

An important corollary of this is that a hearer creates a meaning for an utterance by a speaker. This corollary is not entirely an advocation of the Humpty Dumpty argument (Carroll, 1939: 196; see also Kjolseth, 1972) because the hearer creates *a* meaning, not *the* meaning. In conversation there is no unique meaning to an utterance. The speaker intends his utterance to express a particular proposition and tends to try and ensure that the proposition received by the hearer is as close to this as possible, hence the number of resolved misunderstandings in which devices are used by S to be certain that realization is effected and that H correctly understands the origin.[9] Being understood correctly appears to be important to speakers and therefore when they are aware or suspect that their utterances have been misunderstood they strive to amend their hearers' understandings. The speaker is reluctant to concede the hearer's understanding of an utterance to him if it differs from what he himself intended of that utterance. It must be remembered, however, that the negotiation of the meaning of an utterance does not commence until one of the participants realizes that a misunderstanding has occurred, or suspects that there is a problem in the conversation.

In the examples discussed above participants are involved in misunderstandings of particular utterances, the majority of which are resolved for all participants. These misunderstandings represent the observable surface of a much deeper and potentially more disruptive phenomenon. One can correctly understand another's every utterance but nevertheless fail to understand correctly the underlying motive or intention which has prompted and directed these utterances. It is these deeper, often unspecifiable misunderstandings which tend to constitute the major communication problems which can give rise to serious disharmonies between people.

It is to be hoped that by turning increasingly more attention to what hearers do, and to what they have to do in order to understand correctly, we shall become more aware of the immense difficulties a hearer can face in endeavouring to understand what a speaker is endeavouring to communicate. Communication is a process fraught with difficulties. It is wrong to assume that language is a well-structured medium which, if used in accordance with syntactic, semantic, pragmatic and phonological conventions, is sufficient to engender successful communication. Such an assumption derives from undue emphasis being placed on the speaker's role. Once one considers the hearer's role as well, it becomes apparent that successful communication depends on the behaviour of language-users, in terms of intentions, expectations, understandings and so on, at least as much as on the language they use. Language-users can engineer successful communication. Awareness of the potential or possible occurrence of a misunderstanding ought to encourage more speaker–hearers to draw on the resources which their language-system provides in order to avoid or resolve misunderstandings. Successful communication requires speakers and hearers to monitor their intentions and understandings as an integral part of the communication process. The framework for such monitoring exists; all that remains is for speakers and hearers to make use of it and to be prepared to discuss the possibilities of problems in understanding.

Notes

1. This discussion of hearers and misunderstandings largely derives from a study of how misunderstandings are structured (Humphreys-Jones, forthcoming) and develops some of the issues raised therein. I am particularly grateful to Graham McGregor and John Pellowe for their constructive and challenging comments.

2. Cf. the work of, e.g., Milroy (1984) and Gumperz and Tannen (1979), which focuses on cross-dialectal and inter-ethnic misunderstandings.

3. An exception is an intentional misunderstanding in which H realizes before he produces his manifestation; he chooses to respond as though he has misunderstood the origin, having already understood it correctly.

4. The reason that S is said to *suspect* what H's p^r might be is that he can realize that H has misunderstood the origin without necessarily *knowing* what H's p^r is, although such knowledge generally does accompany realization.

5. The reason for this distinction is that a "y" utterance can contribute to the development of a misunderstanding, whereas a "z" utterance does not affect the misunderstanding, though it does develop the conversation in which a misunderstanding occurs.

6. The following abbreviations are used for devices cited in the examples presented throughout this chapter: "p^r exp. incmp.": incomplete explanation of p^r; "p exp. prtl.": partial explanation of p, that is, with ellipsis; "p^r err. sig.": signal of an error in p^r; "p exp.": explanation of p; "mus. ack.": acknowledgement of the misunderstanding; "p^r qued.": query of the p^r; "p^r exp.": explanation of p^r; "x exp.": explanation of x; "p^r exp."; explanation of p^r; "p^r ref.": refutation of p^r.

7. Out of 19 examples of misunderstandings in which O is a participant, O shares H's misunderstanding in 3 and understands the origin correctly in 14 examples; in 1 example O's p^r cannot be determined and in another O is appealed to subsequent to the origin and may not have heard the origin.

8. A clear example of an indirect manifestation is the response "Yes" or "No" without further comment to an origin utterance which is a polar question. In such an example S could not possibly realize that H had misunderstood the origin unless the indirect manifestation was cognitively inappropriate and S had expected "Yes" rather than "No", or vice versa.

9. Out of 72 fully realized misunderstandings in a corpus of 100 data, S realizes first and effects "+ H real." by the use of devices in 53 examples. In 11 examples H realizes first and effects "+ S real." by the use of devices, in 1 S and H realize at the same time and in 3 O realizes first and uses devices to effect "+ S real. + H real.". The remaining 4 examples are intentional misunderstandings in which S realizes directly after H's manifestations.

References

Carroll, L. (1939) *The Complete Works of Lewis Carroll*. London: The Nonesuch Press.

Chafe, W. (1976) "Givenness, contrastiveness, definiteness, subjects, topics and point of view". In Li, C. (ed.) (1976) *Subject and Topic*. New York: Academic Press pp. 25–55.

Clark, H. and Carlson, T. (1982) "Hearers and speech acts, *Language* **58** (2), 332–73.

Clark, H. and Clark, E. (1977) *Psychology and Language: An Introduction to Psycholinguistics*. New York: Harcourt Brace Jovanovich.

Fromkin, V. (1971) "The non-anomalous nature of anomalous utterances". *Language*, **47**, 27–52. (Reprinted in Fromkin, V. (ed.) (1973) *Speech Errors as Linguistic Evidence*. The Hague: Mouton, pp. 215–242.)

Garfinkel, H. (1964) "Studies of the routine grounds of everyday activities", *Social Problems*, **11** (3). (Reprinted in Sudnow, D. (ed.) (1972) *Studies in Social Interaction*. New York: Free Press, pp. 1–30.)

Goffman, E. (1976) "Replies and responses", *Language and Society* **5** (3), 257–313.

Goodwin, C. (1981) *Conversational Organization: Interaction Between Speakers and Hearers*. London: Academic Press.

Greene, J. (1972) *Psycholinguistics: Chomsky and Psychology*. Harmondsworth: Penguin Books.

Grice, H. P. (1975) "Logic and conversation". In Cole, P. and Morgan, J. (eds) (1975) *Syntax and Semantics Vol. 3: Speech Acts*. London: Academic Press, pp. 41–58.

Grimshaw, A. D. (1980) "Mishearings, misunderstandings and other nonsuccesses in talk: a plea for redress of speaker-oriented bias", *Sociological Inquiry*, **50**, 31–74.

Gumperz, J. and Tannen, D. (1979) "Individual and social differences in language use". In Fillmore, J., Kempler, D. and Wang, S.-Y (eds) (1979) *Individual Differences in Language Ability and Language Behaviour*. London: Academic Press, pp. 305–325.

Humphreys-Jones, C. (1986) *A Study of the Types and Structure of Misunderstandings*. Unpublished Ph.D thesis, University of Newcastle upon Tyne.

Kjolseth, R. (1972) "Making sense: natural language and shared knowledge in understanding". In Fishman, J. (1972) *Advances in the Sociology of Language*, vol. II. The Hague: Mouton.

Lyons, J. (1977) *Semantics* (2 vols). Cambridge: Cambridge University Press.

McGregor, G. (1984) "Conversation and communication", *Language and Communication*, **4** (1), 78–83.

Matthei, E. and Roeper, T. (1983) *Understanding and Producing Speech*. London: Fontana.

Milroy, L. (1984) "Comprehension and context: successful communication and communicative breakdown". In Trudgill, P. (ed.) (1984) *Applied Sociolinguistics*. London: Academic Press, pp. 7–31.

Moore, T. & Carling, C. (1982) *Understanding Language: towards a post-Chomskyan linguistics* London: Macmillan Press.

Pellowe, J. (1980) "Establishing variant intonational systems", *York Papers in Linguistics*, 8 October 1980, pp. 97–144.

Pellowe, J. and Jones, V. (1978) "On intonational variability in Tyneside speech". In Trudgill, P. (ed.) (1978) *Sociolinguistic Patterns of British English*. London: Arnold.

Pirandello, L. (1954) *Six Characters in Search of an Author* (trans. F. May). London: Heinemann.

Prince, E. (1981) "Towards a taxonomy of given–new information". In Cole, P. (ed.) (1981) *Radical Pragmatics*. London: Academic Press, pp. 223–255.

Shannon, C. E. and Weaver, W. (1949) *The Mathematical Theory of Communication*. Urbana, IL: University of Illinois Press.

8

A social approach to propositional communication: Speakers lie to Hearers

JAMES BRADAC, EVAN FRIEDMAN and HOWARD GILES

Introduction

In everyday life, people lie about their aspirations, intentions, and credentials, about their groups' capabilities, attributes and potential, not to mention their close relationships' authenticity, strengths and influences. They also evade difficult questions; they keep secrets; and sometimes they tell the truth. By the same token, we must as Hearers oftentimes be second-guessing other Speakers' lies, evasions and secrets (cf. Hewes and Planalp, 1982). As Giles and Wiemann (in press) claim, communication can sometimes be complex and exhausing work as we attempt to "pull the wool over the ears of others" whilst debugging their messages at one and the same time. Thus, these theorists develop a model of Speaker–Hearers as "crafty–sceptical" communicators. But what is meant by the terms "lying", "evading", "secret-keeping", and "truth-telling"? How are these concepts interrelated? Are there other concepts which bear a family resemblance? This paper addresses these questions by presenting models which focus upon the beliefs or "states of mind" which underlie such communicative acts, and it attempts to outline when and why these beliefs are constructed. We describe cognitive structures which communicators must exploit in order to engage in propositional communication.

It is worth emphasizing at the outset that the notion of Hearer or audience looms large in our presentation; it is essential to our thinking. Speakers do not lie or evade in a social vacuum. Rather, they lie to a particular audience and evade the questions of a real Hearer or Hearers. Communicative actions are thus contextualized, and a very important aspect of the communication context is the Speaker's *beliefs about* the Hearer, including beliefs about the latter's beliefs concerning the former.

Initially, the scope of our theory is described in a discussion of propositional communication. Then the essential structure of the theory is offered in two sections – one which describes axioms and the other which describes theorems derived from these. Some implications of this structure are discussed in subsequent sections, including the ways in which it can be elaborated modestly by attending to questions of message selection and motivations for encoding.

Propositional communication: stating beliefs versus expressing affect

Several theorists have distinguished between analogic and digital displays (see Berger and Bradac, 1982; Watzlawick, Beavin and Jackson, 1967). This distinction is usefully invoked here as the issue of theoretical scope is addressed. Briefly, analogic displays are characterized by *continuous* features which vary exclusively in terms of duration or intensity. Thus, a human scream has starting and ending points yet is not segmentable; it is simply longer–shorter, or louder–softer. Or, a blush begins and then ends, although the precise points of on- and offset may be difficult to determine; sometimes blushers turn beet-red, while at others they become slightly pink only. Typically, a louder scream and deeper blush will signal stronger affect on the part of the perpetrator.

Contrarily, digital displays are composed of discrete segments or elements which are combined according to rules which permit some combinations while precluding others. An important feature of such a display, or more generally digital systems, is that they exhibit generativity; the elements which are combined according to rules yield potentially novel structures. They also allow for transformability; some novel structures generated preserve the meaning of an original structure. Thus $1 + 1 = 2$; $1 + 1 + 1 = 3$; $(1 + 1 = 2) + 1 = 3$; "John is an ape" = "An ape is John", but not "Is John an ape?"

The analogic/digital distinction suggests that a blush, for example, is a very different entity than is the sentence: "I believe I am blusing". The blush and the sentence *about* blushing are of different orders or logical types (Bateson, 1979). Non-humans (e.g. sticklebacks) can produce colouration changes, but with one or two possible exceptions non-humans cannot *claim* to be cutaneously changing (although the character, "Litmus", in the film *Escape from Alcatraz* might suggest untapped potential here!). Such claims demand a digital system for their formulations, and non-humans, we presume, do not have access to this kind of system.

Our approach is all about claims or propositions of the form, "A = B" ("John is an ape"; "I believe I am blushing"). To make or offer such claims, Speaker must have *beliefs* (to be discussed below). Thus, it is a theory rooted in digitality, concerned essentially with belief-based communicative actions which are directed to Hearer. We are *not* interested here in utterances produced by a person stranded alone on a desert island; such a person (albeit capable of complex cognitive machinations so as to make the best of a rotten situation) cannot really lie to, or keep secrets from, herself. More particularly still, we *are* concerned primarily with those beliefs which Speakers have which allow them to offer propositions which may be lies, evasions, instances of truth-telling, and so forth.

The "paradigm message" which would fall within our domain is the type where Speaker signals the message's essentially propositional nature explicitly by saying, "I *believe* that X is Y", or "I *claim* that X is actually Y". However, in many situations Speaker will simply assert that "X is Y" without metacommunicatively indicating that s/he is believing or claiming. Also, where Speaker and Hearer have attained high levels of mutual knowledge or intersubjectivity, messages representing propositions may be further truncated or abbreviated: "X" may stand for "X is Y", or even, "X is Y because C" (cf. *pars pro toto* principle; Hermann, 1982).

This observation regarding message abbreviation leads to the more general, yet nonetheless important, point that there is no necessary connection between overt utterances and underlying beliefs. This not only makes it possible for Speaker to lie, evade, etc. but also makes it impossible for Hearer to know with *certainty* where a given utterance accurately or inaccurately represents Speaker's propositional belief. Indeed, as many Speakers represent their beliefs extremely idiosyncratically and in ways that conventional Hearers find at best ambiguous, efforts at lie detection are very hazardous. In other words, only Speaker can know for sure whether s/he has lied or told the truth.

The axioms and theorems which are offered in subsequent sections describe beliefs which Speaker can have as s/he communicates propositionally. We will argue that a particular constellation of beliefs constitutes a lie, whereas another cluster defines evasion, etc. Communicative action is viewed from the standpoint of the Speaker's cognitions, which of necessity include those pertaining to Hearer. We offer a portrait of what Speaker *plans* to do as s/he communicates propositionally with Hearer, not what is actually uttered. As with the attitude–behaviour debate in social psychology, such intentions are only part of the input into message selection. Other factors such as contextual norms can also play a prominent role in the actual production of messages (cf. Ajzen and Fishbein, 1980). Moreover, our standpoint allows us to say nothing directly concerning the evaluative or attributional consequences of particular communicative acts. In a sense we are describing a general cognitive code which Speaker must employ when rendering the truth, or a lie, when keeping a secret, etc. Hearer may indeed employ this code also when attempting (again, hazardously) to infer whether Speaker is acting veraciously or is "lying through his teeth". In truth(!) then, our theoretical aims are quite modest yet realistic at this stage of theory-building in a very complex area of communicative endeavour.

Elemental beliefs and four axioms

Beliefs are propositions which link an object to some attribute (Fishbein and Ajzen, 1975), and they demand a digital system such as language for their formulation (Bradac, Bowers & Courtright, 1979). Individuals have beliefs about real and abstract entities (labelled "direct" beliefs), and they have beliefs about beliefs (and we term these "indirect" (Wimmer and Perner, 1983)). Therefore "Nixon is a liar" is direct, whereas "I believe that you think Nixon is a liar" is indirect. In the case of indirect beliefs, the attribute is a direct belief and the object is "I" (Speaker) or "you" (Hearer). The clearest example of the former is when a high subjective probability of correctness is assigned to the direct belief (i.e. high belief strength *à la* Ajzen and Fishbein, 1980), e.g. "I am pretty certain that I'm hot stuff!". For our purposes the most compelling instance of the latter exists when Speaker has a belief (however strong) about Hearer's direct belief, e.g. "I think you may love me(?)".

There are four major types of direct and indirect beliefs which enter into propositional communication: (1) beliefs about self ("I dislike Nixon", or "I am very certain that I dislike Thatcher"); (2) about the world ("Nixon is a liar", or "I believe that stereotype about all Welshmen being good singers is actually quite right"); (3) about the Hearer ("you voted for Reagan", or "I think you sympathize with Arthur Scargill"); and (4) about communication ("Tricky Dick is a term understood by most Americans over eighteen years of age", or "Most Britons would probably consider the Californian exclamation, 'that's awesome' as grating as Americans find the British evaluation, 'brilliant!' "). Each or all of these four types of beliefs may become a belief about the topic of discourse, which is the belief about which one lies, tells the truth, keeps a secret, etc. The topic of discourse can be established by Speaker, or Hearer, or by third parties (cf. Tracy, 1985). A paradigm case would be where Hearer asks Speaker the question "Do you think Nixon is an honest or dishonest man?" Assuming participants are playing the "communication game" (see Higgins, 1980), that is if Speaker is being sincere, Hearer attentive, and Hearer accurately perceives Speaker's sincerity, the topic of discourse would be consensually defined as "Nixon's veracity". Indeed, it would be with regard to Nixon's veracity that Speaker would respond to Hearer's question.

Two more specific types of beliefs should now be mentioned. First, a particular type of direct belief about self can be labelled an "intention" (Fishbein and Azjen, 1975). Here, the object is self and the attribute is an intended action, "I intend to buy British, not foreign goods". Second, beliefs about Hearer and beliefs about communication combine to generate "perlocutionary beliefs about Hearer". A perlocutionary belief is that which pertains to the consequence of an utterance. A perlocutionary belief about Hearer is a belief about the consequence of an utterance for a particular

Hearer: "John will understand that I mean 'Thatcher' when I say, 'the Iron Lady' in this context" (as he believes this also). A particular belief about Hearer, namely the belief about Hearer's belief about the topic of discourse, necessarily is a part of any perlocutionary belief about Hearer; minimally, one believes that Hearer has *no* belief about the topic. Perlocutionary beliefs are potentially distinct from perlocutionary knowledge (Searle, 1969), which is part of one's knowledge of communication. That is, it is possible for one to know tacitly how to impress a Hearer while holding an incorrect belief about how this Hearer is typically impressed. Similarly, one can possess a knowledge of the world, self, or Hearer, which is independent of beliefs about the world, self and Hearer. This knowledge can, in conjunction with or apart from beliefs, be one of the important determinants of communicative actions alluded to above. But in any case whilst recognizing the ultimate theoretical importance of knowledge, we must focus upon beliefs exclusively at the present time.

Both "intentions" and "perlocutionary beliefs", along with the other belief types described above, allow us to make four claims having the status of axioms in our theory.

Axiom 1 Given a topic of discourse and Hearer's demand for a Speaker response, Speaker will intend *either* to produce an utterance which will satisfy this demand *or* to withhold this utterance. With respect to the latter intention, the paradigm case might be where Hearer asks, "What is your sex life like?", and Speaker intends to remain silent.

Axiom 2 Speaker has a belief regarding the *accuracy* of a potential utterance in the sense that Speaker believes Hearer would construe the utterance either correctly or incorrectly from the standpoint of Speaker's topical belief. Of course, as suggested by Axiom 1, Speaker may intend to withhold the potential utterance, whether accurate or inaccurate. Speaker may believe that "the man lacks veracity" would have the consequence of creating in Hearer an accurate or inaccurate belief regarding Speaker's belief, "Nixon is a liar". This is a particular perlocutionary belief which entails that topical belief (i.e. "Nixon is a liar") and another perlocutionary belief about how the Hearer will interpret the utterance *vis-à-vis* Speaker's topical belief.

It should be emphasized that *accuracy* refers to a belief regarding the correctness of Hearer's belief regarding Speaker's belief, and not to correctness of Hearer's belief regarding the world. Thus, Hearer can hold an inaccurate belief about the world which is at the same time an accurate belief about Speaker's belief. It should also be emphasized that Speaker's beliefs regarding Hearer interpretation of Speaker's utterances are crucial here. For example, Speaker may believe that "Nixon is truthful" will accurately represent the belief, "Nixon is a liar", *if* Speaker believes that Hearer will infer the *opposite* of what Speaker's utterance indicates when attempting to construe Speaker's true belief. Accuracy in our terms therefore does not reside in any simple, logical correspondence of utterance to topical belief.

Axiom 3 Speaker has a belief regarding the *relevance* of the potential utterance. Speaker may believe that a given utterance is relevant (or irrelevant) to the topical belief, and that Hearer would construe this in the same manner. This belief regarding relevance is related to Grice's (1975) well-known "Cooperativeness Principle" in a general way only. "Relevance" in our scheme and in the latter's are potentially orthogonal. Grice asserts that communicators agree tacitly to make fitting remarks; that is, those which are relevant to the topic and conversational flow (see Tracy, 1983). We are suggesting, more particularly, that a potential utterance (whether it is expressed or withheld) may be relevant or irrelevant from the standpoint of the specific Speaker belief (e.g. "Thatcher is anti-Union"). Thus, a remark may be appropriate and fitting yet *not* "relevant" to the specific belief at issue (e.g. Hearer queries: "Speaker, do you think that Thatcher is intent on destruction of the Trade Union movement, or not?" Speaker: "Thatcher is Thatcher!"). Speaker's belief in the relevance or irrelevance of the utterance depends upon Speaker's having a belief regarding what belief is at issue ("I believe that Hearer wants access to my belief, *Thatcher is anti-Union*"), having beliefs regarding how the specific features of the utterance reflect the belief at issue (e.g. "The woman wishes to take power away from working people" *relevantly* reflects the belief at issue – for the authors at least – since "woman" refers to Thatcher and "wishes to take power away from working people" is equivalent to "anti-Union"), and having perlocutionary beliefs regarding Hearer's likely interpretation of utterance (i.e. Hearer will infer in this context that "The woman wishes to take power away from working people" indicates that Speaker believes Thatcher is anti-Union).

Axiom 4 Speaker has a belief regarding the extent to which s/he will be *accountable* for the intended utterance if it is produced, or if it is withheld. In line with the beliefs regarding accuracy and relevance, accountability is a belief which is based upon the topical belief and a perlocutionary belief. Where Speaker believes s/he would be *accountable* for an intended utterance ("Britain has squandered her North Sea oil assets"), the perlocutionary belief indicates that Hearer would infer that the Speaker believes that statement, and that Hearer will understand that it is the *only* plausible interpretation from such a remark uttered in that context. This perlocutionary belief entails the topical belief and beliefs regarding Hearer and the communication, e.g. a belief regarding Hearer's understanding of ambiguity, and a belief regarding the ambiguity or non-ambiguity of the intended utterance or silence.

When Speaker believes s/he is *not* accountable (e.g. by use of a foreign accent, or joking frame of reference), Speaker must believe that Hearer can be made to see that there is more than one plausible inference which can be made from the utterance (or non-utterance). Thus, if neither Speaker believes Thatcher cares about the unemployed, nor Speaker believes Thatcher does not care about the unemployed can be precluded by the utterance (Hearer), "Does Thatcher care about the unemployed?", with Speaker's reply being "I won't say she doesn't", Speaker would not perceive him- or herself responsible were Hearer to infer one belief rather than the other. This would be true even where it would be advantageous from Speaker's standpoint for Hearer to make one inference rather than the other. The term "devious message" has been used to describe utterances which "trick" Hearer into holding a particular belief regarding Speaker's belief where other beliefs can plausibly be inferred from the utterances (Bowers, Elliott and Desmond, 1977). The essence of deviousness is Speaker's lack of accountability for Hearer's making a particular inference regarding Speaker's belief.

When Speaker intends to withhold an utterance, s/he is accountable if s/he believes that the non-utterance will be construed in one way only, namely, as an intentional avoidance of an utterance which would have the consequence of informing Hearer about Speaker's topical belief. Speaker is not accountable if s/he believes there will be more than one plausible interpretation of the non-utterance.

The four Axioms above regarding intention to utter or withhold utterance, accuracy–inaccuracy, relevance–irrelevance, and accountability–nonaccountability together generate 12 Theorems which describe discrete Speaker belief states which exist prior to the undertaking of communicative actions of a propositional sort. Our assumption is that each of these 12 states is formed from the lower-order beliefs regarding accuracy, etc., which in turn are formed from lower-order, elementary indirect and direct beliefs regarding topic and various perlocutionary beliefs regarding Hearer. This hierarchical ordering is endemic in our detailed description of Axiomatic structure above. The relationships among the elemental beliefs, Axioms and Theorems are summarized in Figure 1.

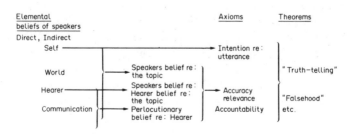

FIG. 1. Relationships among the theoretical concepts.

Twelve theorems: belief states for propositional communication

Our four Axioms generate 12 Theorems which can be grouped into three Families: A "truth-telling", a "falsehood", and an "evasion" Family (see Figure 2). The Families are distinguished on the basis of the criterial beliefs regarding accuracy and relevance, and within Families, membership varies with changes in the criterial beliefs regarding intention to utter or to avoid utterance, and accountability. The Families represent three sets of belief states for communicative action and we will briefly outline each Family in turn.

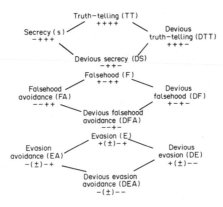

FIG. 2. Families of belief states for propositional communication. Order of +'s and −'s: intention to utter; accuracy; relevance; and accountability (− = "not").

The "truth-telling" Family

Some theorists have argued that the presumption of truth-telling is essential in human communication (Ehninger, 1977), and for this reason we discuss this Family first. Accordingly, intentional communication systems would disintegrate were it the case that communicators could not assume veracity unless given reason to believe other (cf. Kursh, 1971; Brandt, Miller and Hocking, 1982). Other theorists have noted that departures from truth-telling are frequent in everyday talk (e.g. Bok, 1979; Knapp, Hart and Dennis, 1974). For instance, Camden *et al.* (1984: 321) argue that "People lie a lot, and they justify their white lies with some ease – especially in certain social contexts . . . as a practical effective way to cope with certain situational demands . . .". These apparently opposing positions are not necessarily at odds, for it is certainly possible to conceptualize forms whose most typical manifestations are deviant from the standpoint of the defining prototype (Jackson and Jacobs, 1983). Quite simply, communicators may normally assume veracity even though real instances of *non*-veracity are ubiquitous.

"Truth-telling" entails Speaker's intention to produce an utterance which is believed to be accurate and relevant to the topical belief. Speaker must also believe that s/he will be accountable for said utterance. Thus, moving to a non-political realm for our examples, "your dress is hideous" is an instance of "Truth-telling" given Speaker's belief, *The dress = ugly + the dress → Susan* if (1) Speaker believes "your dress is hideous" accurately represents for the Hearer (Susan), *The dress = ugly + the dress → "Susan"*; (2) Speaker believes that "your dress is hideous" is relevant to *The dress = ugly + the dress → Susan* and that Hearer will believe this; and (3) Speaker believes that *The dress is ugly + the dress → Susan* is the only plausible inference from "your dress is hideous".

"Secrecy" arises when Speaker's intention changes from producing the above utterance to deciding to withhold it; "your dress is hideous" would be accurate and relevant, yet Speaker decides to remain silent. Moreover, Speaker believes that s/he is accountable for this non-statement and this act will be construed only as an intentional withholding of accurate, relevant information. Perhaps Speaker is intending to act politely by planning to withhold this utterance, or perhaps s/he fears an insulting reciprocation from Hearer. In any case, "secrecy" can have many different motives, as can each of the other belief states.

If Speaker intends to produce an utterance and believes that this utterance will have the consequence of causing Hearer to hold an accurate and relevant belief regarding Speaker's topical belief by virtue of Hearer's inference, *but* believes that Hearer can be made to see other inferences can be made plausibly from the utterance, then the belief state of "devious truth-telling" exists. This state undergirds the planned deeds of crafty squealers who desire to leak the truth about events with a degree of impunity (e.g. "but I didn't *say* your dress was hideous").

The fourth member of the Family (see Figure 2) is "devious secrecy". Here, Speaker intends to withhold an utterance which s/he believes is relevant and accurate, and s/he believes s/he will not be accountable for this withholding. In this case, the avoidance could be construed as keeping a secret, but could also be interpreted in other ways (e.g. preoccupations, inattentiveness).

The "falsehood" Family

When Speaker's belief changes from accuracy of a planned utterance *vis-à-vis* the topical belief to *in*accuracy, we move to the Family of "falsehood". Simple "falsehood" entails the intention to produce an utterance which is believed to be relevant to the topical belief. Further, Speaker must believe that the utterance will create in Hearer an inaccurate belief regarding Speaker's topical belief, and that s/he is accountable for that utterance. A straightforward example could be afforded with ease but instead we will provide a more complex instance which calls attention to the primacy of our thinking of Speaker's beliefs *about Hearer*; Speakers lie to Hearers. Suppose Speaker's topical belief is, *John loves Sara*, and suppose further that Speaker believes that Hearer always infers the opposite of what Speaker's utterance denotes. Speaker believes the statement "he adores Sara", is relevant to the belief. Speaker believes that this utterance can be interpreted by Hearer in only one way; namely, as *Speaker believes John despises Sara*. Then, Speaker's intention to utter "He adores Sara", would constitute the belief state "falsehood".

If Speaker's intention to utter "He adores Sara" changes to the intention to withhold this utterance, then the belief state changes to "falsehood avoidance", assuming no further changes in the accuracy, relevance and accountability belief states. Here, Speaker intends to withhold an utterance which s/he believes would create in Hearer an inaccurate belief regarding Speaker's belief. On the other hand, assuming no change in Speaker's intention to utter "He adores Sara", and no change in the accuracy and relevance beliefs, but given a change from a belief in accountability to a belief in *non*-accountability, Speaker's belief state would become "devious falsehood". This is apparently the belief state which Bowers, Elliott and Desmond (1977) have in mind when they discuss "devious messages". But the concept of deviousness is broader than this, as we saw in the "truth-telling" Family above and will see in the "evasion" Family below. The fourth member of the "falsehood" family is termed "devious falsehood avoidance" and occurs when Speaker intends to withhold an inaccurate utterance which is relevant, with its absence having more than one plausible interpretation. Of course the relative frequency of occurrence of these belief states will vary considerably within and between societies and across time, and in this sense, devious falsehood avoidance is probably not that commonly construed.

The "evasion" Family

When Speaker's belief changes from relevance of the utterance *vis-à-vis* the topical belief to irrelevance, we move to the Family of "evasion". Here, the belief regarding accuracy–inaccuracy of the intended utterance is moot; the utterance may accurately or inaccurately reflect *some* belief, but this is arguably unimportant if the utterance is irrelevant. Indeed were accuracy and inaccuracy deemed to be important in conjunction with irrelevance we would have proposed four Families of belief states for propositional communication, and not three. Thus, the criterial beliefs for "evasion" are: Speaker intends to produce an utterance, believes it to be irrelevant as regards topical belief, and feels accountable should it find expression. If Speaker believes that the topical belief is *I dislike Hearer's bright socks*, perhaps because Hearer has indicated a desire for Speaker's evaluation by saying "I bought these just yesterday at The New Trend Shoppe"; if Speaker says "The food at this party is just marvellous, don't you think?" (believing that party food is not relevant to the belief, *I dislike Hearer's bright socks*, and if Speaker believes that this utterance can be taken in only one way by Hearer (viz., as a comment upon food in lieu of a non-comment on Hearer's dress sense), then this belief state is "evasion". Speaker may or may not believe that Hearer will believe that the utterance is irrelevant. But Speaker must believe that the irrelevance of the utterance is unambiguously discoverable by Hearer for Speaker is subjectively accountable for the utterance (a situation which differs from that of "devious evasion" below).

When Speaker withholds an irrelevant utterance and is accountable for this action, the belief state is "evasion avoidance". When Speaker plans to produce an irrelevant utterance believing that s/he is not accountable for this, the belief is "devious evasion". Typically, in this case, Speaker will hope that Hearer will take the utterance as relevant to the topical belief at issue, but Speaker must believe that Hearer could be made to see that the utterance is *ir*relevant in fact. For example, Speaker might reply to Hearer's "I bought this just yesterday at The New Trend Shoppe", with "Wow, The New Trend Shoppe has so many terrific things". When Speaker withholds an irrelevant utterance while believing s/he is not accountable for this intended non-utterance, the belief state is "devious evasion avoidance". This state is logically compelled by our axiomatic machinery but is almost certainly a rare state for real communicators. Perhaps this state is experienced now and then by the press agents of Presidential candidates, especially when they talk to other press agents.

Motivating and encoding propositional communication

Our theorems describe 12 states of mind which constitute a cognitive code exploited by Speaker as s/he communicates propositionally. Several of the particular belief states, and more generally, the three Families, appear to us to be very basic to human communication. Whether or not Speakers actually utilize subjectively these belief states in their encoding of communicative acts in a manner isomorphic with our axiomatic analysis is an important empirical question. But in any case our approach only tells part of the story. The situation is much more complex. We will not try and reveal all of the complexities in this single chapter, of course, but in this section we will suggest other factors which enter into propositional communication.

For one thing, Speaker plans to lie, evade or tell the truth for a reason; that is, propositional communication is motivated. Many particular motivating influences can be imagined, but generally there are probably two main primary motivators from the perspective of the Speaker; namely, Hearer and the communication situation. In one case Speaker believes that Hearer is the cause of Speaker's potential lie: *that guy cannot be trusted with the truth*. On the other hand, many types of situations will predispose Speaker to plan one sort of an act instead of another. For example, a child's impending birthday may often predispose parents to withhold information from their child regarding a gift they will give him or her even if the child asks them directly about it: "I'm sorry, that's a secret!" If asked to explain the keeping of a secret in such circumstances, Speaker will doubtless say, "It's supposed to be a surprise". That is, the situation dictates non-informativeness in order to achieve a particular effect on the child's birthday.

In addition to beliefs about causes of propositional acts, Speaker has beliefs about their potential consequences: *If I lie to Hearer, I will win the money and she will lose*. This particular belief regarding the likely consequences of a propositional act can be labelled "selfish" (good for Speaker/ bad for Hearer) (cf. Hample, 1980). Three other beliefs regarding consequences seem plausible: "altruistic" (bad for Speaker/good for Hearer), "generally malefficient" (bad for Speaker and Hearer), and "benign (neither good nor bad) (cf. Hopper, 1981). These four beliefs regarding consequences of propositional action constitute very general motives for communication. In the following we speculate about the whos, whens and whys of our 12 Theorems in more detail.

It may be that the 12 propositional acts could be usefully located in multidimensional space in ways quite independent of the Three Families notion. Two (Speaker) continua strike us as particularly promising in this regard as a starting point. These are the directness–indirectness of the propositional acts (see Baxter, in press) and their implied cognitive effort. Hence some acts assume an explicit verbalized form as Speaker plans them (e.g. truth-telling, falsehood and devious truth-telling) whereas others are not explicit at all (e.g. falsehood avoidance, devious secrecy and devious falsehood avoidance). At the same time some actions usually involve little cognitive effort to encode in most contexts (e.g. truth-telling, evasion and secrecy), whereas others are typically far more cognitively demanding to deliver (e.g. devious evasion, devious falsehood avoidance and devious secrecy). Figure 3 represents the 12 Theorems in this two-dimensional space.

To add meat to this skeletal structure, we would wish to superimpose two further continua on these dimensions, viz. high–low Speaker value for talk, and high–low Hearer attributional confidence. Wiemann (personal communication) has suggested that some individuals place greater or lesser weight on the affective and cognitive utility of talk. Put another way, some might say "my word is my bond", whilst others on the other hand might say "talk is cheap". In this way individuals with a high value for talk would be

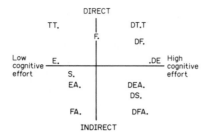

FIG. 3. Theorems in speculative two-dimensional space (see Figure 2 for nomenclature meanings).

more prone to be direct in their propositional acts, whereas those who possessed a negative set of such beliefs would be more indirect. Attributional confidence is a construct utilized, amongst other places, in cognitive uncertainty theory (Berger, 1979; Berger and Bradac, 1982). Its essence in our context is the extent to which Speaker believes Hearer will be sure or wary about how the latter will attribute the intent of the former. Hence, a deliberately ambiguous message, or set of speech markers (Brown and Fraser, 1979), would constitute an act presumably inducing attributional non-confidence in the Hearer, and a good half of the theorems veer in this direction. We would argue that those propositional acts which instill attributional confidence in their Hearers are more often than not likely to be cognitively effortless, whereas those infusing non-confidence are likely to involve more cognitive difficulty. By a comparison of Figure 3 with Figure 4 below, the theorems can be placed into four quadrants. For example, the "indirect" acts of devious evasion avoidance, devious secrecy and devious falsehood avoidance (the lower, right quadrant) are utilized when Speakers (a) experience low concern for talk, (b) experience high cognitive difficulty, and (c) desire to induce attributional non-confidence in Hearers.

The model thus far is an admittedly embryonic attempt to specify the whos and whens of propositional acts. We still have, however, the whys with which to contend. Camden, Motley and Wilson (1984) have provided a list of the types of social motivations underlying "white lies". Whilst we feel that these very same motives (albethey less mutually exclusive than these authors imply) may also be intricately involved in the underlying causes of our Three Families too, there is some reason to believe that they are biased in a uni-polar direction given their reliance on inter*personal* data. We shall argue that a more complete picture can be provided by moving towards a *bi*polar model which takes into account *intergroup* behaviour as well.

Camden *et al.* procured their data by means of "interpersonal communication diaries" where respondents were asked to record instances over a couple of weeks when they believed *they* had been told white lies. Interpret-

ation of these data suggested four motives: *tact* to save the Hearer embarrass-
ment, e.g. "what a pretty dress" (when it is ill–fitting); *relational stability*
when Speaker wishes to avoid conflict with the Hearer, e.g. agreeing with
Hearer's valued beliefs on the economy in order to maintain the friendship;
psychological compensation in order to present a favourable social image to
another, e.g. "sorry, I can't join you tonight I have so many other friends to
see" (when you will be bored and alone all night!); and *power deference* in
order to avoid being made dependent on a controlling other, e.g. "sorry, I
can't come to your office right now, I have an important buyer on the other
line ringing from Hamburg" (when there's not).

To us, and despite the fact that these motivations exude a sense of
creating, maintaining or repairing a positive self-esteem which can be
interpreted in a personally beneficial way, they nonetheless appear a little
too "socially agreeable" for our theoretical tastes. Surely many of us can
recount instances when we or others have deceived or lied so as to be, for
example, tact*less*, or have lied to create *in*stability in a particular relationship
(Baxter, in press; Reagan and Hopper, 1984), or even have in high-status
positions lied (e.g. about people's future opportunities) in order to bolster
our perceived control. Such tactics of "tactlessness", "instability" and
"control induction" are of course the converse of tact, stability and power
deference respectively.

Why then did not these motives surface in the Camden *et al.* study? One
answer may lie in the particular methodology used. Informants were asked
to uncover *others'* lies to them personally, some of which may have escaped
them entirely and others of which may have produced misattribution. An
equally plausible, if not more significant, answer might lie in the fact that the
student diaries were "interpersonal". Elsewhere, one of us has argued,
following on from Tajfel and Turner (1979), that much of interpersonal
communication is overly individualistic and that much theory suffers as a
result (e.g. Giles and Street, 1985; Giles and Wiemann, in press). Much of
our social lives is spent in *intergroup* encounters between socioeconomic
classes, age groups, religious communities, occupational categories, etc. In
such encounters our social identities can be of supreme importance, and in
such cases we use language to create, maintain or bolster our sense of
distinctive and valued ingroup identity (Giles, 1979). In other words, we do
not treat each other as individuals with unique temperaments and per-
sonalities but as undifferentiated representatives of social groups; we act
stereotypically ourselves in ways consistent with our beliefs about our
ingroup (Turner, 1982). Under these conditions it would seem that tactless
lies and deception which "put down" linguistically an outgroup and or
elevate an ingroup (cf. Taylor and Jaggi, 1974; Hewstone and Jaspars, 1984)
are rational choices for maintaining a favourable group identity. Instantiat-
ing an unstable intergroup relationship by deception or control induction

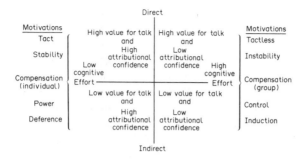

FIG. 4. Motivational and superimposed two-dimensional space.

also represent creative tactics of this ilk. Furthermore, the Camden *et al.* tactic of "psychological compensation" could also be seen to operate at the intergroup as well as at the individualistic level.

As we intimated previously, these opposing tactics can be seen in inter-personally differentiating encounters where rivalry between individuals is rife. Yet it is our belief that they are most prevalent in intergroup encounters. Hence in a "socially cloistered" student (intragroup) environment where the emphasis is on intimate relationships, the opportunities for mixed-category interactions (where even male and female identities may be less salient than elsewhere) are far reduced. In sum, then, we argue that the 6 Theorems clearly located in the *right-hand* quadrants of Figure 4 will be utilized most often in encounters where group relations are *subjectively* salient and where social identifications are at issue. As Stephenson (1981) pointed out, it is often the case that interindividual *and* intergroup relations coexist. In other words, an individual might strive for a valued group identity whilst wishing to maintain the personal relationship at some level. Hence the need for instilling attributional non-confidence in the Hearer as a "let out" (e.g. "did you hear me *say* that? I meant . . . How insensitive of you!") is paramount in such situations. Again, Speakers' experience of cognitive difficulty is a necessary condition for their referent occurrence, and Speakers' different levels of value for talk will determine whether direct or indirect propositional acts are deemed most appropriate. Obviously situational constraints, relational norms, and the sociostructural relationship operating between different groups will determine which particular Theorem in a quadrant will establish a basis for action. Additionally, the extent to which the Axioms, Theorems, and attending motivational structure are historical and cultural artefacts is a sobering issue. In any case, should this model have sufficient external validity in elaborative expansion with doubtless other important theoretical constructs, then more precise predictions per Theorem might be possible in the very long term. In any case the present framework illustrates well Giles and Wiemann's (in press) view of the Speaker–Hearer as a "crafty–sceptical" communicator.

By the same token the less differentiating, more socially cohesive motivations of tact, etc. can be seen to underlie the two left-hand quadrants in Figure 4. Arguably, these more habitual orientations where the Speaker believes that attributional confidence is being instilled in the Hearer require little conscious effort and self-motivating to achieve (cf. Roloff & Berger, 1982) given standard Western, conversational norms of truthfulness (Grice, 1975; Higgins, 1980). In other words they require less cognitive effort. Needless to say, the homogeneity implied in the contextual notion of any monolithic theorem, such as for example "falsehood", will render the above theoretical framework simplistic in all cases. For instance, sometimes truth-telling (e.g. delivering bad news), or being evasive (e.g. when a loved one desperately requires confidential information you possess), can require tremendous amounts of cognitive activity. Nonetheless, we would subscribe to the view again that whether a direct or indirect Theorem establishes the basis for meeting the demands of the situation will be determined to some degree by the extent to which Speakers value talk.

The belief states and their expression

Regardless of Speaker's reasons for planning propositional actions, s/he must plan to encode the falsehood, the evasive manoeuvre, etc. in a particular verbal and non-verbal form. There are many different ways to construct propositional acts. The beliefs constituting the various members of the three Families of propositional communication are necessarily joined with other beliefs about expression. These expressive beliefs are particular direct beliefs about communication – that is, beliefs about grammatical form, stylistic effects, and so forth. Coherent sets of these expressive beliefs can be labelled "expressive genres".

Irony, for example, is a widely understood genre for expressing propositions. Speaker may decide to convey a belief ironically and do so by engaging in truth-telling in such a manner that Hearer will infer the opposite of what the utterance literally proposes. For example, Speaker believes *Hearer will infer Speaker believes X from "I believe non-X"*, and Speaker's belief is in fact, *X*. Speaker has various beliefs which allow him/her to perform ironically; the ironic speaker uses exaggerated intonation, and is loud, etc. Thus, in a given case, Speaker will believe that Hearer will believe that Speaker is behaving ironically, and that Speaker will for this reason come to hold a correct belief about Speaker's beliefs. But in another case Speaker can exploit the ironic genre in order to commit a falsehood. That is, Speaker can behave in a sufficiently ironic manner as to create in Hearer a false belief regarding Speaker's belief. At this point it appears to us that expressive genres and the three Families (and the 12 belief states comprising them) intersect orthogonally such that any propositional belief state can be coupled with any particular set of expressive beliefs. (To be sure, some couplings would be odd, for instance, a secret rendered in the form of a tall tale or a bluff.)

We postulate that normal communicators engage in propositional acts which reflect a wide variety of expressive genres. These genres have a cultural basis; they are part of the standard equipment which speakers use when communicating propositionally. But there is an idiosyncratic basis as well. If Speaker and Hearer have a long-term relationship they will probably develop special expressive devices (and beliefs about these) which constitute derivations from the culturally standard forms (Hopper, Knapp and Scott, 1981). And they may even develop private expressive genres for expressing propositions which are completely baffling and alien to third parties.

It would be useful in future research to elicit judgements from a wide variety of communicators which can be used to construct a general, expressive-genre typology, perhaps using the multidimensional scaling strategy of Hopper and Bell (1984). Indeed, these researchers have performed a cluster analysis of respondent judgements of deception-related terms which suggests a preliminary typology. Their obtained structure has six types: *Fictions*: irony, tall tale, make believe, etc.; *Playings*: joke, tease, bluff, etc.; *Lies*: dishonesty, fib, cheating, etc.; *Crimes*: disguise, con, counterfeit, etc.; *Masks*: masking, back-stabbing, two-faced, etc.; *Unlies*: distortion, mislead, false implications, and misrepresent. Rather clearly, some of the general forms and specific representative terms are more closely related to mode of expression than are others; yet this typology is constructively suggestive. We speculate that *Fictions* and *Playings*, for example, are general categories which include expressive genres widely understood by persons communicating in Western countries, at least.

Discussion

We have offered four Axioms which generate twelve Theorems representing belief states for propositional communication. We have also produced a model speculating about some of the motivational bases for these types of communication and about the ways in which propositions are encoded for Hearers. In this concluding section we raise several issues which seem important to us, and which reinforce our earlier claim that communicating propositionally is indeed a complex activity.

The role of time: stasis versus process

In its current form "time" is of little importance to our theory. The point of view is that of a Speaker planning to communicate propositionally. The attempt has been to describe belief states which exist *prior* to Speaker's engaging in communicative action. The interval between Speaker's accessing the cognitive structure which we have described and the production of an overt utterance will be measured in microseconds in some cases, and even years in others. Our approach currently is "Cartesian", which is certainly not a clear virtue in our minds (Rommetveit, 1983). The Theorems are constitutive rules (Sanders and Martin, 1975) which specify the essential components of lies, secrets, etc. Although admittedly we have speculated about a motivational structure attending them, in and of themselves they are not causal statements which specify relationships among variables. Nor are they regulative rules which specify appropriate and inappropriate actions.

But a few suggestions about "time" can be offered here. First, it is worth noting that two or more of the propositional belief states cannot exist simultaneously. One cannot plan to commit a falsehood and plan to engage in truth-telling in the same moment (although perhaps depending on the "mixed" nature of the audience present, the phenomenon of "linguistic inversion" might be an exceptional case in point – Holt, 1972). But the belief state can change rapidly; Speaker plans to keep a secret; Hearer threatens torture for non-revelation; then Speaker plans to exude the truth.

Second, it is also the case that the propositional beliefs of Hearers are often, even usually, contingent upon those of Speaker to some extent, although the nature of this contingency cannot be described here. (Its nature is rendered complex by virtue of the non-necessary connection between Speaker's actual utterance and Speaker's belief state prior to utterance, and by virtue of the fact that Hearer must interpret Speaker's utterance). And when Hearer assumes the role of $Speaker_2$, $Speaker_1$'s propositional beliefs are to an extent contingent upon those of $Speaker_2$. Thus, we can think potentially of chains of belief states which can be described as Markov processes. For example, in many situations there may be a greater likelihood that $Speaker_2$'s intention to produce an evasive act will follow from the identical state in $Speaker_1$ compared to the state of, say, truth-telling. Similarly, the state of secrecy in $Speaker_1$ may be quite likely to be followed by secrecy in $Speaker_2$. This suggests that belief states may be reciprocal to some extent (Roloff and Campion, 1985).

An interesting, albeit difficult, set of questions arises when propositional communication is viewed from the perspective of history (Gergen & Gergen, 1984). Were the beliefs which now constitute "falsehoods" and "secrets" the beliefs which constituted the same propositional forms in second-century Rome or fifteenth-century England? Were some of the 12 possibilities indicated by the Theorems non-existent in the past? Did other forms of propositional communication, which may now have disappeared, exist in antiquity? Are the forms which we have described evolving? These temporal, and cultural, questions will probably be best saved until the basic validity of the theory is probed empirically.

Psychological reality: mindful versus mindless activity

The belief states described by the Theorems are logically compelled combinations of more basic beliefs. How do these logical constructions relate to the *psychological* reality of real liars and truth-tellers? We can of course only speculate at this point.

Implicit in the argument has been the conception of a Speaker who is highly mindful (Langer, Blank and Chanowitz, 1978) in the sense of being extremely aware of his or her plans for utterance or non-utterance. And certainly in some very important situations which Speaker anticipates weeks in advance, the careful planning of communicative acts will occur (e.g. many guest lecturers). Speaker may even test planned utterances against his/her beliefs by asking self "would this *really* be a truthful statement?" or "Why might this utterance be construed as a lie – which it *is*, in fact".

But in many other situations, Speaker will function mindlessly (Langer, Chanowitz and Blank, 1985), creating spontaneous falsehoods, evasions, and so forth. We postulate that, even in mindless situations, Speaker will access in some way the belief structure which we have described; perhaps in a way analogous to that in which Speaker accesses a grammar of the language in order to create sentences. The belief structure may be a particular cognitive scheme which is available to Speaker. Various situational codes may elicit from Speaker immediate, reflexive, mindless utterances of a propositional sort. For example, Speaker may always act evasively in response to questions of a sexual nature. But even these reflexive sorts of utterances must be based on a cognitive scheme of some kind; that is, some kind of structure must enable Speaker to evade spontaneously. Our Theorems might well be a description of what this cognitive structure would look like.

Testing the theory: formal tests versus naive construals

As suggested earlier, our theory in its present preliminary form is a logical structure having psychological implications. The major tests of a logical structure are to (1) probe its internal consistency, and (2) discover whether it can be simplified without loss of information. In other words, are there inherent contradictions, and how parsimonious is the structure? We are satisfied for the moment on both counts, particularly given the tortuous history of the emergence of our theory into its present far more simplified format. Yet we are well aware of the fact that this theory is still one very much in process; elements will be added to it, others subtracted away.

Quite apart from any formal tests, the theory can be tested empirically against the judgements or intuitions of naive liars, evaders, and tellers of truth. This could be achieved in a way which is analogous to that used to test formal grammars of a natural language (Ringen, 1975). The "analogous" in the preceding sentence is seriously intended because the particular utterances in context which can be formed on the basis of our Theorems are clearly less rigorously derivable than are sentences generated by a putative grammatical rule.

Although difficult, it should be possible in future research to construct a naive theory of propositional communication on the basis of untutored persons' responses to a variety of structured stimuli, One could, for example, produce many examples of particular, hypothetical utterances-in-context, each of which could be offered to respondents with a specification of the Speaker's relevant beliefs prior to utterance. The utterances-in-context would be designed to reflect the 12 belief states. (Respondents would be instructed to assume that utterances were true reflections of Speaker beliefs.) The task would be for a respondent to group the utterances on the basis of perceived similarity. For example, they could be provided with many cards each displaying a different utterance and they could be instructed to form from one to twelve card groups on the basis of their perceptions of similarity. They could further be asked to characterize each group with an appropriate term or word. Multidimensional scaling analyses of the similarity data could then be performed (see for example, Forgas, 1983) and the labels generated by the respondents could be used to interpret the obtained dimensional structure.

There would be a great deal of interest in seeing how the "naive" structure corresponds to our formal one. A good analogue here is the attempt of Sternberg *et al.* (1981) to compare formal theories of intelligence which are reflected in standard intelligence tests with informal or naive theories of this concept. This scholar has found evidence of some similarities and some differences between the two sets of theories, and we might well find a similar outcome. If differences were to be found, we would attempt to account for these, and this would be a very tricky business potentially (Ringen, 1975; Bradac *et al.* 1980). Naive theories may differ from formal ones for a variety of reasons; but we would be compelled to examine again those Theorems which consistently failed to correspond in any way to any part of the judgements of most evaders, liars, and truth-tellers.

The issue of validity: what is a good theory for?

Implicit in our argument has been the assumption that making sense of propositional communication is a worthwhile goal. Apparently, reasonable others share it, and we are comforted by this fact. Lying, evading, and truth-telling are ubiquitous human activities, and they sometimes have enormous import for propositional communicators. Sensible statements about these activities would seem to be useful on the face of it. Also implicit in our exposition has been the assumption that formal integration is desirable. We have suggested that the states of mind undergirding planned falsehoods, devious messages, etc., are related to each other. They hold membership in one of the three Families of belief states for propositional communication. But certainly one can argue that integration is not desirable, or that it is premature in a given domain.

We have chosen to explore propositional communication from a particular perspective, that of the *beliefs* of Speaker as s/he plans a message for Hearer. There are other plausible points of attack. On the basis of the literature (cf. Knapp and Comadena, 1979), one could construct a data-based theory using the empirical research available on truth-telling and deceptions. This theory (and unfortunately many of the findings are at least superficially "inconsistent") would be about classes of behaviour varying as a function of personality or situation, a very different sort of theory than ours. Alternatively, a theory of behaviours which constitute various propositional acts could be formulated. One of the problems we have with this latter approach is that it seems to us that *any* behaviour (i.e. utterance) *can* count as a lie, evasive act, etc. Much hinges upon what the Speaker is *intending*. On the other hand it would seem to be valuable to construct a theory of utterances *and* non-utterances in context which are categorized by Hearers as falsehoods, evasive acts, etc. This would be a form of attribution theory (Hewstone, 1983), the goal of which would be to explain why a particular utterance form in context is taken to be a particular propositional act. Whereas our theory takes the viewpoint of the Speaker – the planner of propositional acts – this approach would take the Hearer's; it would focus upon *attributed* intentions and beliefs.

Actually, we expect that our theory could inform the "attributional" theory of propositional communication. For example, Hearer may try to assess whether Speaker has been truthful or not. Where Hearer is mindfully attentive to Speaker's utterance, Hearer may ask "Did Speaker believe that I would hold an accurate belief regarding her belief?", "Did she believe the utterance was relevent to the belief at issue?", and so forth. Thus, not only may Speaker access our hypothetical cognitive code for propositional acts, but Hearer may *also* do so when interpreting Speaker's utterance. Hearer will make inferences about Speaker beliefs regarding the accuracy, etc., of Hearer beliefs regarding Speaker beliefs on the basis of Speaker's verbal and non-verbal communicative behaviours and various contextual cues. For example, if Speaker avoids eye contact with Hearer and if the situation is one where Speaker would be expected to lie (the situation of some used-car salespersons comes to mind), then Hearer might infer that Speaker intends to produce in Hearer an inaccurate belief regarding Speaker's belief (Speaker: "This car is in *perfect*, *mint* condition – only been driven once a month for the last year by a very timid person"). This suggestion implies that Hearer holds a naive theory of propositional acts which connects a situational typology and a typology of communicative behaviours to Speaker belief states.

But as we have claimed frequently throughout this chapter, in the final analysis only Speaker knows for sure whether s/he intended to tell the truth or to lie. This has been a clear implication of our theory of *belief states*; Hearers will have beliefs regarding Speaker beliefs and Speakers will have beliefs regarding Speaker beliefs, but they need not be isomorphic, of course. If Hearer's beliefs appear not to correspond to those of Speaker, recourse to magical devices such as polygraphs will not help Hearer to achieve certainty about Speaker's veracity. The connection between a polygraph report and Speaker's belief state is necessarily indirect according to our theory. A polygraph report is merely another indicator, along with low levels of Speaker eye contact and other behaviours. Clear arguments can be made for the connection between a polygraph report and Speaker's physical state of arousal, but high arousal does not directly reflect the belief state of "falsehood", for example. The tellings of "truth" can be highly arousing if Speaker's motive is "selfish", perhaps to injure Hearer by candid revelation. Nor can Hearer trust Speaker's characterization of Speaker's belief state, for Speaker's characterization may reflect the belief state, falsehood. Yet again, there is no necessary connection between Speaker self-report and Speaker belief state.

In conclusion, we feel that much language and communication research is based on false premises of human veracity, and consequently the deviance of deception, and that we should work backwards from behaviour to cognition given the implicit primary afforded the latter in our data. We feel that our largely converse approach is an initial foray moving us beyond the rule-bound dominance of communication-based information processing.

Moreover, it also will allow us to grapple empirically more with concepts of "identity", "negotiation" and "transaction" to which for the most part we have only afforded lip service (see however, Scotton, 1980; Gumperz, 1982). Whether the essential fabric of our approach lives for long or dies is incidental and unimportant to our prime goal of thinking along these lines – namely, to provide an *initial* set of cognitive structures pointing the way forward to examining the true complexity of human communication which of necessity affords belief states, social motivation and deception primary roles. Put differently, it allows us embryonic access to that caricature of the individual with which we commenced this paper, viz., the "crafty–sceptical" communicator. Finally, we hope that our Speaker-oriented, and the outline of our "attributional" Hearer-oriented, frameworks will be coalesced in due course into a more rounded view of communicators as negotiative, identity- and information-driven animals in social transaction who are reflexive, *Speaker–Hearers* (cf. Farr, 1980).

References

Ajzen, I. and Fishbein, M. (1980) *Understanding Attitudes and Predicting Behaviour*. Prentice-Hall, Englewood Cliffs, NJ.

Bateson, G. (1979) *Mind and Nature*. Bantam, New York.

Baxter, L. A. (in press) "Accomplishing relationship disengagement". In Duck, S. and Perlman, D. (eds), *The Sage Series of Personal Relationships*. Sage, Beverly Hills, CA.

Berger, C. R. (1979) "Beyond initial interaction: uncertainty, understanding, and the development of interpersonal relationships". In Giles, H. and St. Clair, R. N. (eds), *Language and Social Psychology*, pp. 122–144. Blackwell, Oxford.

Berger, C. R. and Bradac, J. J. (1982) *Language and Social Knowledge*. Edward Arnold, London.

Bok, S. (1979) *Lying: moral choice in public and private life*. Pantheon, New York.

Bowers, J. W., Elliott, N. D. and Desmond, R. J. (1977) "Exploiting pragmatic rules: devious messages", *Human Communication Research*, 3, 235–242.

Bradac, J. J., Bowers, J. W. and Courtright, J. A. (1979) "Three language variables in communication research: intensity, immediacy, and diversity," *Human Communication Research*, 5, 257–269.

Bradac, J. J., Martin, L. W., Elliott, N. D. and Tardy, C. H. (1980) "On the neglected side of linguistic science: Multivariate studies of sentence judgment", *Linguistics: An interdisciplinary Journal for the Language Sciences*, 18, 967–995.

Brandt, D. R., Miller, G. R. and Hocking, J. E. (1982) "Familiarity and lie detection: a replication and extension", *Western Journal of Speech Communication*, 46, 276–290.

Brown, P. and Fraser, C. (1979) "Speech as a marker of situation". In Scherer, K. R. and Giles, H. (eds), *Social Markers in Speech*, pp. 33–62. Cambridge University Press, Cambridge.

Camden, C., Motley, M. T. and Wilson, A. (1984) "White lies in interpersonal communication: a taxonomy and preliminary investigation of social motivations", *Western Journal of Speech Communication*, 48, 309–325.

Ehninger, D. (1977) "On inferences of the 'fourth class'," *Central States Speech Journal*, 28, 157–162.

Farr, R. (1980) "Homo loquiens in social psychological perspective". In Giles, H., Robinson, W. P. and Smith, P. M. (eds), *Language: social psychological perspectives*, pp. 409–414. Pergamon, Oxford.

Fishbein, M. and Ajzen, I. (1975) *Belief, Attitude, Intention: an introduction to theory and research*. Addison-Wesley, New York.

Forgas, J. P. (1983) "Language, goals and situations", *Journal of Language and Social Psychology*, 2, 267–294.

Gergen, K. J. and Gergen, M. (eds) (1984) *Historical Social Psychology*. Lawrence Erlbaum Associates, Hillsdale, NJ.

Giles, H. (1979) "Ethnicity markers in speech". In Scherer, K. R. and Giles, H. (eds), *Social Markers in Speech*, pp. 251–290. Cambridge University Press, Cambridge.

Giles, H. and Street, R. L., Jr. (1985) "Communicator characteristics and behaviour: a review, generalizations, and model". In Knapp, M. and Miller, G. R. (eds), *Handbook of Interpersonal Communication*. Sage, Beverly Hills, CA (in press).

Giles, H. and Wiemann, M. (in press) "Language and social comparisons". In Chaffee, S. and Berger, C. R. (eds), *Handbook of Communication*. Sage, Beverly Hills, CA.

Grice, H. P. (1975) "Logic and conversation". In Cole, P and Morgan, J. L. (eds), *Syntax and Semantics*, vol. 3: *Speech Acts*. Academic, New York.

Gumperz, J. J. (ed.) (1982) *Language and Social Identity*. Cambridge University Press, Cambridge.

Hample, D. (1980) "Purposes and effects of lying", *Southern Speech Communication Journal*, 46, 33–47.

Hermann, T. (1982) "Language and situation: the pars pro toto principle". In Fraser, C. and Scherer, K. R. (eds), *Advances in the Social Psychology of Language*, pp. 123–158. Cambridge University Press, Cambridge.

Hewes, D. and Planalp, S. (1982) "There is nothing as useful as a good theory. The influence of social knowledge on interpersonal communication". In Roloff, M. E. and Berger, C. R. (eds), *Social Cognition and Communication*, pp. 107–150. Sage, Beverly Hills, CA.

Hewstone, M. (1983) "The role of language in attribution processes". In Jaspars, J., Fincham, F. D. and Hewstone, M. (eds) *Attribution Theory and Research: conceptual, developmental and social dimensions*, pp. 241–260. Academic Press, London.

Hewstone, M. and Jaspars, J. (1984) "Social dimensions of attribution". In Tajfel, H. (ed.), *The Social Dimension*, pp. 379–404. Cambridge University Press, Cambridge.

Higgins, E. T. (1980) "The 'communication game': implications for social cognition and persuasion". In Higgins, E. T., Herman, C. P. and Zanna, M. P. (eds), *Social Cognition: the Ontario symposium*, pp. 343–392. Erlbaum, Hillsdale, NJ.

Holt, G. (1972) "Inversion in Black communication". In Kochman, T. (ed.), *Rappin' and Stylin' out: communication in urban Black America*, pp. 152–159. University of Illinois Press, Urbana, IL.

Hopper, R. (1981) "The taken-for-granted", *Human Communication Research*, 7, 195–212.

Hopper, R. and Bell, R. A. (1984) "Broadening the deception construct", *Quarterly Journal of Speech*, 70, 287–302.

Hopper, R., Knapp, M. L. and Scott, L. (1981) "Couples' personal idioms: exploring intimate talk", *Journal of Communication*, 31, 23–33.

Jackson, S. and Jacobs, S. (1983) "Generalizing about messages: suggestions for design and analysis of experiments", *Human Communication Research*, 9, 169–181.

Knapp, M. L. and Comadena, M. E. (1979) " 'Telling it like it isn't': a review of theory and research on deceptive communication", *Human Communication Research*, 5, 270–285.

Knapp, M. L., Hart, R. P. and Dennis, H. S. (1974) "An exploration of deception as a communication construct", *Human Communication Research*, 1, 15–29.

Kursh, C. O. (1971) "The benefits of poor communication", *Psychiatric Review*, 2, 189–208.

Langer, E. J., Blank, A. and Chanowitz, B. (1978) "The mindlessness of ostensibly thoughtful action: the role of 'placebic' information in interpersonal interaction", *Journal of Personality and Social Psychology*, 36, 635–642.

Langer, E., Chanowitz, B. and Blank, A. (1985) "Mindlessness – mindfulness in perspective: a reply to Valerie Folkes", *Journal of Personality and Social Psychology*, 48, 605–606.

Reagan, S. L. and Hopper, R. (1984) "Ways of leaving your lover: a conversational analysis of literature", *Communication Quarterly*, 32, 310–317.

Ringen, J. D. (1975) "Linguistic facts: a study of the empirical scientific status of transformational generative grammar". In Cohen, D. and Wirth, J. R. (eds), *Testing Linguistic Hypotheses*. Hemisphere, Washington, DC.

Roloff, M. E. and Berger, C. R. (eds) (1982) *Social Cognition and Communication*. Sage, Beverly Hills, CA.

Roloff, M. E. and Campion, D. E. (1985) "Conversational profit-seeking: Interaction as social exchange". In Street, R. L. Jr, and Cappella, J. N. (eds), *Sequence and Pattern in Communicative Behaviour*, pp. 161–189. Edward Arnold, London.

Rommetveit, R. (1983) "Prospective social psychological contributions to a truly interdisciplinary understanding of ordinary language", *Journal of Language and Social Psychology*, 2, 89–104.

Sanders, R. E. and Martin, L. W. (1975) "Grammatical rules and explanations of behaviour", *Inquiry*, 17, 65–82.

Scotton, C. M. (1980) "Negotiating social identity". In Giles, H., Robinon, W. P. and Smith, P. M. (eds), *Language: social psychological perspectives*, pp. 359–366. Pergamon, Oxford.

Searle, J. R. (1969) *Speech Acts*. Cambridge University Press, Cambridge.

Stephenson, G. M. (1981) "Intergroup bargaining and negotiation". In Turner, J. C. and Giles, H. (eds), *Intergroup Behaviour*, pp. 168–198. Blackwell, Oxford.

Sternberg, R. J., Conway, B. E., Ketron, J. L. and Bernstein, M. (1981) "People's conceptions of intelligence", *Journal of Personality and Social Psychology*, 41, 37–55.

Tajfel, H. and Turner, J. C. (1979) "An integrative theory of intergroup conflict". In Austin, W. G. and Worchel, S. (eds), *The Social Psychology of Intergroup Relations*, pp. 33–53. Brooks/Cole, Monterey, CA.

Taylor, D. M. and Jaggi, V. (1974) "Ethnocentrism and causal attributions in a Southern Indian context", *Journal of Cross-Cultural Psychology*, 5, 162–171.

A social approach to propositional communication 151

Tracy, K. (1983) "The issue–event distinction: a rule of conversation and its scope", *Human Communication Research*, **9**, 320–334.
Tracy, K. (1985) "Conversational coherence: a cognitively-grounded rules approach". In Street, R. L., Jr and Cappella, J. N. (eds), *Sequence and Pattern in Communicative Behaviour*, pp. 30–49. Arnold, London.
Turner, J. C. (1982) "Towards a cognitive redefinition of the social group". In Tajfel, H. (ed.) *Social Identity and Intergroup Relations*, pp. 15–40. Cambridge University Press, Cambridge.
Watzlawick, P., Beavin, J. H. and Jackson, D. D. (1967) *Pragmatics of Human Communication*. Norton, New York.
Wimmer, H. and Perner, J. (1983) "Representation and constraining function of wrong beliefs in young children's understanding of deception", *Cognition*, **13**, 103–128.

9

The hearer as 'listener judge': an interpretive sociolinguistic approach to utterance interpretation[1]*

GRAHAM McGREGOR

This paper is addressed to analysts of speech in social scenes and asks for a theory of utterance interpretation that incorporates the listener's point of view. The difficulties of providing such a theory, however, require that we proceed with some caution since our role as analysts and as creators of interpretive theories does not allow us privileged status in providing interpretations of talk that other speaker–hearers of the same language would share.

Because talk comprises a significant part of language use, it is for this reason, if for no other, that it has become an important area of research not only for linguists but also for a wide variety of other scholars whose professional concerns are related to the study of the nature and functions of human communicative behaviour (Kreckel, 1981; Gumperz, 1982a,b; Brown and Yule, 1983; Levinson, 1983; Stubbs, 1983).

However, current models of interpersonal communication have tended to neglect the interactional dynamic of contexts that help to determine the nature of the variables and the kinds of variation that everyday language use involves. From a linguistic point of view, the orientation of such models has largely been geared to the study of written and spoken discourse and the elucidation of its content and structure within a wide variety of different discourse types (see, for example, Coulthard and Montgomery, 1981; Edmondson, 1981; Brown and Yule, 1983; Stubbs, 1983).

Since successful communication has to depend on the contingent satisfaction of enforceable conditions on particular occasions of use, we suggest that models of this type provide but one possible approach for studying linguistic variability in interactional contexts. By focusing on possible discourse

* Superscript numbers refer to notes at end of chapter.

patterns in spoken and written texts, what such models tend to ignore are the kinds of communicative responses that listeners need to undertake in order to formulate their responses.[2] This work is fundamental to and necessary for, successful communication because everyday talk is a joint production and involves individuals in trying to make communicational sense of others, in order to know what to say next.[3] Hence neglect of the listener's role is liable to trivialize both the kinds of variables and great complexity of principles which mesh interactionally and help to determine how what is said becomes communicatively significant.

In order to confront the problem of how to "make sense" of what any speaker is saying, then, we must take into account how listeners "make sense" of what is said. But accounting for the interpretative work of the listener is not as obviously straightforward as we might imagine, for reasons that we will need to consider in some detail.

At least three major areas of difficulty face the analyst.

(i) in the first place, and to the best of my knowledge, it is impossible to determine exactly what it is a listener understands in the moment-by-moment sequencing of taking turns at talk. Unlike the grammarian who can "view a sentence as an enduring structure to be scanned at leisure", the listener is "exposed to an utterance just once and is forced to register its ingredients in just the temporal sequence in which it reaches him" (Hockett, this volume p. 50). Not only that but the listener "cannot know for sure part way through an utterance just what is going to be said next; he can at most have an array of expectations derived from earlier experience (that is from his knowledge of the language) and from what has been said so far this time" (Hockett, this volume p. 50).

Given that the interpretative strategies of listeners are context-specific, the analyst cannot know for certain which utterance or utterances may have been of particular salience in leading to the communicative sequences created by the participants. As Dore and McDermott (1982: 396) point out:

All utterance interpretation is public and subject to negotiation between persons. it is also collusional; i.e. it is subject to the constraints of contexts which are reflexively maintained and are made possible in part by the utterances to be interpreted.

Consequently, as Dore and McDermott go on to argue, it takes the *cooperative* effort of the individuals concerned to arrange a conversation that makes sense.

The need for such cooperation is intrinsic to even the most banal forms of talk as the following exchange demonstrates. The exchange took place in a snack-bar queue between two students recently returned from vacation; the two were obviously acquainted but clearly not close friends.

A Hello
B   (Kinetic response – smile plus head nod)
A   Did you have a good
   holiday
B   No
A   End of conversation
B   Would you if you had had bloody exams
   to sit
A   The weather has brightened up any way

B's initial abruptness (one might have expected him to elaborate in this particular social context) is only justified when A indicates his rejoinder might reasonably have been expected to prompt further conversation. However, by arguing that one could not, by definition, enjoy one's holidays if one had exams to face, B succeeds in preventing the conversation from developing topically because A, obviously feeling snubbed, continues the exchange in the same phatic vein.

My point is that there are an extraordinarily large set of possible linguistic and extra-linguistic permutations which either speaker in the exchange could have invoked and which could have determined a very different kind of interaction. The interpretative work of the listener would seem to have particular relevance in this respect since his response clearly affects the communicative success of the exchange. In order to offer any assessment of what is going on, that goes beyond his or her own subjective platform, the analyst must therefore take the listener's response(s) into consideration.

However, notwithstanding our willingness to take into account the nature of the listener's responses, we are faced with the further difficulty of determining the reciprocal "intentions" of speaker–hearers and the necessary forms of knowledge that their exchanges imply. This second difficulty arises because there would seem to be many levels of contextual frames which affect the interpretation of speaker "intent".

(ii) If we consider for a moment the role of the analyst as the creator of an interpretative theory, we can begin to elucidate something of the responsibility that he or she faces. Adelman (1981, p. 7), for example, reports on the procedure of "triangulation" as a method that "resuscitates intended meanings and interpretations allowing the researcher to elucidate the significance of the talk for the talkers". As the substance of the work reported in Adelman is concerned with interpreting the interactional success of teacher–pupil exchanges, there is little doubt of the care that must be taken. Quite simply, no matter how painstakingly thorough work of this kind is, the analyst is faced with the difficulty of stating with even a fair degree of certainty what a speaker "meant" by some utterance or specifying precisely what the communicative effect of the utterance was for the listener. The problem arises partly because of the asymmetry between utterance production and utterance comprehension.

Straight (1976, 1982), for instance, argues that any processually neutral account of language knowledge is problematic.[4] It is problematic because research from various different disciplines (Straight cites work in semantics, syntax, phonology, historical and developmental linguistics, sociolinguistics and neurolinguistics) indicates that the kinds of information processed by the comprehension mechanism are qualitatively different from those processed by the production mechanism. These differences suggest that there may be a gap in the communicative interface between "intention" and "effect".

Something of the nature of this gap has been explored in the context of Grice's work on conversational implicature. By focusing on the nature of what it is to "mean" something, in the non-natural sense of the word, Grice is able to distinguish between

what a speaker has *said* . . . and what he has "implicated" (e.g. implied, indicated, suggested etc.), taking into account the fact that what he has implicated may be either *conventionally* implicated (implicated by the meaning of some word or phrase which he has used) or *non-conventionally* implicated (in which case the specification of the implicature falls outside the specification of the conventional meaning of the words used). (Grice, 1968: 225)

Within this schema of what it is to "intend" something, the utterer of some linguistic string (be it word, phrase or utterance) is given the potential of creating some kind of propositional attitude. The interpretation of this attitude lies in the characterization of what Grice termed the "M intended effect", that is, ". . . for some audience A, U intended his utterance of X to produce in A some effect (response) E, by means of A's recognition of that intention" (Grice, 1968: 230). The nature of the M intended effect of some utterance is determined by how that utterance is heard. Thus for imperative type utterances, Grice claims that the speaker intends that the hearer should do something, that is, that the hearer should go on to do the act in question. On the other hand, for indicative type utterances, the M intended effect will be to induce the hearer to think that the utterer *believes* something; the hearer may then act accordingly.

Grice's achievement in making the distinction between "what is said" and "what is implicated" is to demonstrate that intention is a dynamically manipulable variable. By examining the processes involved in the interpretation of different types of utterance, Grice raises the problem of how listeners assign implicatures to what is said on some given occasion of utterance. These implicatures may be thought of as indirectly conveyed "understandings"; they provide the difference between locutionary content and illocutionary force.

Yet, whilst speech-act theory of the kind put forward by Grice and others recognizes that listeners take into account the essentially reflexive nature of "intention" (Bach and Harnish (1979: 15), for example, note "the intended effect of an act of communication is not just any effect produced by means of the recognition of the intention to produce an effect, it is the recognition of that effect"), it must be the case that something more complex is going on because we cannot really recover "intention" except through effect and reaction to it. Consequently, we need to account not only for the perform-ance and recognition of various acts of speech but also for circumstances in which alternate meanings are imputed. In other words, we cannot simply *assume* unanimity between some speaker's utterance and the way in which it has been heard as Goffman (1976: 261) is prepared to assert:

(If speakers and hearers were to file a report on what they assumed to be the full meaning of an extended utterance, these glosses would differ, at least in detail). Indeed, one routinely presumes on a mutual understanding that doesn't quite exist.

The reasons why this mutual understanding does not quite exist are presum-ably also related to the individual and social differences that occur within contexts that help to determine the nature of everyday verbal exchange. Lesley Milroy (1984), for example, cites various instances of "miscommuni-cation" which can arise due to syntactic, contextual and inferential dis-parities that may exist between speakers from different dialect backgrounds. In order to avoid such disparities, individuals must do communicative work to inform themselves of what they are doing together. However, "the momentary and often fragmentary understandings which people must share in order to organize their concerted behavior" (Dore and McDermott, 1982: 386) are not entities that exist in either time or space. They are the result of what Dore and McDermott refer to as "working consensuses". The problem facing the analyst is how to assess the kinds of consensus that have been reached (if any) as the talk is in progress. As Goffman (1976: 278) neatly puts it, "How individuals arrive at an effective interpretation on all those occasions when the stream of experience makes this easy and instantaneous is not much explored, this exploration being rather difficult to take from a sitting position." The question thus arises as to how we can ascertain "what is going on" in the talk of others such that we can provide evidence for our claims.

Appeal to the interactions of context and utterance is one approach to facilitating analysis of what speakers are "doing" through talk (Dore and McDermott (1982), for example, provide a pragmatically based framework for examining how talk becomes determinate for the participants). Another is to form and test hypotheses about the perceived effectiveness of verbal exchange by asking participant and non-participant judges how they interpreted utterances in various different conversational extracts and then requiring them to specify what linguistic features led them to their interpretations. This approach is taken by Gumperz and Tannen (1979) whose research is concerned to provide "concrete evidence for hypotheses about the ways in which speakers expect meaning to be communicated" (Gumperz and Tannen, 1979: 307).

But asking for the judgements of (non) participants in this particular way raises new problems for the analyst, problems that might best be considered in the context of the third major difficulty which we shall consider, that is, that the attentional and interpretative skills of individual listeners would seem to vary.

(iii) In undertaking the work which they do, Gumperz and Tannen (1979: 307) conclude, "any utterance can be understood in numerous different ways, and that people make decisions about how to interpret any given utterance or gesture based on their definition of what is happening at the time of interactions". This conclusion clearly has important ramifications for analysts of talk but is based on the rather large assumption that judges know in some straightforward way which "linguistic features led to their interpretations" (Gumperz and Tannen, 1979: 307). In the first place, judges may not be aware that *that* feature led them to *that* interpretation. Secondly, we cannot assume that the utterance or utterances chosen as being salient by the analyst would be "heard" to be salient in the same way by (non) participant judges. Indeed, it would be quite wrong to suppose that the kinds of "message" being communicated in some exchange were those that the analyst selected to work upon. Goffman makes something of the same point in explicating his notion of "keying", which is a central concept of his frame analysis. He explains that "key" refers to "the set of conventions by which a given activity, one already meaningful in terms of some primary framework, is transformed into something patterned on this activity but seen by the participants to be something quite else" (Goffman, 1974: 43–44). We must therefore be aware that the "keyings" of listener judges, whether lay or professional, are likely to affect how they interpret any particular stretch of talk. Furthermore, we must expect that the nature of individual listening behaviour will differ quite markedly. After all, listener judges may or may not choose to attend to some piece of data that they have been asked to comment on. They may choose rather to focus on non-linguistic information about the participants rather than on the communicative content that some piece of talk involves. And even though judges may have listened to the data in question, we have no way of ascertaining if the comments offered have simply been invented in order to fulfil the informant role in which they have been placed.

Presumably, however, participants in various different kinds of talk may be supposed to know "what is going on" and this knowledge, in turn, presumably influences and is displayed in how they participate in "what has gone on". What is at issue for the analyst is that the communicative effect and results of what has gone on are, in participant terms, "always an EMERGENT phenomenon, explicitly specifiable only in retrospect (and then by way of simplifying procedures that may well distort their experience)" (Dore and McDermott, 1982: 386). Nonetheless, it is possible to investigate the ability of participant and outside observers to recover and interpret "what has gone on" in some stretch of talk from their own point of view. Indeed, Kreckel (1981) maintains that one of the main objectives of any study of face-to-face interaction ought to be the conceptualization of the interaction by both outside observers and the participants themselves. This is not to argue that what (non) participant judges have to say about "what is going on" in some linguistic exchange will necessarily match their experience as speaker–hearers (what they have to say may reveal only peripheral aspects of various underlying complex processes as Dore and McDermott (1982) suggest) but rather to suggest that an examination of what the lay-individual has to say about "what is going on" in their own and other people's verbal exchanges promises to be at least as interesting as theoretical introspection about what such an activity might constitute.

The present study

By comparing the interpretative remarks of lay listener judges with those of two professional linguists, we hope to account for some of the differences that occur in judgemental work which seeks to establish "the significance of the talk for the talkers". Discussion and explanation of these differences will be used as a basis for determining criteria that may contribute to a theory of utterance interpretation that more fully embraces the communicative and interactional complexity of everyday language use.

Possible explanations for variation in judgements across and within speakers and analysts have begun to emerge in the context of research which I have undertaken to examine the listening behaviour of participant and of non-participant "eavesdropper" judges, that is, individuals who have been asked to listen to and comment on various different tape-recorded extracts of talk (see, for example, McGregor, 1983, 1984).

Unlike the judges used in other work of this nature (Gumperz and Tannen, 1979; Kreckel, 1981), however, the individuals who were asked to participate as informants were not given specific instructions of what I wanted them to comment on or to listen for. Thus, by pointing out to my informants the need not to prejudice the outcome of the research by providing them with information whose significance one could not predict in advance, I hoped to circumvent the dangers of either imposing regularities

on the data or undertaking the kind of speculative glossing work which
Cicourel (1974: 1573) warns against. He notes,

Linguists prefer to live with different kinds of conveniently constructed glosses, while the
ethnomethodologist prefers to treat the glossing as an activity that becomes the phenomenon of
interest while recognizing that no one can escape some level of glossing in order to claim
knowledge about something. But this claim to knowledge, this use of some level of glossing for
communication, is also a claim for a privileged position. Different levels of glossing provide
different self-validating circles and hence different claims about what is known. We can perhaps
achieve glimpses of our glossing activity by making it clear that every attempt to stimulate or
avoid the glossing activity is itself a glossing operation. This means showing the absurdity of
efforts to be uncompromisingly literal in out description of observed events or the activities in
which we participate.

In order to evaluate the kind of glossing work that one might undertake as
an analyst of talk, I compared the interpretative remarks of two professional
linguists with those of non-participant eavesdropper judges who listened to
the same data extracts. The extracts used in the study that I would like to
present were taken from tape-recordings made by Crystal and Davy (1975)
as part of their corpus of conversational English. The recordings were made
for the most part surreptitiously and in circumstances which Crystal and
Davy describe as "a normal domestic environment". The data were of
particular interest to me because they were accompanied by "a commentary
dealing with points of pronunciation, syntax, lexis and usage which might
cause temporary difficulties of interpretation as one listens to the conversation" (Crystal and Davy, 1975: 13).

I should explain that the commentary and text are intended for non-native
students of English who wish to improve their conversational skills. However, in providing the comments which they do, Crystal and Davy have
clearly made important decisions about those utterances or stretches of
utterance that led them to interpret the data in a particular way. The nature
of these decisions is presumably determined by the respective experience(s)
of the analysts as native listeners to English, and consequently we might
compare their listening behaviour and subsequent glossing work with that of
other members of the same language community.

**A comparison of analyst and lay listeners' comments on
conversation**

In order to make such a comparison, six extracts of conversation were
selected from different exchanges in the corpus. The extracts were selected
on the basis that they were accompanied by "clarifying remarks" provided
by Crystal and Davy. All the exchanges in the corpus are transcribed in
ordinary orthography with accompanying analyses of the main prosodic
features. Where Crystal and Davy deem it appropriate, students referring to
the text are advised of "important prosodic effects that require elucidation
in order to clarify what is being signalled". I was, therefore, curious to

discover whether (a) the eavesdropper judges I used as informants would focus on the same or similar stretches of utterances and effects, and (b) the extent to which the interpretation of the data given by Crystal and Davy would match that provided by eavesdroppers.[5]

The chosen extracts were played on different occasions to seven pairs of eavesdroppers. The idea of using pairs of informants, rather than individuals on their own, arose because in previous work of this nature, I felt that my personal involvement with individuals may have restricted what they had to say (compare McGregor, 1983, 1984). By using pairs of informants, then, I hoped to minimize my influence as analytic observer and thus encourage greater spontaneity of comment.

Each pair of informants were given the following verbal instructions:

I am going to play you a number of short extracts of talk which have been tape-recorded. At the end of each extract, I will switch the machine off. If you have any comments to make about the extracts, I would like to note them.

If clarification of these instructions was requested, I simply explained the need not to prejudice the outcome of the research and further assured informants that *any* comments they made would be welcome.

Whilst comments were noted as far as possible, tape-recordings of each session were also made in order to check the accuracy of what was said. Transcripts of each set of comments were made in ordinary orthography to facilitate a comparison of eavesdroppers' remarks with the Crystal and Davy glosses.

The analysis that follows is based on eavesdroppers' commentaries for each extract in turn. The first extract is taken from Crystal and Davy (1975: 22–23).

C | I went to
     'Stamford ↑ BRÌDGE last year ÓNCE | –
B | all ↑ fifty 'thousand have
     got to get ↑ ÒUT through THÉRE |

C   I'd | never ↑ BÈEN BEFÓRE | · | CÒR | – | CÒR | the
     | CRÒWDS | · | ÒOH | and you | WÒNDERED | if you were
     going to be | trampled to DÈATH | they | started to SHÒVE | · do
     you | KNÓW | it's | quite ↑ FRÌGHTENING | (A: | where was ↑
     THÌS TÓNY | B: | YÈAH |) | carrying 'Justin – | Stamford
     BRÌDGE | where I | went to see CHÈLSEA | | play ↑ LÈEDS |
     (A: | oh YÈS | | M̀ |) – and | Leeds 'played SHÒCKINGLY | – |
     worst 'game they ↑ ever PLÀYED |

B   well | some of the 'gates 'might be a'bout as WÍDE as ↑ that
     ↑ RÒOM | as the | RÒOM | | MÌGHTN'T they | | RĚALLY |

C | ÒOH | there were | KÌDS |
| sitting on 'that ↑ great HÒARDING |

B   a|bout as 'wide as THÁT | – and a|bout ↑ thirty
↑ THÒUSAND have to 'go out through ↑ THÉRE | (C: |
CÒR |) you | KNÓW | I mean er (A: | M̀ |) – oh it's |
TÈRRIBLE |

C | ÒOH | the | sea of – ↑ bodies in ↑ front of you ↑ MÒVING |
and | people 'started to PÙSH | BE|HÌND you | it got | quite
FRÌGHTENING | cos you | couldn't have 'done 'anything you'd
have been | absolutely ↑ HÈLPLESS |

In this extract, Crystal and Davy note the importance, for interpretation, of the following prosodic and paralinguistic features in respect of two utterances; both utterances are realized by the same speaker.

Utterance 1

| Leeds 'played SHÒCKINGLY | – | worst 'game they ↑ ever
PLÀYED |

C & D commentary: "Note the husky tone off voice indicative of disparagement."

Utterance 2

| ÒOH | the | sea of – ↑ bodies in ↑ front of you ↑ MÒVING | and
| people 'started to PÙSH | BE|HÌND you | it got | quite
FRÌGHTENING | cos you | couldn't have 'done 'anything you'd
have been | absolutely ↑ HÈLPLESS |

C & D commentary   "Note the extra prosodic features as C gets more involved in his story, marked glissando movement, and increasing speed towards the end."

The following remarks in respect of these two utterances, or parts of them, were recorded in the course of eavesdroppers' comments.

Pair 1

"Shockingly" really stood out. Yeah it sounded really affected. It was the way he said it "shockingly".

In both realizations of the word *shockingly*, the eavesdropper attempted an imitation of the original. A fuller prosodic and paralinguistic analysis of the utterance concerned reveals that *shockingly* carries: (a) a wide falling nuclear tone, (b) receives a high booster at onset, (c) is drawled on the first syllable and (d) has the paralinguistic feature "husky". A comparison of the imitations with the model utterance is interesting in terms of the features by which the eavesdroppers realized it. The nature of the glosses, and the fact of the imitation, suggest that the co-occurrence of prosodic and paralinguistic features in the original utterance is intentional, that is, both in respect of signalling the speaker's "intentions" and his determination to gain the attention of his audience. Notice too that one of the pairing also makes a bare judgement about the effect of this realization, at least from her own point of view – "it sounded really affected". This comment may be compared to the remarks of the second pair of eavesdroppers in respect of the second utterance (Pair 1, by the way, made no reference to the second utterance and Pair 2 made no reference to the first).

Pair 2

"All those people" and "it got quite frightening" didn't sound natural at all.

Perhaps this remark is responding to what C & D note as "C getting more involved in his story", though to what extent we could claim that the extra prosodic features are integral to the interpretation "non-natural sounding" is problematic. However, we can speculate that since one of the eavesdroppers in the first pairing considered that *shockingly* **sounded** affected and at a different point one of the eavesdroppers from the second pairing judged that what was said did not **sound** natural, the comments offered are presumably based on the relative quality of these notions based on the eavesdroppers' own interactional experience, either real or imagined.

How eavesdroppers apply the nature of this experience in making the judgements that they did is not obvious but suggests the use of some kind of inferencing framework which is sociolinguistically based. What the analyst considers is communicatively significant, for example, will differ from the eavesdroppers' sense of what is communicatively significant because of the different roles that they fulfil as an "audience". The comments offered by Crystal and Davy must be determined, at least in part, by their sense of what it is to be professional linguistic analysts. What they have to say, as a result, is likely to be governed by their knowledge of the situation and of the individuals whose talk they seek to characterize. Thus, just as there are different listeners to talk (as Goffman (1976: 260) indicates), there are also different kinds of eavesdroppers.

In the data in question, Crystal and Davy indicate their familiarity with the domestic environments in which the recordings were made. It also seems likely, from the comments given about both participants and situation, that they had participated in some of the exchanges. We need, therefore, to distinguish between different kinds of eavesdropper according to their

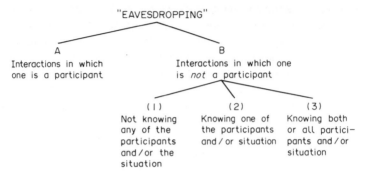

FIG. 1

knowledge of who was involved and what went on. The relevant distinctions are presented in Figure 1.

The non-participant eavesdroppers used in the study were all of the B (1) category. Despite this fact, Pair 3 were to give relatively detailed comments on the utterances concerned.

Pair 3

A guy who was trying to make a point kept saying, "it was really quite frightening". It was like talking to somebody who wasn't really listening . . . he kept repeating things.

They're talking about Chelsea and Leeds. He didn't sound so pleased about it. He said "Leeds played shockingly" like he had an interest in it.

He was quite vehement about it when he said "Leeds played shockingly".

At one point it seems that they're not talking about the same thing. One guy is talking about the gates and the other is talking about the sea of bodies. ..

The second guy is quite sympathetic and doesn't seem to know what it is like. The other guy has kind of experienced it all.

Whilst these comments report in part what was actually said, they also involve comments that are *imposed* upon the data. The first member of the pairing suggests that "it was *like* talking to somebody who wasn't really listening". The second member *guesses* that the speaker had "an interest" in the way in which Leeds played and whilst one of the speakers is judged to be "quite sympathetic" to the story that is being related, he does not "seem to know what it was like". The speaker's interlocutor, on the other hand, is sensed as having "kind of experienced it all". These "attributions" of speaker involvement are remarkable because on this occasion, there would seem to be a reasonable match between eavesdropper comment and the Crystal and Davy glosses.

C & D, for example, note "disparagement" in C's tone of voice. Compare the sense of "displeasure" and emotional content, with respect to the topic of conversation, reported by the eavesdroppers. Though "vehement" goes rather beyond the notion of "disparagement", the adjective does suggest that the utterance concerned has been invested with a particular emotional stance. Indeed, C's "sense of involvement" (C & D) is clearly established for at least one of the eavesdroppers in the pairing because he is described as "if he's kind of experienced it all".

These comments may be compared with those offered by the fourth pairing who were both to describe the communicative effect of *shockingly*.

Pair 4

He was definitely posh when he said "shockingly".

I wouldn't have said that. I thought he was a Northerner.

The nature of these comments is worth comparing with Pair 1 ("It sounded affected") and Pair 5 below ("I loved his expression of the word *shockingly*. It sort of represented upper bourgeoisie middle class"). The reactions of the eavesdroppers here suggest a degree of sociolinguistic stereotyping which may relate to the backgrounds of the eavesdroppers concerned. All three eavesdroppers who remarked on the varietal "affectedness" of *shockingly* came from London. Of these three, the informants from Pair 1 and Pair 4 were both speakers of "cockney" or localized London speech, whilst the informant from Pair 5 was an R.P. speaker. The second member of Pair 4, who contradicted the judgement offered by her partner, came from South-port on Merseyside. In terms of accuracy, it is the notion of "northerness" which comes closest to identifying the region of origin of the speaker. Crystal and Davy (1975: 19) inform us, "C is a primary school teacher, who has lived in Berkshire for many years, but whose accent has remained predominantly that of his county of origin, Yorkshire". This information also gives C's occupation as primary school teacher, which presumably does not generally carry the stereotypes of "poshness" or indeed "upper bourgeoisie middle class". Since the eavesdroppers who made these statements did not know the individual(s) concerned, the attribution of non-linguistic information of this kind has to be based purely on guess work. The guesses, as in this case, are often wrong but indicate the willingness of eavesdroppers to generalize about who and what the speakers are. It is perhaps interesting to note that the eavesdropper who attributes a negative class stereotype to the speaker was in fact a psychiatric social worker and may have been reflecting her own personal/professional judgemental norms in assessing C as she does.

However, despite the disagreement between the members of Pair 4, they do seem to concur in their assessment that there was something "odd" about the realization of *shockingly*. Their response to the second utterance, "it got quite frightening", is comparable to the remarks made by Pair 2 about the same utterance (cf. Pair 2, "it got frightening didn't sound natural at all" and

Pair 4, "quite frightening sounded quite artificial"). The artificiality, in this case, is attributed to a stylistic rather than varietal source. One informant from Pair 4 explained, " 'Quite frightening' actually sounded quite artificial as if he was reading it rather than speaking". The notion of "naturalness" was also implicit in the remarks made by Pair 5 about the realization of *shockingly*.

Pair 5

I loved his expression of the word *shockingly* (imitated). It sort of represented upper bourgeoisie middle class.

Yes it's inflected "shockingly" (imitated).

Mm he certainly emphasizes the word doesn't he.

Whilst the speaker is judged to be marking the utterance in some fairly obvious way for both these eavesdroppers, the markedness is not specified as being "disparaging" as Crystal and Davy suggest.

Indeed, Pair 5 were to further contradict the glosses offered by Crystal and Davy for the second utterance "it got quite frightening". Crystal and Davy consider that the extra prosodic markers here are indicative of "greater involvement". Pair 5, on the other hand, said, "He was talking about a situation which he considered frightening and yet there didn't seem to be any real emotion." This remark would seem to suggest that the set of cues marking "involvement" are not only to be interpreted from Crystal and Davy's point of view. Perhaps then, C & D's gloss is based on something more than the interpretation of the features specified in their analysis. If either of the analysts was a participant in the exchange in question, as would appear to be the case, then their judgement has to be affected by this fact and would help to explain something of the differences in their assessment of the communicative effect of the utterances in question.

The second extract was taken from Crystal and Davy (1975: 40).

A   oh and | one 'pig DÌED | be|cause it ÀTE too 'much | (B: |
ooh RÉALLY |) | ÒH | it was RE|VÒLTING | | oh they
were ↑ TÈRRIBLE | the | PÌGS | (C: oh ~) they made a |
dreadful ↑ row in the ↑ MÒRNING | when it was | FÈEDING
'time | – and | ÒNE PÍG | it was erm · a | YÒUNG 'pig |
a|bout · THÀT size | you KNOW | m | MÌDDLING | –
| and erm – it was ↑ DÈAD | and it was | LÝING 'there | I'd |
never SÈEN a 'dead 'pig BEFÓRE | | absolutely STÌFF |

B   di the | children SÀW it DÍD 'they |

A | oh they were ENGRÔSSED | you | KNŌW | (C: | oh
YÈS | ~ it was | MÂRVELLOUS |) erm they | thought this
was ↑ WÒNDERFUL | · | and erm · they ~ they 'asked 'why it
was DĒAD | – and er · the | farmer · ap ↑ parently · ↑ didn't 'want
his ↑ wife to KNŌW | be|cause · he'd over'fed them BEFÔRE |
· and she'd been | "FÙRIOUS | – and of | course he was ↑ trying
to 'keep it FRÒM her | but | all the KÎDS | were a|gog a'bout
this 'dead ↑ PÌG | and ~ was | telling them 'not to 'tell the farmer's
WĪFE | (D: | YÉAH |) and | all THÌS | – so this | pig was ↑
absolutely DÈAD | so they · | put it on · they | have a 'sort of
'smouldering HÈAP | that | smoulders all the ↑ TÌME | so
they | went to ↑ burn the ↑ PIG | – and | all the ↑ KÌDS | |
~ *laughs* (C *laughs*) – hanging 'over the ↑ GÀTE | | watching
this ↑ PÌG | ~ | and they were ↑ very er ↑ very 'taken that the ↑
pig had ↑ DÌED | be|cause it had ÈATEN too 'much | you |
KNŌW |

D | what a 'marvellous DÈATH |

The utterance which Crystal and Davy comment on is realized by Speaker A.

| ÒH | it was RE|VÒLTING | | oh they were ↑ TÈRRIBLE |
the | PÌGS | they made a | dreadful ↑ row in the ↑ MÒRNING |

C & D commentary;   "Glissando pitch movement is very expressive of A's intense feelings
here. It occurs at various places during the extract."

The relevant eavesdropper comments reveal that four out of the seven pairs
of eavesdroppers were to describe A's contribution as "excited". In so far as
"excitement" may be thought of as "intense feeling", there is general
agreement with the gloss provided by the analysts.

Pair 1

There's a sense of excitement. It gets faster as she gets carried away. It's very animated.

Whilst Pair 1 link this sense of "excitement" to the effect it has on the
speaker's "speed" of delivery, Pair 3 attribute the "excitement" to part of the
speaker's "non-surface" communicative intent.

Pair 3

It's the sort of tone of voice you use where you're trying to engage people you know you are
trying to interest.

Excitement in her voice made it seem as if it was going to be terribly amusing but it never really
finished.

For this pair, prosody would seem to be salient in helping to signal that the speaker, on the one hand, is trying to "engage" and "interest" her audience and that on the other, she is preparing to tell an "amusing" story. Notice that the second eavesdropper is prepared to evaluate the communicative success of the story telling by judging that "it seemed as if it were going to be terribly amusing but it never really finished". This evaluation is presumably based on the eavesdropper's notion of what constitutes the successful telling of an "amusing" tale.

The comments of Pair 4 and Pair 6 are comparable to those offered by Pair 1 and Pair 3 respectively. Both Pair 4 and Pair 6 remarked that the sense of excitement was linked to a perceived increase in speed.

Pair 4

Did you speed it up? She seemed to be speaking really fast.

Her voice seemed a bit high. She was getting more excited as it went on.

Pair 6

It's a racey sort of exciting delivery. She sort of gabbles it out.

It's fastly said, bubbly.

The nature of A's delivery is, however, further evaluated by one of the eavesdroppers from Pair 6 as "a very immature kind of speech". This particular speech style helps to characterize what is said as more like a "lecture" rather than a "story" for the eavesdropper concerned but nonetheless reflects the speaker's "non-surface" intent to "engage" with and "interest" her audience. "It's a very immature kind of speech. She sounded as if she was giving a lecture and was trying too hard to get their interest" (Pair 6).

More detailed prosodic analysis of the utterance in question reveals that there is considerable speech variation to "allegro" as well as a step up in pitch. The "widened" pitch range with the feature "glissando", mentioned by Crystal and Davy, would seem to account for the following remarks which relate to the extract in general.

Pair 7

She uses different expressions in her voice and emphasizes some things.

She is laughing kind of playfully as if she is sort of excited by it.

The notion of "playful humour" can be compared with the remarks of Pair 3 who said "it seemed as if it were going to be terribly amusing but it never really finished". Pair 5 also report "humour" but this is related to the nature and quality of the speaker's voice as much as anything else.

Pair 5

There is a kind of lightness in her voice and a definite raising in pitch.

It was a very speedy delivery suggestive of humour.

Again the communicative effect of particular features seems to be open to interpretation, though eavesdroppers' comments were not always evaluative. One eavesdropper from Pair 2, for example, simply stated "Her voice pitch ranged very widely."

The comments given for this extract indicate something of the eavesdroppers' ability to not only describe the kind of prosodic criteria that may be of salience for listeners in interpreting the talk of others (they reported variations in "pitch", "speed" and "rhythmicality", for example) but also their willingness to establish or impose a view of their own on the "non-surface" content of a particular utterance and/or exchange in general. Different inferences are obviously likely to be made about different kinds of exchange and the nature and detail of comments offered would seem to be partially determined by what eavesdroppers found to be of interest in the exchanges they listened to. We must therefore consider both what eavesdroppers did and did not say about the extracts they listened to as is clear from their remarks about the third exchange in the series.

Extract three was taken from Crystal and Davy (1975: 41).

B | ÀH | well · | we ↑ took a | we 'took some 'children on a ↑
VÌSIT | to er · | Enfield's en ↑ viron ↑ mental · ↑ STÙDY
'centre | · the | other DÁY · and | they have 'various 'animals
a'round THÉRE | | one of · WHÍCH | is a | PÌG – er |
PÌNKY | · | PÌNKY | | that's RÌGHT | · and | all the
CHÌLDREN | (C *laughs*) | stood 'round the 'OUTSÌDE | – –
(C: | M̄ | | like THÍS | at the | FÉNCE you 'see | and | this
'large 'slobbering PÍG | (A *laughs* | YÈAH |) was al|lowed
ÓUT | · | into the MÚD | – (C *laughs*) and | each 'child was ↑
given a 'slice of ↑ CÀRROT | you | SÉE | (A: | oh ↑ NÒ |)
and | they · ↑ poked it THRÓUGH | – and er | this PÍG | |
twice a DÁY | you | SÉE | cos | they had ↑ two VÍSITS |
a | DÁY | (A & B *laugh*) so | twice a DÁY | | this 'pig was
FÉD | | by ↑ twenty – 'slices of ↑ CÁRROTS | *laughs* (*All
laugh*) and | Pinky 'looked a VÈRY 'happy 'pig | (D *laughs*)

Crystal and Davy comment on two utterances taken from this exchange. The first utterance with accompanying commentary is as follows:

| Enfield's en ↑ viron ↑ mental – ↑ STÙDY 'centre |

C & D commentary: "Note that B pronounces the noun phrase *Enfield's environmental study centre* with a mock refined accent, perhaps because she feels she has introduced a note of academic formality into the conversation."

The second utterance is realized later in the extract and is spoken by B.

| this 'large 'slobbering PÍG | was al|lowed ÓUT | · | into the MÚD |

C & D commentary: "An expressive description, with tempo variation playing the main part in producing the effect (note especially the clipped syllable in mud)."

The "mock refined accent" which Crystal and Davy describe is not referred to by the eavesdroppers as such. Perhaps this is because of different regional norms relating to the stereotyping of particular varieties: though we recall the comment of Pair 4 and Pair 5 about Speaker A in the first extract. Crystal and Davy seem to be suggesting that the speaker on this occasion affects a hypercorrection of her own variety in order to "introduce a note of academic formality". The eavesdropper comments which were given about the speaker do not specifically mention the hypercorrection but they do suggest regional and class stereotypes that are judged to characterize her speech.

Three pairs of eavesdropper were to attribute prestige or status to the variety. They were Pair 1, who came from London and Bradford (Yorkshire), Pair 6, who came from Banbury (Oxfordshire) and Edmonston (Nottinghamshire) and Pair 7, who came from London and Macclesfield (Cheshire). All of these eavesdroppers used localized rather than R.P. varieties of English. Their comments were:

Pair 1

I get that middle class aura about it.

There isn't much accent. I'd say it was Southern.

Pair 6

She is much more genteel in speech than the other two. There is almost no dialect at all, very little inflection.

Pair 7

This is the aspiring middle class I think. They have got quite high status. There are traces of background.

It sounded pretty middle class. Midlands, middle of the road. They have some intellectual status.

The kind of stereotyping these comments reflect has no doubt as much to do with other features of the exchange (phonological, syntactic, lexical) as it has to do with non-segmental features but they are no less interesting for that. I draw attention to the remarks of Pair 1 and Pair 6 particularly because of how they attempt to locate the speaker in terms of regional origin. The eavesdropper from Bradford (Pair 1) comments that there "isn't much accent". Establishing where the speaker comes from is consequently problematic and the eavesdropper applies the general variety label "Southern" in contrast to her own speech which she would presumably characterize, in general terms, as "Northern". The eavesdropper from Pair 6, on the other hand, said "There is very little dialect at all, very little inflection." This eavesdropper came from Edmonston in Cheshire. His perception of "little dialect" is presumably taken as a measure of the fact that the speaker is using a variety which he also finds difficult to localize. The eavesdropper goes on to suggest that the lack of "dialect" can be accounted for, at least in part, by the relative lack of "inflection" in the speaker's voice. To what extent the eavesdropper is relating this perception to his own use of non-segmental phonology is unclear (the degree of intonational variation between the speech patterns of the speaker and the eavesdropper were not particularly marked to my ears). However, the eavesdropper had spent the last two years of his life as a student in Newcastle upon Tyne and it is possible that his judgement was based on a comparison with Tyneside speech, where he might reasonably have perceived much more inflectional variety than in the "South".

Compare now the comments of the eavesdropper from Pair 7 who characterized the speaker's variety as "Midlands, middle of the road". Though this judgement is wrong (the speaker we are informed came from Liverpool, though having lived in the South of England for some years – Crystal and Davy (1975: 39)), it is worth mentioning that the other female participant in the exchange did come from the Midlands. As a result, the eavesdropper may have assumed that they both originated from the same area, an area which indeed he was not unfamiliar with since he himself came from Macclesfield in Cheshire.

These attempts to specify the speaker's regional background seem to be closely related to other non-linguistic information that is provided by the same three pairs of eavesdroppers. The speaker is judged to be, for example, "genteel" (Pair 6) and like her fellow interlocutors "aspiring middle class"; "pretty middle class" (Pair 7). Pair 1 aver that the exchange has "that middle class aura" about it. Regional background and socioeconomic status are further associated with stereotypes of prestige by Pair 7. We are told that the speakers have got "quite high status", they have "traces of background" and that they might have "some intellectual status". The social/psychological attitudes which may have prompted this kind of assessment are clearly shared by the three pairs. All six eavesdroppers were undergraduate students from the University of Newcastle upon Tyne and we suggest that some kind of group norm is clearly exhibited in this case. However, the extent to which such non-linguistic information is central to what goes on in some particular interaction is uncertain, and has not received as much attention from researchers as the fact that we, in Britain, tend to derive such information about our interlocutors as a natural consequence of our every-day linguistic behaviour. For the record, Speaker A is described by Crystal and Davy as a "housewife". The other female participant was also a housewife "who does some primary school teaching". The two male particip-ants were the spouses of the women and are both "university teachers". Perhaps on this occasion the stereotypes offered by the eavesdroppers were more familiar than they knew!

The second utterance which Crystal and Davy comment on concerns the description of "the pig" and prompts them to describe the speaker's realiz-ation as "expressive". The "tempo" variation which they mention was remarked upon by only one eavesdropper. He said "It was a bit slow, with some bits slower than others" (Pair 1). Another eavesdropper, from Pair 3, described the utterance as "a very dramatic presentation". This sense of "drama" was shared by one of Pair 4 but the nature of the latter's inference is based on a quite different strategy. The strategy involved the eavesdropper in "imagining" what the speaker was doing. She comments, "I think I imagine her talking with her hands a lot. When she said 'large pig', I could imagine her showing how big it was" (Pair 4). A different strategy again was employed by one of the eavesdroppers from Pair 7. The message which comes across, however, appears to be much the same: "Again she was trying to impress people with her wit by her way of expressing things like her emphasis on the words *mud* and *pig*" (Pair 7). Different listening strategies, then, need not always lead to different interpretations of what went on. What might differ are the details which are provided.

The fourth extract which was played to eavesdroppers was taken from Crystal and Davy (1975: 59).

D | I didn't 'realize you'd ↑ let those
   things ↑ loose in the ↑ GĂRDEN | no | ''wonder we're in'fested
   by MÍCE |

A | well they er it was a | very 'cold NÍGHT | and they'd | never
   been 'out · BEFÓRE | and I thought (D: well they'd | been 'out
   in the GĂRAGE | · which | wasn't particularly WÁRM |) and it
   was | very DÀMP | and I | thought they'd ↑ soon be DĒAD |
   of pneu | monia if 'nothing ↑ ELSE | – | HOWÈVER | · there
   was the | mother 'UNACCÓUNTED for | and | one who'd es'caped
   we'd ↑ SÈEN 'go 'out |

D   ~ at | LÈAST 'one | at
   | LÈAST 'one | ·

A | one · | I'm st · I'm | being FÀCTUAL DĀVID |

D   ~ well it | could have 'been – – | YÈS | well it | could
     have 'been 'far ↑ MÔRE | – be | cause there were
                                                    | HOWÈVER
     | | we 'thought it's 'in the GĀRAGE | | so · | then ↑ one
     'Sunday MÓRNING | | David ↑ cleaned 'out the 'garage
     COM ↑ PLÈTELY | and they're | TÈRRIBLY 'clever | | we
     'had – to ↑ matoes in there RÍPENING | · | wrapped up in ↑
     NÈWSPAPER | · | each 'one 'indi ↑ vidually ↑ WRÀPPED | –
     and · | ''every 'one that was RÌPE | that had | really TÚRNED |
     – the | mice had ↑ ÈATEN | the m | mouse or MÍCE | had
     | ÈATEN a 'little 'bit of | · and the | ones that HÁDN'T
     'turned | they | hadn't | TÒUCHED | (C: | Ṁ |) · you |
     KNÓW | they | hadn't even | nibbled at the | PÀPER | ·

The commentary for this extract concerns the function of a single word
which is used twice in the exchange with differing degrees of stress and a
falling tone.

↑ HOWÈVER |

C & D commentary: "*however:* used to indicate a return to the main theme."

The use of *however* to achieve a reorientation in the exchange was remarked
upon by five out of the seven pairs of eavesdroppers.

Pair 1

However receives an emphatic stress.

She just dismisses his argument and his interruptions "however" (imitated) as if she wasn't
going to listen to him anymore.

These comments suggest that in communicative terms, the eavesdroppers
construe the effect of *however* as an "intentional" strategy to "dismiss" or
"ignore" the speaker's interruption. It is not only that the speaker is heard
to be "dismissive" but also that she seems singularly determined to retain her
turn, even at the expense of ignoring her interlocutor(s). The same communicative effect is gleaned by Pair 2 who said, "I notice the way she said
'however'. When somebody did interrupt her she just continued and then
said 'however' (imitated) and then just continued." "She didn't want her
flow to be interrupted." For this pair, the speaker is judged to use the word
however as a means of both revoking any attempt to take over her turn and
also to indicate that she does not wish to be interrupted. In order to hold the
floor, she has to dismiss any attempt to take over the turn space. She does

this by "refusing to listen" and "by refusing to be side-tracked" in the eyes of Pairs 4 and 5.

Pair 4

Every time he tried to interrupt her she kept going.

She kept saying "however". She is not going to listen to him. "However" (imitated) she says.

Pair 5

There again you've got this woman telling the story and she's not prepared to give in on her story. Despite various comments which could side-track her from the discussion she seems to be ignoring them.

A couple of times she just sort of talked over him.

The use of *however* can also be interpreted as a means of signalling the speaker's "non-surface" intention that she *wishes* to continue the turn and *will* continue it until she decides it is time to relinquish it. Thus we get the comments of Pairs 3, 4 and 7.

Pair 3

Earlier on where he says "the whole place will be overrun with mice" she cuts him off with "however".

Pair 4

Every time he tried to interrupt her she just kept going.

Pair 7

Her husband tries to get in a few times and is summarily dismissed.

The strategy "dismiss" or "ignore" would seem to be glossed as being achieved in a number of different ways then. It can be achieved by refusal to yield the turn; the speaker can simply continue talking or actively rebut attempts to take over the turn slot. It can be achieved by disattending any attempt to take over the turn slot and it can be achieved by directly intimating that the turn slot is not negotiable. The difficulty facing the analyst is to decide which of these strategies is most likely to have led to the communicative sequence that resulted. Comments like the above may help to establish which assessment is *more* likely. We do not have to be right, only more circumspect in the analyses we offer.

The "non-surface" effect of prosody is further described by Crystal and Davy later in the same extract for the utterance.

| · | I'm st · I'm | being FÀCTUAL DĀVID |

C & D commentary: "Note the effect of the level tone as the second element of a compound tone: a 'warning' is introduced into the dialogue. A presumably wants to get on with the story, and not be side-tracked into a point of detail: the tone is one of mild irritation."

The interpretation of A's attitude as being one of "mild irritation" can be compared to the much more forceful and emotive glosses of her behaviour offered by the eavesdroppers.

Pair 2

She sounds indignant. The man kept trying to break in and contradict her.

She kept just not listening and carrying on which is infuriating for a person.

Speaker A is judged to be "indignant" by the first eavesdropper, who is prepared to suggest a reason for her indignation; it is because her interlocutor "kept trying to break in and interrupt her". The second eavesdropper would appear to be rather more sympathetic to the other participant in the exchange and judges that A simply was not listening. Such behaviour she tells us "is infuriating for a person" and consequently she felt that "the man had no control over her irritated burst."

One member of Pair 3 shared the opinion of the first eavesdropper (above) and described the speaker's tone as "indignant".

She was very indignant with the bloke and very keen to get on with the story (Pair 3).

The notion that she is "keen to get on with the story" provides evidence for C & D's claim that she is not going to be "side-tracked into a point of detail".

Rather different interpretations of the same point are offered by three pairs of eavesdroppers. Pair 4, for example, considered that her state was one of "excitement" rather than "indignation". Consequently, when the speaker is prevented from continuing her story she reacts accordingly.

Pair 4

Her voice gets more excited when he starts interrupting. She sounded nagging really. She makes it more dogmatic.

She definitely knows what she wants and what she wants is to get on with her story.

In intimating her wish to get on with the story, the speaker's tone is interpreted as "indignant", "irritated" and "excited", perhaps even "patronizing". Compare the comments of Pairs 5 and 6.

Pair 5

It sounds to me as if she has told the story several times. It's almost as if she is telling a bedtime story to the children. They are going to listen and that was that.

Pair 6

She seemed to get the point over very forcefully. She gives a very detailed account of what the mice were doing.

Clearly, participant roles are very different. Crystal was a participant in the exchange in question and is presumably able to infer that "a warning is introduced into the dialogue" because he recognizes the speaker's tone from previous interactions with the same individual. Non-participants, on the other hand, do not have access to the same kinds of information or experiences and their judgements, as a result, are often singularly evaluative in nature. Pair 7, for instance, said:

Pair 7

The thing that struck me most of all was the way she dictated the conversation. She was a bit kind of woman's lib.

Yes, it all sounds rather peremptory to me.

Pair 7, by the way, were both male eavesdroppers and their evaluations here might arguably be said to indicate sex stereotyping. In other words, women who dominate conversations are judged by these males to belong to a particular female group type, who as a consequence of their group membership and beliefs, behave in a particular way interactionally. In this case, the woman is judged to "dictate the conversation" and is therefore attributed to the group type "women's lib".

The fifth extract was taken from Crystal and Davy (1975: 75) and involved the exchange which follows.

B | ÀNYWAY | – | Susie SĀID | – that · there were | no such 'things as FÁIRIES | | ÉLVES | | this 'that and the ↑ ÒTHER | – | WÈLL | · the | night she ↑ PÙT her 'tooth 'under the PÍLLOW | we for|got to 'put the ↑ MÒNEY there | and | take it A ↑ WÀY | we for|got all A ↑ BÒUT it | (A *laughs*) so she got | ÙP in the MÓRNING | – my | TÔOTH'S all 'gone | and there's | no MŎNEY | – | Dave said well 'there you ↑ ÀRE you SÉE | | YÔU said | you didn't BE|LÌEVE in FÁIRIES | so | how can you ex'pect the ↑ fairies to ↑ come and ↑ SÈE you if | – – | ÔH | but I | "DÔ believe in FÁIRIES | (D *laughs*) you | know | I | really DÓ | (A *laughs*) so | Dave said well · ↑ try a'gain TONÌGHT | – – so | that NÍGHT | | thank 'goodness we RE|MÈMBERED | (A *laughs*, C: | M̂ | ~) so the | next MÓRNING | she | gets ÚP | | all HÁPPY | | "oh they've | BĒEN | they've | BĒEN | I've | got my MŌNEY | and | Dave said well ↑ there you ÁRE | – – that | just SHÒWS | that

you i if you | they hear you 'saying you 'don't BELÍEVE **|** · | no ↑
MÒNEY **|** she.| SĀYS **|** – she says | well · I ↑ know you're 'only
↑ SÀYING 'that **|** be|cause you for ↑ got to ↑ PÙT it THÉRE **|**
(*all laugh*)

The utterance commented on in the extract was realized by speaker B.

| ÔH **|** but I | "DÔ believe in FÁIRIES **|**

C & D commentary: "The louder and slower pronunciation signals the quotation."

Four pairs of eavesdroppers commented on the realization of this utterance, which was perceived to be an imitation of the child who is the subject of the narrative. In giving the imitation, the speaker was not only heard to be quoting what the child said, she was also judged to be "a good story teller". This evaluation is based partly on what she does intonationally.

Pair 1

She was very emphatic when she was repeating the story and what the little girl said. She is very good at telling stories.

The second pair of eavesdroppers, however, considered that the speaker's use of intonation was "excessive".

Pair 2

She was very excessive in her use of intonation. She uses it mainly to imitate the child. "Oh but I do" (imitated) she said.

Pair 5 thought that the style of delivery was "expressive" rather than "excessive". They said:

Pair 5

There is more expression in her voice when she imitates the child. It's very expressive when she changes her tone.

It's not just the tone though. It's the way she emphasizes things. Her voice goes up.

There was some disagreement between this pair as to whether or not the speaker "intended" the imitation. The first eavesdropper comments, "There are bits where she seems to be talking like a child." The second eavesdropper replied, "Surely she is imitating what the child said. 'I do believe in' (imitated). There is a sort of inflection on *do*." For Pair 6, the imitation was "intentional" because it is marked stylistically. The effect of the imitation is also judged.

Pair 6

It's a story telling style. She really loves story telling. She establishes an effect upon the audience, "I do believe in fairies" (imitated).

Yes, she becomes emotionally involved with it. It's also a very indulgent way of speaking. She talks very indulgently about the child.

A more detailed analysis of the utterance reveals that it is not only "slower" and "louder" but also makes use of wide fall rises, extra strong stress on *do* and is accompanied by the paralinguistic features "whisper", "tremulousness" and "giggle". The "non-surface" effect of these features is judged to be "greater emotional involvement" and the fact that the speaker is using "a story telling voice." How this voice is evaluated would seem to be dependent on how the eavesdroppers rate the qualities of "a good story teller". Individual preference and/or taste would seem to be the determining factor here and the speaker is evaluated with both positive and negative results (cf. the comments of Pair 1, Pair 5 and the first eavesdropper of Pair 6 with those of Pair 2 and the second eavesdropper from Pair 6). What is of salience for Crystal and Davy, on the other hand, is not so much the qualities of the speaker as a story teller but the fact that she uses specific features to indicate that she is now "quoting" directly what was actually said for whatever narrative purpose she might have in mind.

The final extract which the eavesdroppers were asked to listen to and comment on was taken from Crystal and Davy (1975: 78).

```
B      I│MÈAN │ │"CÌNEMA │ have b for a│LÒNG time │
       has│been in TRŌUBLE │ – I mean that's why well│you 'got ↑ all
       these ↑ SÈX 'films │ – it was a│kind of a ↑ desperate at ↑ tempt to

C                                          sh it's a│sure 'sign of
       FÀILURE │ │ÌSN'T it │

B      │YÈAH │

C      │ once they're 'sort to THÁT │ │RÈALLY ~

B              they're · they're│TRỲING to │ get them ~

A                                                  │WHAT │
       │once you re'sort to ↑ SĚX │ · you│MÉAN │ (all laugh)

C      well it's · │some 'people re ↑ sort to ↑ BÈER │ laughs│NÒ │
       but you│KNÒW what I MÉAN │ i it to│MÉ │ it's│ÀLWAYS
       been a con'fession of 'failure │

B & C │YÈAH │
```

C   you│KNÓW │ tha the i it's│CHÈAP .│ is'n it's a│cheap way of
    − − I er

B   it's│trying to 'get the ↑ CRÒWDS in │

C   it's a CON│FÈSSION │ − −
    er│YÈAH │ − to│MÈ │ it's a con│fession of a ↑ lack of a ↑
    STÒRY │ │ÌSN'T it │ a lack of er (B:│YÈAH │) − you KNÓW
    │ │any ↑ DÈPTH RÉALLY │ I've│ÀLWAYS 'thought THÍS
    │ with · with│THÉSE 'things │

The utterance we shall consider from this final piece is spoken by participant
C.

│NÒ │ but you│KNÒW what I MÉAN │ i it to│MÉ │ it's│
ÀLWAYS been a con'fession of 'failure │

C & D commentary: "Note the change in speed as C tries to make a serious point."

The change in speed was not mentioned by any of the eavesdroppers.
However, C's "non-surface" intention "to make a serious point" drew the
attention and comments of eavesdroppers from three of the pairs.

From Pair 1, one of the eavesdroppers noted, "Having talked about beer
and sex they go back to the argument again. They say 'no but seriously'
reinforcing the fact that I've always thought this for years." This is an
interesting comment because the eavesdropper had either misheard what
was said, the quotation does not match the actual words used by C, or he has
interpreted the speaker's "non-surface" intent as signalling "now I am being
serious". The speaker's change of attitude is also linked to the change in the
topic of conversation, "having talked about beer and sex they go back to the
argument again". By convincing his interlocutors that his opinion on the
subject has been held for some time, B is further judged to be seeking their
"agreement".

Pair 4

He's giving off very high flown ideas. He wants the others to agree with him.

Pair 6

He is trying to come over as the educated opinion on these things and his mates agree with him.

Given the number of possible functions of the utterance suggested by the
eavesdroppers, the problem that faces the analyst once again is to decide
which function is most operative at that moment.[6] Is the speaker giving off
"high flown ideas"? Is he trying to "come over as the educated opinion"? Is
he attempting to "make a serious point"?

The very fact that different possibilities of interpretation may be entertained in answer to these questions merits serious consideration. Indeed, any theory of utterance interpretation must needs take these differences into account if the interactional and communicative functions of everyday language use are to be more fully understood.

Concluding remarks

The conceptualizations offered by Crystal and Davy have been shown to present but one possible view of what has gone on in some discourse in communicative terms. In the absence of an adequate conceptualization, and other supporting evidence from (non) participant listener judges, the analyst who wishes to make claims about the "non-surface" intentions of speakers, or indeed the communicative effect of some interactional sequence, always runs the risk of oversimplifying or falsifying the data.

However, in considering the kind of inferencing work that was undertaken by eavesdroppers, we must take great care to distinguish the nature of listening behaviour that one might employ as a focused participant in talk from the listening behaviour that one might employ in the circumstances which we have described. Whilst the participant listener can seek ratification from his or her interlocutor that something has been "intentionally" signalled, for example, the eavesdropper has no such opportunity and can therefore only attempt to guess at what has gone on. In attributing the kinds of information that they did, we must also remember that what eavesdroppers described may only involve a low-level frame analysis of what they believed was going on, or, for that matter, of what processes were actually going on. The ways in which (non) participant eavesdroppers assess these processes is obviously difficult to ascertain, but some attempt to explore the kind of work that might be undertaken has been explored in the context of psychological research concerned with the perception and attribution of some individual's behaviour. This work has essentially involved comparing the views of actors and naive observer informants about the perceived causes of an actor's behaviour (Jones and Nisbett, 1972; Storms, 1973). Given that the views of actors and observers seemed to differ, the nature and significance of these differences was explored. Jones and Nisbett (1972: 80), for example, found that there was a prevailing tendency for actors "to attribute their actions to situational requirements, whereas observers tend to attribute the same actions to stable personal dispositions". The variance in attribution is explained by Jones and Nisbett (1972: 85) in two major ways. Firstly, actors and observers operate with different background data; that is, they have different kinds of information available. We can compare, in this respect, the different kinds of information that are available to the different kinds of participant and of non-participant eavesdroppers. Secondly, the same information would seem to be differentially processed; that is, both actor and observer will find different aspects of the available information salient. This differential salience, Jones and Nisbett argue, "affects the outcome of the attibution process". In other words, "The actor and the observer are both reaching for interpretations of behaviour that are sufficient for their own decision-making processes" (Jones and Nisbett, 1972: 85). Presumably, this pattern of decision-making is also true for analysts of talk and for eavesdroppers of the kind that were used in the study.

What was evident from eavesdroppers' comments was the fact that they appeared to be making decisions about the data in different ways; they employed different kinds of listening behaviour. The differences, evidenced in the remarks that were offered, would seem to suggest that it is not possible to draw listeners of this type into the same listening framework without directing their attention in some artificial and pre-determined way. But even on those occasions when it might be argued that eavesdroppers were attending to the same or similar stretches of utterances and/or the same or similar linguistic features, contrasting descriptions of the communicative effect of those utterances/features were often provided. We might now try to summarize why these differences occurred.

They occurred, perhaps, because the features concerned were: (a) differently ranked with respect to one another, (b) differently interpreted as to their co-occurrence, or (c) differently "heard", in the sense in which what was understood to be going on from one eavesdropper's point of view may not have been shared by others. The reasons for this would appear to be fundamentally related to the individual and social differences that led to the interpretations that were given. These differences included: (i) familiarity with the participants in the exchanges that were used, (ii) varying regional and social norms concerning the perception and attribution of non-linguistic stereotypes (e.g. class, education, status, sex), (iii) varying social, psychological and interactional histories of the informants (including, for example, their age, educational background, sex, affective states and attitudes), (iv) different interpretations of what was expected in terms of the instructions that were given, (v) the relative willingness of eavesdroppers to say anything at all whether on the basis of stereotype, invention of memory, (vi) differences in informant roles between professional analysts and lay observers.

There is, too, the possibility raised by Labov and Fanshel (1977) that the intonational signals themselves are inherently ambiguous. The nature of such ambiguity would thus enable speakers to escape accountability for what they said/"meant". Labov and Fanshel (1977: 46) note, "In our view, the lack of clarity or discreteness in the intonational signals is not an unfortunate limitation of this channel, but an essential and important aspect of it. Speakers need a form of communication which is deniable." The gap, then, between speaker "intention" (even if this is recoverable) and listener "interpretation" would seem to create a number of potential thorn-beds for the would be analyst of talk. Indeed, if, as Goffman (1976: 261) suspects, "one routinely presumes on mutual understanding that doesn't quite exist", then we need to take a great deal of care in offering the glosses that we do.

What this care would involve is the recognition of the work participants jointly undertake to provide "a working consensus" that enables everyday activity to be successfully negotiated. As part of this activity, the listener's role is absolutely crucial. We can no longer afford to ignore "the mystery of his achievement" because in providing a framework within which inferencing can be seen to be made, we can only contribute towards the kind of theory that will provide in Firth's (1957: 32) terms "a key to the questions of what language really is and how it works". Such a contribution would, therefore, have to include not only an account of speech acts and Gricean maxims but also, as Gumperz (1982: 29) suggests, "a sociolinguistics which accounts for the communicative functions of linguistic variability". Our understanding of these functions, in turn, can only be satisfactorily explored in the context of a sociolinguistics which incorporates a theory of "listener" effect and the kinds of variation that occur as a result.

Notes

1. This is a revised version of a paper which was originally published in *Language and Speech*, **28**, 1985 under the title of "Utterance interpretation and the role of the analyst". I am particularly grateful to Lesley Milroy for her encouragement and insightful comments on earlier drafts, and to John Wilson and John Dore for their positive criticisms.

2. Grimshaw (1980: 32) complains along similar lines that "attention to Hearer (H) has only been modest in the literature on language use in social contexts and that attention has been attentuated by a speaker-oriented bias in most treatments".

3. Cf. Clark (1985: 179) who notes,

Language is a social instrument. When we talk, we direct our words not to the air but to other people. Our aim is not to express our thoughts aloud but to affect the people we are talking to. We intend our listeners to recognize certain of our goals in saying what we say, and they listen intent on recognizing them.

4. See also Straight, this volume, chapter 5.

5. Schaffer (1983, p. 243) suggests that "the majority of studies which discuss prosodic cues . . . still do so from the point of view of what speaker behaviours can be observed, without verifying that the 'cues' so identified are actually used by *listeners* in the predicted way". By undertaking a series of listening tests, based on different conversational extracts, Schaffer examines how intonation is used as a *perceptual* cue for turn taking.

6. Cf. Brown *et al.* (1980: 15) who argue that

One of the main problems which confronts the student of intonation is finding external evidence to bring to bear to justify one analysis rather than another. Obviously this problem is particularly acute when one tries, as we have tried, to describe the effect of the interaction of several different systems in spontaneous speech.

In order to resolve difficulties "in interpreting their data confidently", Brown *et al.* adopt the policy of appealing "to other judges, not only phonetic colleagues but also to native speakers" (1980: 15). Whilst the use of judges in this way is redolent of my own research approach, notice that Brown *et al.* make what is almost a classic error of reference by failing to acknowledge that it is of course the native speaker–*hearer* or *listener* whose skills they call upon.

References

Adelman, C. (ed.) (1981) *Uttering Muttering*. London: Grant McIntyre.
Bach, K. and Harnish, R. M. (1979) *Linguistic Communication and Speech Acts*. Cambridge, Mass.: MIT Press.
Brown, G. and Yule, G. (1983) *Discourse Analysis*. Cambridge: Cambridge University Press.
Brown, G. Currie, K. L. and Kenworthy, J. (1980) *Questions of Intonation*. London: Croom Helm.
Clark, H. H. (1985) "Language use and language users". In Lindzey, G. and Aronson, E. (eds), *The Handbook of Social Psychology*, 3rd edn, pp. 17–229. New York: Knopf.
Cicourel, A. V. (1974) "Ethnomethodology". In Sebeok, T. A. *et al.* (eds), *Current Trends in Linguistics*, vol. 12, pp. 1563–1605. The Hague: Mouton.
Coulthard, M. and Montgomery, M. (eds) (1981) *Studies in Discourse Analysis*. London: Longman.
Crystal, D. and Davy, D. (1975) *Advanced Conversational English*. London: Longman.
Dore, J. and McDermott, R. P. (1982) "Linguistic indeterminacy and social context in utterance interpretation". *Language*, **58**, 374–398.
Edmondson, W. (1981) *Spoken Discourse*. London: Longman.
Goffman, E. (1974) *Frame Analysis*. Harmondsworth: Penguin.
Goffman, E. (1976) "Replies and responses", *Language in Society*, **5**, 257–313.
Grice, H. P. (1968) "Utterer's meaning, sentence meaning and word meaning", *Foundations of Language*, **4**, 225–242.
Grimshaw, A. D. (1980) "Mishearings, misunderstandings, and other nonsuccesses in talk: a plea for redress of speaker-oriented bias". *Sociological Inquiry*, **50**, 31–74.
Gumperz, J. J. (1982a) *Discourse Strategies*. Cambridge: Cambridge University Press.
Gumperz, J. J. (ed.) (1982b) *Language and Social Identity*. Cambridge: Cambridge University Press.
Gumperz, J. J. and Tannen, D. (1979) "Individual and social differences in language use". In Fillmore, J. *et al.* (eds), *Individual Differences in Language Ability and Language Behaviour*, 305–325. New York: Academic Press.
Jones, E. E. and Nisbett, E. N. (1972) "The actor and observer: divergent perceptions of the causes of behavior". In Jones, E. E. *et al.* (eds), *Attribution: Perceiving the Causes of Behavior*, pp. 79–94. New Jersey: General Learning Press.
Kreckel, M. (1981) *Communicative Acts and Shared Knowledge in Natural Discourse*. London: Academic Press.
Labov, W. and Fanshel, D. (1977) *Therapeutic Discourse: Psychotherapy as Conversation*. New York: Academic Press.
Levinson, S. C. (1983) *Pragmatics*. Cambridge: Cambridge University Press.
McGregor, G. (1983) "Listeners' comments on conversation", *Language and Communication*, **3**, 271–303.
McGregor, G. (1984) "Conversation and communication", *Language and Communication*, **4**, 71–83.
Milroy, L. (1984) "Comprehension and context: successful communication and communicative breakdown". In Trudgill, P. (ed.), *Applied Sociolinguistics*, pp. 7–31. London: Academic Press.
Schaffer, D. (1983) "The role of intonation as a cue to turn taking in conversation", *Journal of Phonetics*, **11**, 243–257.
Storms, M. D. (1973) "Videotape and the attribution process: reversing actors' and observers' points of view", *Journal of Personality and Social Psychology*, **27**, 165–175.

Straight, H. S. (1976) "Comprehension versus production in linguistic theory", *Foundations of Language*, **14**, 525–540.
Straight, H. S. (1982) "Structural commonalities between comprehension and production: products of monitoring and anticipation". In Lowenthal, F., Vandamme, F. and Cordier, J. (eds), *Language and Language Acquisition*, pp. 177–180. New York: Plenum Press.
Stubbs, M. (1983) *Discourse Analysis*. Oxford: Blackwell.

Index